ELDER
WISDOM

EUGENE C. BIANCHI

ELDER WISDOM

Crafting Your Own Elderhood

WIPF & STOCK · Eugene, Oregon

Wipf and Stock Publishers
199 W 8th Ave, Suite 3
Eugene, OR 97401

Elder Wisdom
Crafting Your Own Elderhood
By Bianchi, Eugene C.
Copyright©1994 by Bianchi, Eugene C.
ISBN 13: 978-1-61097-544-5
Publication date 7/1/2011
Previously published by Crossroad, 1994

Acknowledgments

I am particularly grateful to the Georgia Humanities Council for a grant that helped make possible the earlier phases of this project. I also thank Emory University for a recent leave period that permitted a concentrated effort to write the book. But I am specially grateful to Ms. Carol B. Pitts, a doctoral candidate at Emory, who spent long hours culling and logging on a computer the best insights from the interview tapes. Hers was not simply a task of copying, but of selecting and classifying, a work that called for patience, intelligence, and good judgment. And a sincere final thanks goes to the elder participants who share with us many facets of their creative eldering.

Preface to the 2011 Reprint Edition

The reprinting of this book several years after its first publication gives me a chance to add a few new thoughts. Two decades after starting work on *Elder Wisdom*, I wondered about its relevance for today. Discounting some author prejudice, I think it holds up pretty well. One reason is that the ideas and experiences expressed by the hundred elders seem to be deeply rooted in human nature. My aging interviewees were speaking from core issues in their lives. Another reason for relevance is the great expansion of elderly populations in the United States and other industrialized countries. For years to come, the Boomer cohort born after the end of World War II will continue to swell the ranks of older people in America. Similar projections can be made for great nations like India and China as they enter into the league of economically developed countries. Advances in health care will further lengthen the lives of people around the world. If the central topics of *Elder Wisdom* can be adapted widely, the book could help many people.

Another benefit of the book is that it explores the spirituality of aging in a humanistic idiom. Its themes can be related to traditional religious language, but they don't have to be. For example, topics like community, nature, gratitude, acceptance, contemplation, compassion, friendship, humor, celebration, transformation, suffering, and death are taken up by all historical religions. Too many people still think of the secular and profane as separate categories. We can make distinctions, but real separation is misleading. We live in one interlinked world.

In my recent memoir *Taking a Long Road Home*, as well as in earlier writings, I have tried to point to a closer relationship between what we think of as the secular and the sacred. Their intimate connections are not arbitrary or insignificant. In the first chapter of the *Tao Te Ching*, we are told that the invisible ultimate is present in its manifestations. The sacred infuses the secular. Or, in the voice of Simone Weil, the world is the language of God. As I launch into my ninth decade, I become more convinced of this reality, especially while meditating. As an elder, I recognize the real tragedies and evils that accompany our lives, but these do not negate the sacredness of our secular lives.

As society focuses more on aging populations, there will be more need for individual- and group-counseling toward creative aging. Chapter 8 provides some techniques or guides for the contemplation of aging. Questions for personal reflection cluster around key themes of the chapters. Meditative and graphic techniques invite an individual or group to deepen their immersion into the aging journey. These meditative forays provide a way of turning discursive sections of the text into a workbook.

I'm optimistic about developing our later years into a valuable time for personal growth and for elders to make contributions to the wider community. Yet I want to stay aware of the inevitable downsides of aging. Life after eighty brings home for me some of these challenges. In this light, I'd like to end this preface with a recent statement from Stephen Hawking, the brilliant physicist who has contended for years with A. L. S. (Lou Hehrig's Disease), which greatly limits his mobility and speech: "My advice to other disabled people would be, concentrate on things your disability doesn't prevent you from doing well, and don't regret the things it interferes with. Don't be disabled in spirit as well as physically." (*New York Times*, May 10, 2011) Aging will in various ways disable us all. It's particularly impressive to hear such elder wisdom from someone like Hawking. I hope the reappearance of this book will help keep that spirit alive.

Eugene C. Bianchi
Athens, Georgia
May, 2011

Contents

Acknowledgements   *v*

2011 Preface   *vii*

Introduction: Finding Your Elder Voice   1

Chapter 1: Integrating Family Histories   9

Chapter 2: Learning from Work and from Turning
           Points   37

Chapter 3: Empowering Your Elder Self   63

Chapter 4: Expanding Your Elder Self   87

Chapter 5: Reaching Out from the Elder Self   114

Chapter 6: Encountering Personal Mortality   141

Chapter 7: Developing Personal Spirituality   169

Chapter 8: Crafting Your Own Elderhood   195

Chapter 9: Sharing Gifts of Wisdom   223

Appendix A: Questions for Interview   233

Appendix B: Participants in the Elder Wisdom Project   234

Index   237

Introduction:
Finding Your Elder Voice

Are you aging? People answer that question in various ways, depending on how the word "aging" strikes them at the moment. If they are walking out of a nursing home after a visit, they might respond with some relief that they are not aging. If they are seeing their last child off to college, they might sense the inevitable hand of senescence on their shoulders. But in general the word "aging" has negative connotations, especially for Americans and others living in technologically advanced cultures. Our technologies tend to remove us from the natural patterns of life with their seasonal rhythms. We confide in medicines and machines that will or should solve our problems, even the problem of aging. Aging is something to be resisted and denied in a culture that deifies youthful vigor. In advanced industrial societies, aging depresses us in special ways. It mocks our sense of superiority and the potentials of our splendid machines. Yet it is ironical that the more developed our technologies, the larger our aging populations.

Dramatic statistics of exponential growth in elderly populations confront us as we approach the new millennium and beyond. For the most part, aging depresses many people and yet we are promised much more of it. The "baby-boomer" cohort is approaching fifty. The Roper Organization projects that by 2010 more than ninety-six million Americans will be older than fifty. Those who are sixty today, because of improvements in healthy lifestyles, are twice as likely to live to be eighty-five than were people a generation ago. When active lifespans stretch into the seventies and eighties, the traditional view of retirement tends to lose its meaning.

We are on the cusp of an aging revolution. On the level of material standards, economic hard times are impacting the older worker with particular intensity. In recent years, the rate of unemployment for people over fifty-five in the United States was seven times that of younger people. Workers who cannot keep pace with the shifting job market may be permanently locked out of the work force. Many of these people are unprepared for retirement. It is estimated that two out of every five Americans in their fifties will retire with no pension income other than social security. The loss of siblings, spouses, and workplace friends can leave many older adults with the prospect of isolation in later life. All these factors demand that we reflect deeply on what it means to grow old in a society that does not encourage new roles of respect for its elders.

This book is about taking a new look at our individual aging experiences and finding paths that will help us move toward elderhood in more promising ways. The book has clear limits. It will not assist directly in providing financial security or other material benefits in later life. It won't help with legal issues, housing, or transportation for the old. It will not give advice on retirement homes and leisure activities for the elderly. It offers no panaceas for perfect health, nor any cure for death in old age. Rather, the book invites us to reexamine our personal visions of aging, conditioned as they are by our family and societal backgrounds. It summons us to experience a more positive wisdom about aging that emerges from the lives of over one hundred creative elders who are the subjects of our story. These men and women act as our mentors, inviting us to reflect on their lives so that we can come back to our own autobiographies with pertinent questions about how we are eldering. These aging mentors will not promise us an "ageless body" or a "timeless mind," as the title of a modern bestseller does. The goal of elder wisdom in these pages is more modest. The sagacity of these elders shows us that we can grow inwardly and reach out to the world during later life in exciting and rewarding ways.

A key impetus for the book is the conviction that too many of us shut down on life as we move into our fifties and sixties. In the modern corporate mind, one is already perceived as getting old during the sixth decade. Too many late middle-agers accept and incorporate destructive stereotypes about aging. They start to view themselves as mindless, useless, and even sexless. Seeing themselves as relatively worthless people, they plod on through leisure and other activities in semiconscious resignation. They try not to show it externally, but down deep they feel that life "has passed them by," that they are "over the hill." Such persons may have decades of life still ahead of them. This book attempts to challenge this widespread social reality. By walking the modern candidate for elderhood through the experiences of creative elders, the book says that things don't have to be so dire. It declares that the present vast waste of energy and talent among the old can be reversed. It announces that there are ways of truly enriching the personal life of each elder, and of helping him or her to find satisfying ways of contributing skills and wisdom to society.

Over a two-year period, more than one hundred older people were interviewed for this book. Their ages range from the mid-sixties to centenarians. The average age of these men and women was about seventy-seven. There are a few celebrities among them like President Jimmy Carter and Archbishop Desmond Tutu. But many, though less known, are outstanding persons in various fields. (See appendix B for a brief identification of each participant.) The purpose of the book may have been better served by not filling it with celebrity figures. Celebrities, while objects of great popular curiosity, tend to become too removed from ordinary life. For many, they represent distant icons whose attainments may overpower rather than inspire. The book aims to draw readers into lives that are not too unlike their own, so that they can apply its elder wisdom to themselves. The selection process of these creative elders is not the result of a scientific random sample. It represents a careful choice of older people by the author through suggestions from his wide network of colleagues in the area of psychological and spiritual development in later life. An attempt was made to select persons from different educational and occupational backgrounds, as well as from diverse religious, national, and ethnic traditions. The author also tried to maintain some geographic balance by interviewing elders in different parts of the country.

For the most part, interviewees were sent a list of "pump-priming" questions well in advance of the interview. (A sample list of such questions is given in appendix A.) Not all of the questions would be asked in the tape-recorded interviews, but a general pattern of inquiry developed in keeping with the life experiences, feelings, and thought patterns of each participant. In general, the interviews followed a "life-review" format, allowing the participants to remember significant events and persons, and weave these together into a tapestry of their lives. The process is more circular than linear; it becomes a circumambulation of the past for the sake of the present and the future. Interviewees also filled in gaps by sending written materials by and about themselves. This large body of material was arranged into themes or topics that seemed to derive from the data. To allow the participants to speak in their own voices, particularly appropriate quotes are used throughout the book.

The book is arranged to go from their lives to our lives, from the experiences of vital older persons to our own experiences as we attempt to shape a richly satisfying elderhood for ourselves. Viewed from the widest angle, the book tries to immerse us in other people's stories from chapters 1 through 7 for the purpose of coming back to our own story in chapter 8, the personal workshop chapter of the volume. When seen from this perspective, the volume strives to be more of a stimulus for our own reflection than a discussion about other people. It is not meant to be used as a spectator sport of being passively entertained or inspired by elder athletes, as it were, who know how to play the game. Rather, the book wants to get us into the play action by helping us realize that we can't be mere spectators, that we are already on the field, and that the clock is running in our own game of aging.

For the most part, this book is aimed at the still active elder. Only about 5 percent of the elderly population at any one time would be classified as infirm or frail in the sense of nursing-home inhabitants or those living at home with greatly reduced mental or physical capacities. The sick and frail elderly form a very important topic for our attention, study, and care. But the main audience for this volume is that much larger population of relatively healthy middle-aged and older persons who seek more rewarding elderhoods.

The trajectory of chapters 1 through 7 starts off by first plunging us into concrete histories. Chapter 1 leads us into examples of diverse family backgrounds, both in families of origin and in adult families formed by the participants. Our later life is strongly influenced by the environments of our childhood and youth. A number of elders had to struggle against the odds when they were young, because of dysfunctional family situations or other problems. Others learned to shape more personally successful lives out of the failures of past marriages. Still others enjoyed the advantages of encouraging family milieus to launch them into creative directions, even though these paths were not seen until later in life. Whatever the positive or negative impacts of early formation, each elder had to learn to become his or her own person, often enough in contrast to expectations of their families.

Chapter 2 focuses on important turning points in specific lives, as elders look back on their long journeys. Women, for example, had to discover modes of balancing home responsibilities with involvements in the world of work. Sometimes this happened as a result of marital breakup; in other situations, individuals discovered their callings to careers later in life. Some elders can point to major events that turned their lives in unforeseen directions. Such turning points resemble revolutions of thought and experience, accompanied by significant inner turmoil. Again, just as with family backgrounds, diversity is also a theme in exploring turning points. Some elders were set on a career course in youth from which they would not diverge.

Chapters 1 and 2 immerse us in concrete lives. We wanted to establish the life-review or life-history aspect of the enterprise as a basis for discussing the eldering themes of chapters 3 through 5. It is important to understand that the themes for developing the elder self do not flow from abstract speculation about older people, but rather from their authentic life experiences. Thus the eldering themes of chapters 3 through 5 move in concentric circles from the inner life of a developing elder to the ring of family and friends, and on to the wider circle of worldly engagements. Chapter 3 invites us to reflect on how elders develop inner resources in a society still filled with negative stereotypes about old age. Participants talk about the value of strengthening self-reliance, self-esteem, and self-acceptance. They stress the importance of humor and play for empowering the inner self. And they realize that inner growth must be linked with reinvigorating purposes and goals in later years. Although the inward journey is emphasized in chapter 3, the participants know that inner power is not shaped in isolation from outward interactions.

Chapter 4 presents themes that expand the elder self beyond his or her self-containment in the present. How are people helped or hindered by reminiscing? Can indulgence in past memories cease to be an escape from life and become a motor for new directions? What memories need to be healed so that the elder can become unstuck from fruitless repetitions of past hurts? A strong theme among the participants concerns lifelong education to keep one's mind alert, informed, and challenged. They talk about learning to welcome surprises, even painful ones, and turning them into possibilities for deeper living. All of this forms a milieu in which the elder liberates himself or herself from soul-narrowing confinements of the past. Elder freedom becomes a reality in ways they hadn't suspected. A remarkably constant theme among creative elders is living with gratitude, if one hopes to expand the self in later life. And they are grateful not only for the benefits of the past, but also for the lessons they learned through hardships.

In chapter 5, the themes for a wise elderhood broaden into wider rings of involvement. We hear the voices of elders talking about fostering deeper contacts with members of their own families. An important task of the old is to work out mutually benefiting relationships with younger generations of their families. Elders insist on the importance of cherishing old friends and forming new ones. Sometimes friends are more important to older people than are members of their own families. A number of participants find special meaning through their involvements in "intentional communities" that both encourage richer friendships among members and also pursue focused goals as a community. Disengagement from the great concerns of humanity is not a theme of creative aging among these elders. Rather, they view older age as a time for renewed commitment to social causes: local, national, and international. The elder is seen as one freed from past burdens, inward and outward, to be able to follow the special calling of elderhood to mentor and advocate for peace, justice, and environmental caring. This vision of a contemporary elder goes against the cultural emphasis on the old as mainly passive consumers of goods and as a market for leisure activities. Developing a social conscience and reaching out in altruistic service were mentioned often by elders in commenting on what contributed to a rewarding old age.

The next two chapters take up overarching themes that were implicit in the preceding chapters. Although the reality of our own death lingers like a shadow just a step behind us throughout life, it looms up with particular intensity in our middle and late years. Chapter 6 examines the encounter with mortality as a crucial process for continued growth in elderhood. We take up the challenge of Blaise Pascal who said, in paraphrase, that humans are reduced to fleeing from themselves because in this way they can run away from the thought and the injury of their own deaths. The chapter shows how people stop fleeing from themselves and deal with their "small deaths" of physical hardship and emotional suffering. It portrays elders attempting to face honestly their fears about the process of dying. It depicts these elders as they assess their lives in the context of death, looking for patterns of hope and meaning. Chapter 7 explores another underlying theme for the whole book: how to shape a viable spirituality for elderhood. One's spirituality or "religiousness" is not static; it shifts and develops with each elder's life experiences. Sometimes it requires resistance to inherited traditions or at least it demands a reformist dialogue with one's past heritage of values and purposes. Elders reflect on their inward and outward journeys to create a personalized spiritual life.

Chapter 8 invites the reader to craft his or her own elderhood in light of the wisdom shared in previous chapters by creative elders. This is a workshop chapter that calls for something to be done rather than merely read. It is adaptable to individuals or to groups. The chapter suggests and provides techniques for deeper involvement such as meditation and journaling. It attempts to create an environment of contemplation in order to derive the most benefit from the lists of questions that pertain to chapters 1 through 7. Chapter 8 summons us to our own ongoing work of eldering. It implies at least two things. First, older age is not a time for static disengagement, but rather a special period for dynamic growth into a fuller human integrity. And secondly, the chapter indicates that we have the tools and the capacities for such a journey, if we but find the courage to walk the path. The final brief chapter is a gift-giving from the old to the young. Elders wrap their gifts for the next generations in the form of advice, as pondered from the vista of the final season, about what really counts for living a satisfying and contributory life.

This book is an invitation to reflect on the prospects of one's own aging in the company of a hundred creative elders who share their insights and experiences about getting older. It is not just for the old. It is rather for anyone who wants to think creatively about his or her elderhood. As the statistics indicate, an increasing number of us will live well beyond the limits of what our culture sees as our "work force lives." How can this lengthened period become a time of personal growth and social contribution? In her book *Silences*, Tillie Olsen, one of the participants in this project, talks about the importance of overcoming "unnatural silences" in our lives. She is speaking mainly of would-be creative artists who, because of inner and outer circumstances, are not able to let their voices be heard. But her vision about breaking our unnatural silences applies to each of us in terms of the aging process. Listen to Tillie Olsen:

> These are not natural silences, that necessary time for renewal, lying fallow, gestation, in the natural cycle of creation. The silences I speak of here are unnatural; the unnatural thwarting of what struggles to come into being, but cannot. In the old, the obvious parallels: when the seed strikes stone; the soil will not sustain; the spring is false; the time is drought or blight or infestation; the frost comes premature. (From *Silences*, foreword)

In the chapters that follow, we hear contemporary elders striving to break the silences that stifle their voices, that blunt their desires to become all they can be even into later life. Virginia Davis, an elder playwright whom we will meet in these pages, echoes Olsen's insight about breaking silences. Among the things that give life its deepest meaning for Davis are "the persistence to make my voice heard . . . the desire to become the best human being I can." This is the hope and the promise of elder wisdom.

CHAPTER 1

Integrating Family Histories

Elders carry with them a long legacy of family experiences that in often undetected ways impact on their satisfaction in later life. Families of origin launch us into life, give us our earliest experiences of love and self-worth, and influence our relations with others. Yet our parents and siblings, as psychotherapy knows so well, affect us profoundly in positive and negative ways. Usually our families exercise a mixture of both benign and unhealthy influences. Of course, what we become is not solely determined by how we were "marinated" in childhood. Our personalities in older age are a changing amalgam of the external influences combined with our own genetic propensities and our own decision-making. Moreover, we can change to some extent at any stage of life. The challenge is to understand and integrate family histories so that we can continue to develop toward our fullest human potential.

In this chapter, we look at a number of ways in which creative elders reflect on their families of origin as well as the families they formed as adults. This review of selected experiences is only a sampling of the possibilities for understanding an older person in the context of his or her closest relationships. Yet this selection of family dynamics gives us a picture of the ongoing task of assessing ourselves in terms of who we were and what we may yet become. It is both the task and the privilege of those in later life to reflect on their life histories. Younger people tend to neglect such explorations because they are too preoccupied by the demands of building families and careers. The young may also be too close emotionally to families of origin or to their adult families to get a good perspective on the pros and cons of personal formation. It may be even more important in older age to ponder our beginnings if we want to grow according to our real potential. For we may have been stuck in patterns of thought and behavior that we assumed to please others rather than to develop ourselves.

Against the Odds

Ross Gritts, a Cherokee, was born in an Indian hospital in Oklahoma. His father died when Ross was a child, and he was eventually put in an orphanage during his teen years. Although he learned some discipline in school, he was alienated from earlier friends and developed an attitude of "nobody cares about me." After a little more schooling, he got into construction work and fell into patterns of alcoholism. Ross drifted from place to place, supporting himself on construction sites and also promoting his drinking habit. Among his earliest memories is that of his grandmother, a tribal leader, who told him that he had latent healing abilities. She said that he had been chosen from birth to be a healer. But his mother, a school teacher, would not allow him to indulge in the old ways. Ross remembers the powerful impression that an old faith healer made on him as a child. When his baby sister was very sick in the hospital, doctors said there was little hope for her. The healer brought hot coals into the hospital and performed a ritual that the astonished boy never forgot. His sister recovered, and Ross connected the work of the tribal healer with his own later calling to care for the sick.

He remembered the social prejudice that hurt self-esteem in his formative years. Many times he heard the phrase "lazy, dirty Indian." But he was able to compensate somewhat for these labels by finding support in his closely knit Indian community. He claims that black people had a harder time than Indians. "The whites tolerated us to an extent, and we could always find spiritual help in tribal rituals such as stomp dances," he says. But blacks, he recalled, were more isolated. They couldn't come to the front door of a restaurant, and they had to sit on rough benches, not padded ones, in bus stations. They had to go to different toilets. Gritts's reflections on prejudice speak eloquently about the need to rethink earlier life situations. "I didn't know I was experiencing prejudice, because I didn't know the word 'prejudice' until I was completely grown." There is more in this statement than merely knowing a word. It also reveals our gradual awakening to the harm that early life milieus cause. Often we are so immersed in negative family or community conditions that we cannot take full stock of them. We can't get at enough distance from them to see them for what they are.

It took Ross Gritts many years and many miles of riding the rails in box cars to understand his deeper self as healer over against his boyhood conditioning. About fifteen years ago, a strange train ride carried him where he had no intention of going. "I fell asleep drunk on my way to Stockton to work in the fields and ended up in San Jose," he says. It was in San Jose that he would turn his life around, meet his wife, and become a leader in the local Indian community. Toward the end of his time as an active alcoholic, he had been working in a Phoenix hospital and came to understand "what it was like to be nice to people." He claims that his conversion from alcoholism came from his own decision, the support of the Indian community, and the prayers of his mother and friends.

An insulin-dependent diabetic, Gritts has realized the vocation of healer that his grandmother envisioned. Much of his energy goes into caring for his wife who is wheelchair-bound from multiple sclerosis. "I take care of her, and she sort of takes care of me. Responsibility is a great thing to have in one's life in order to be productive," he says. He also operates his own janitorial service, and is in charge of a group of Indian elders who assist the community connected to the San Jose Indian Center. He speaks in local schools about the dangers of drugs and alcohol, citing his own experiences. Gritts had to terminate one of our interview sessions early to take a wheelchair shut-in to her doctor in his janitorial van.

Gritts understands himself as a healer-mediator who was given a special gift at birth. For a long time, he wandered away from his calling, but now he appreciates his vocation as seen from later life. Part of this healing mediation comes from being in touch with nature. He recalls the natural remedies used in childhood such as poultices and herbs. "Healing is living naturally with Mother

Earth." He would love to be living closer to the great redwoods of California, but he finds peaceful moments of renewal when walking in local parks. He has a strong sense of the interconnectedness of the natural world. "Nature is religious. God is in it, in the trees, in the water, and in ourselves," he says.

By reflecting on his journey, Ross Gritts has redefined his sense of self-esteem. While he was "carousing around the country," his sense of self-worth came from fighting hard, conversing effectively, and working for a living. "I did not bum," he says. But now he thinks well of himself for different reasons. "I evaluated my life. I came from an orphanage. Then I was a drunk. Finally, I realized that I was a good person who learned compassion and found a direction in life. I think well of myself now for who I really am and for what I can do for others."

Looking back on family beginnings can give an older person a more complete understanding of his or her journey against the odds. Just as Ross Gritts uses past experiences to appreciate his later years as healer, so Gregory Bergman tells a story of overcoming initial hardships. Bergman was born of immigrant parents in San Francisco. Because of the family's poverty, his parents took a job as caretakers at a wealthy estate, leaving Gregory in foster care for two years. His parents were afraid of losing their job if they disclosed Gregory's existence to their wealthy employer. Well into his eighties, Bergman still suffers from powerful anxiety attacks that he says are connected to the separation anxiety suffered by the absence of his parents. Although he was a very good student, an undiagnosed, severe sinus infection plagued him for years. Because of this condition, he couldn't see well enough to play sports and felt very lost in school.

At fifteen, he became seriously sick from the infection and suffered an emotional breakdown that put him in a mental hospital. He was one of only two people at the institution under twenty-one. "In a way, being in a mental institution saved my life," he says. This comment seems to have a physical and a psychological dimension. His sinus condition was finally diagnosed, and after many operations on his sinuses, eyes, teeth, and gums, he regained a measure of health. He "saved his life" at the asylum on another level. He recalls an early experience of social injustice that launched him into a lifetime of crusading for human rights.

While he was working in the hospital ranch that supplied milk, fruit, and vegetables for the institution, he noticed how the best products went to doctors and other officials. Rejects from the ranch were kept to feed the inmates. This experience sensitized him to social injustice. Like many poorer youngsters of his day, he took whatever jobs he could find to help his family. One of these was delivering papers for the local Hearst newspaper. "I saw how Hearst was exploiting his workers, while he was buying expensive statues and stuff in Europe," he says. This further stirred Gregory's interest in social action and radical politics. He became involved with the Communists until World War II. Because he helped organize farm workers in Arizona, he lost his job with the post office. When his sinus condition returned to some extent, he settled in the California mountains as a bookkeeper for a sawmill, and continued to write social-justice tracts and raise a large family of his own.

Bergman's life from the start has taught him to face suffering, even tragedy. His wife was killed almost before his eyes in an automobile accident in the early seventies. A drunk driver crashed into her car. Though not Bergman's intellectual equal, she had been a very important emotional support for him. After her death, he raised the seven children of a stepson who had committed suicide. As he glances back at the intense challenges of his life, Bergman quotes a saying of his: "Old people are like wine; as they get older, they either mellow or they turn sour." Despite his occasional panic attacks, Bergman has mellowed without losing his intense concern for what he refers to as "the stream of life." Yet perhaps the strongest lesson from this elder has to do with facing suffering creatively. Another of his aphorisms connotes this hard doctrine: "Be happy not in spite of what happens in life, but because of what happens." For him, this has to do with facing events straight on and taking the risk of being hurt by moving closer to people. He had always wanted to be a writer, but in early life it seemed too remote a goal. Now in his ninth decade, he continues to publish and reach people.

Born to a sharecropper family in Louisiana, Gertrude Wilks knows the meaning of struggle, hardship, and well-deserved successes along the way. Her early years were those of a black migrant child, moving from one plantation to another. Gertrude was one of seven children. She remembers her mother as a woman who got things done, even to the extent of plowing fields. She was close to her children, organizing their activities and instilling a sense of discipline. Her father was often away working. He was illiterate, but as a Baptist lay preacher, loved to sing gospel songs and tell stories. Gertrude doesn't recall her father ever saying that he loved her. "But I know he did," she says. Storytelling time was very special for her father, who prepared for it by roasting peanuts for the children. She also recalls her mother reading the Bible to her father, who would memorize and recite it.

She remembers her anger as a child during the Depression when her family had to wait in line for rations of rice until all the whites were served. White people would spill rice on the floor and tell the "niggers" to pick it up. This infuriated Gertrude. But her mother told the strong-willed girl to be quiet about it despite her anger, for her expressed fury might bring reprisals on the family. She recalls that only white children were able to ride buses to school for nine months. Blacks had to walk to shabby school rooms for only four months of the year. During the rest of the year, black children were expected to do physical work or be idle. Wilks says that it has taken her many years to overcome her racial prejudice against whites. "I'm glad to have that gone," she says. It is hard to pinpoint what elements help to diminish prejudice in the aging process. In Wilks's life, some of those factors were her own developing sense of self, contacts with less prejudiced white people, her accomplishments as an educator, and a deepening faith in God whom she sees in all people.

"The school was really the highlight of my life," she says of the alternative schools, called "Nairobi Schools" in East Palo Alto, that she started in 1966. The schools were developed by a group, Mothers for Equal Education, that tutored black kids who often did poorly in the public schools. Wilks was in part prodded into developing these alternative schools by the failure of her older son to learn reading and writing in the public school, even though he had graduated from it. Yet during the twenty years of her work with alternative education, she had to face severe family traumas. Her older son became involved with drugs and died of an overdose. Her husband slipped ever deeper into problems of his own, "which really strained the relationship." And her second son, who had gone on to Harvard to become a physician after finishing in the alternative schools, died suddenly of a heart attack.

To the question of what kept her going under such heavy blows, Wilks responds that her faith in God and the help of psychological counseling were important factors. Still another element in her support system is the joy she experiences from her daughter's family and seven grandchildren. As she ages, she knows she is slowing down. "I can't move my legs as fast as my brain, and that bothers me," she says. She also fears violence in the neighborhood where drugs are still rampant. A strongly built woman, she speaks of not trusting herself any more in self-defense, and she no longer has her sons to defend her. But Gertrude Wilks has cultivated a wider family through her church and the senior center she helped organize. "I look forward to going there as my midweek high," she says. In addition to meals, the senior center offers programs in arts and crafts, Spanish classes, physical education, and opportunities to visit the sick. She is proud of the fact that seniors are on the board of this extended family. "They're active, not passive, even in decision-making," she says. Like Ross Gritts, Wilks not only understands the influence of her family of origin and her personal family, but she has also learned to extend her family-support system through her educational, church, and senior-center work.

Yet it would be a mistake to see her upheld only by these wider families. She has also learned to deal with personal rejection and find self-acceptance. "It's important to stay in charge of yourself," she says. "I've tried to use up my life. The thing that makes me feel good is I know I made a difference in lives. That makes my life more whole."

Learning from Family Failure

Virginia Davis has become a playwright and a director of plays in later life. Now in her seventies, she speaks about her long, troubled marriage as a painful failure. Perhaps a keynote in her commentary about herself is the expression, "I've had a hard time learning how to let go." This caption statement of her family reflections underlies some main directions in her life. But in many ways Davis's family musings touch all of us in terms of the fears we form in childhood and the difficulty of replacing them with hope and with freeing decisions. She remembers as an eight-year-old having her father come home in the middle of the day to tell her mother that he had been laid off. It was the beginning of the Depression. She can still hear her mother's startled remark: "My God, how will we eat?" There were five children to support. Davis refers to this event as her first memory of fear. A second childhood recollection instilling fear was the pounding on the door at night when she was twelve. When she reached the kitchen with her brothers and sisters, she was told that her mother had been in a serious car wreck and might not live. The accident left her mother partially crippled and very angry, a state that Davis says "shaped and changed all of her children."

Davis has been able to let go of experiences in Catholicism that she found stifling and hurtful. This break took a long time, since she wanted to give her seven children a religious background. "I could say I formally left the church when the last one graduated from high school." This decision to leave the church has freed her to pursue her own spirituality. But the struggle with her marriage remains unresolved. She claims to have carried over from her religious past some naive ideas about the power of prayer and love to change another person. Gradually she learned about emotionally crippled persons who deny their problems and resist help from others. "They wear a mask to cover their potential for emotional pain," she says. "After a while, the mask becomes the person." Davis regrets the impact her "blissful ignorance" about the depths of her marital problems had on her family. Yet she is also upheld by the care and love she experiences from her children.

Davis's lifetime task of learning to let go of debilitating fears has expressed itself in her plays. "There is no separation between art and life. Whatever touches me deeply comes out eventually in my plays." Her story can be told, in different modes, about all of us. We can all recall how fearful we have been to step out alone into a perilous world at important junctures of our lives. But Davis also teaches us a lesson about hope that each person must learn on one's own. Reflecting on her family experiences, she expresses this lesson in a polarity between recognizing years of fear and false hope, on the one hand, and on the other hand the dawning of new hope for herself. "I have to admit my unwillingness to accept reality and my indulgence in false hope," she says. "I was too afraid that all would be lost. I was missing the right focus for that hope. What I've learned from it all is that there is now hope, not for changing others, but for me."

Clara Crook is an outspoken octogenarian with a strong streak of no-nonsense independence. "Don't give me that cutesy-wootsey golden age stuff," she says. She has been chair of her California county commission on aging, and before that had a significant career in business education as an administrator. When she reflects on the ups and downs of her family life, the search for balance between independence and dependence stands out. She was the eldest of three daughters born to Russian-Jewish immigrants. She remembers her father as an entrepreneur and a risktaker, who was also a very controlling parent. He wouldn't let her mother learn to drive. He wanted a boy. Clara related closely to her father and "wanted to be a boy, which meant being as independent as possible," she says. She recalls an argumentative household where her parents did not get along. "My father was a spender; my mother was tight; my father was handsome; my mother was jealous." Still, amid the hurly-burly of her home, she attests to receiving enough basic psychological nurturance.

Her first marriage of fifteen years produced two children, and became a lesson in incompatibility through which she learned more about the independence and dependence struggle in herself. During the first years of the marriage, she enrolled in medical school, but left after two years to take care of her hypochondriacal husband who was suffering from a bad case of hemorrhoids. Falling into a more passive woman's role, she decided to be full-time wife and mother, foregoing a medical career. "I had such low self-esteem," she says, attributing it to her desire to be a male and her lack of any assertive feminine role model. "I did not have a high regard for myself as a woman. I didn't find myself attractive, nor did I know anything about sex in my naiveté. I felt very lucky that someone wanted to marry me," she says. The eventual collapse of this marriage further depreciated her self-regard: "I felt this marriage breakdown as a supreme rejection of me," she says.

Her second marriage in the early fifties started off well. She met a Protestant minister who swept her off her feet with the kind of romance she had always wanted but felt she could never have. Clara thought that with a minister she would have a faithful and committed husband. He was handsome, bright, and winsome. But these hopes were not to be realized. The marriage rocked back and forth for ten years, but finally, with the help of therapy, she ended it. Crook looks back on that marriage as a costly learning experience. "He brought me alive as a woman. I saw myself as attractive as well as smart. I was someone to be reckoned with as a woman. For the most part, this feeling has stuck," she says.

She wondered out loud about how she might make sense of these failed relationships in terms of her aging process. Then she answered her own musings. "I figure that everything that happened to me was an experience that I could build on. And I have." The observation is borne out in her career. With a better balance of independence and dependence, of keener self-esteem and appreciation of her talents for working with others, she held important jobs. She was public-relations officer for a university chancellor and became assistant dean of a business school. When she was about to retire at sixty, she was solicited for a position in Hawaii at the Japan-American Institute of Management. "I learned that people would want me for me," she says, "not just because I had a husband. That was so very important for me."

When Lillian Rabinowitz thinks back to childhood, she talks about having few happy memories. She could have said the same thing about her two marriages. Her reflections about her mother's hardships in the Ukraine are harrowing. Her mother, raised by a cold and unloving stepmother, was abused by raiding Cossacks. Coming to America at seventeen with very little education, she lived as an indentured servant to an older married sister. Then she had to work from dawn to dusk in a New Haven armaments factory whence she was liberated by marrying a Latvian immigrant.

Lillian remembers a better educated father, but one who contributed to a marital disaster. As the elder of two daughters, she recalls her mother being physically abused, struggling to abort a third pregnancy, and almost dying at the hands of a cheap abortionist. She could not relate to a very distant father who was bored with his wife and family. Contempt and fear about close human relations were the mother's legacy to her older daughter, who remembers a life of poverty and illness in her family of origin. Outside her home, she found some countervailing influences in appreciating the Bible as literature when she was sent to Sunday school for purposes of upward social mobility. But her most humanizing discoveries in childhood were the public library with its quiet rooms of literature, and especially obtaining free piano lessons from a German immigrant. Music and singing became the great loves of her life.

Her two marriages seemed to follow similar patterns of disappointment. The first was to a religious scholar of Semitic languages who had great difficulty finding employment during the Depression. Lillian recalls the marriage as a bitter experience, in part because her husband lost interest in her. In addition to the two children born to them, she looks back on one positive benefit of the union, her college degree from the University of Cincinnati. She shakes her head, as if she should have known better, when she recounts her second marriage. It was to the much younger brother of the first husband. This brother had served in World War II and subsequently finished a doctoral degree in classical languages. "He had some of the same traits as his brother," she says, "and the same personality problems." She felt constantly depreciated in a relationship where her husband firmly believed that he was the ruler of the house and his wife's purpose was to serve him.

Rabinowitz found it difficult to review some of these memories, but she noted: "I'm grateful to you for helping me put the pieces together in a broader perspective; I want to see my life whole with its sufferings and joys." Her significant career accomplishments are recounted later, especially those of the last two decades in the field of aging. Despite her family of origin and later marital problems, she speaks of an essential personhood that she has known since childhood. "If I were a theist, I'd say God gave it to me," she says. For her this consists in a constant search for beauty. It builds on the excitement she found as a little girl at the piano. She also speaks of it as the creativity she found in the arts that carries over into the organizing work she has done for the elderly. Reviewing her difficult family memories in light of the accomplishments of her later life becomes a testament to human resiliency. The hardships have also made her more understanding of others. "I'm not so rigid in my moral judgments," she says. "I'm more willing to see how life is both evil and good."

Reflections on families of origin and one's own marital family are usually a blend of positive and negative influences. In the above three examples, we observe people coping with painful memories, attempting to integrate them into a healthier pattern of elder living.

With the next four elders, we see how beneficial relationships in marriage help people grow into creative elderhood. In the first two of these families, common work goals were especially important in fostering close ties and personal growth.

Healing Family Backgrounds

For many years in Catholic circles, Patty Crowley's name was synonymous with the Christian Family Movement that she and her husband, Pat, founded. The movement was an example of strong lay leadership to improve the quality of married life and foster a deeper religious spirit in families. Patty Crowley's reflections on her childhood are generally happy ones. As the eldest of five children, she had the benefit of a stable home life and of financial security. "My parents had a good marriage," she says. She remembers her mother, a convert to Catholicism, as a very strict person who ruled the home with discipline, while her father, a success in the textile business, traveled a great deal. Patty was sent to a strict convent school where, she recalls, the girls had to wear white gloves. When time came to place her own five children in grammar school, she chose a school that was less strict and exclusive. Even these decisions reveal a continuous change going on in her own spirituality that would be significantly different from the type inherited from her parents.

She met her husband, Pat Crowley, at the cathedral in Chicago, an auspicious beginning for a couple so dedicated to the church. When she married a man of Irish descent in the late thirties, she had to stand against her mother who "thought the Irish were no good." Pat was a corporate lawyer who had a special interest in Christian lay mission, based on the then rediscovered theology of the Mystical Body of the church. This European theology of the forties and fifties ran counter to the intensely hierarchical and legalistic understanding of Catholicism then prevalent. It emphasized the role of the laity in the life and mission of the church, as a corrective to the exaggerated clericalism of the period. The Crowleys worked as a team to shape such theological teaching into concrete organizations that worked at grass-roots levels. For years they traveled together, spreading the CFM cause. Crowley reflects on the impact such collaboration had on their relationship: "I'm convinced that in marriage you have to have something that is a common interest other than your children, because your children leave you."

Their work together involved travel and study that gradually changed the lifestyle of the Crowley family from that of their families of origin. Their home became a frequent meeting place for groups that were formulating ways of opening up the nuclear family to wider concerns in parishes and neighborhoods. As years progressed, the Crowley home became more ecumenical, interracial, and international. They took in foreign students and as many as a dozen foster children, adopting one of these to add to four of their own. "I think it was hard on our children, but I don't think it hurt them," she says of these changes. She notes that one of her daughters is married to a black man with an adopted black child; another daughter is married to a Japanese.

Crowley's family life, so connected to lay church movements, is an especially good example of changing personal spiritualities. An early influence on her religiousness was having Monsignor John Ryan as a teacher at Trinity College in Washington. He was a well-known thinker who was responsible for an important statement of the American bishops in 1919 about the role of the church in the social order. Until she met him, she had no knowledge about the social-justice teachings of the church, which were to deeply affect both her ministry and her home life.

But the most dramatic change in outlook on the Catholic Church came when the Crowleys were invited to Rome in the middle sixties to be part of the birth-control commmmission established by the Pope Paul VI to guide him in taking a stand on the issue. Here were two dedicated Catholics brought up to believe that birth control was wrong, something to be avoided in the Christian Family Movement. They were about to confront a sea-change moment in their lives. They were asked to obtain information from around the world on the value of the "rhythm" method of natural birth control. The responses "were eye-openers for Pat and me, as they overwhelmingly rejected the rhythm method, and hoped their kids wouldn't have to put up with it." Another eye-opener for the Crowleys were the convincing arguments of progressive theologians who wanted to change the church's teaching on birth control.

Patty Crowley's development in family life reflected her change in religious life, and vice versa. She has become much more independent in relation to her past. Not only did her mother oppose her marriage to Pat, but she was also upset by her involvement in racial issues. Crowley has become much more independent of the dictates of the Catholic Church, which for a long time was her extended family. Her ministry is less connected with the institutional church. She has become deeply immersed, partly through the influence of her children, in the women's movement. After Pat died, she began to realize in her aloneness how women suffered discrimination. At eighty she works at a woman's shelter and makes weekly visits to women in prison. Her home is now a place for women's organizing, reflection, and liturgies. "I think my role now is in the woman's movement. A real change because before everything was focused on married couples." Aging with mindfulness has taught this courageous woman to rethink and to act in new ways. "If you have just your children as an interest, which a lot of older people do," she says, "I think you're lost."

To understand Rose Lucey's story as a very creative elder, it helps greatly to put it in the context of an Italian immigrant family and her marriage to Dan Lucey. On a personal level, her life at one dimension is a journey from her self-image of being a "Guinea-Wop" kid on the outskirts of Boston to a self-loving and caring individual. It wasn't until midlife at a meeting with Margaret Mead that Rose Marciano Lucey first articultated to herself that she was somebody. On her own telling, she "felt no good because I was an Italian kid. We were seen the way racist people see blacks." She remembers wanting to deny all connection with being Italian, because of the negativism ingrained in her by family and community. Only at age seventy-seven could she be induced by a daughter to travel to Italy; even then she almost refused to go.

Of course, the reasons for our emotional revulsions or attachments are never reducible to a single factor. One has to add into the mix a dominant mother with whom Rose did not get along. As a middle child she had to cater to her older brother in the old machismo style, even to the extent of making his bed. Added to this sibling servitude was an awareness that her younger sister was "the apple of her mother's eye." But perhaps the crowning memory of her childhood self-depreciation was her first experience in grammar school. Her given name in the family was Rosaria, a name that was to change by fiat as the child of six approached the daunting Miss Wilson at the school door. In the presence of the child's mother, Miss Wilson declared that "Rosaria" was too complex and foreign; henceforth the child would be known as Rose.

Rose Lucey also recalled how mysterious childhood memories stay with us into old age. When she commented on her fear of being mugged or robbed, she flashed back to that "scared little girl afraid of something dark." There was something threatening or possibly abusive in that darkness, she says. Her mother was terrified of the dark. Rose remembers how she and her siblings would come home from school and sit on the back steps, not venturing into the house until her mother came home from work, because there was something in the house "to be afraid of." Rose Lucey has battled with forces of darkness over a long life both as a reformer within the Catholic Church and as a pioneer peace advocate.

The greatest turning point in her gradual self-acceptance was her long marriage to Dan Lucey. She recalls the chance event that brought them together. She "was sitting around in a very depressed and lonesome mood" when a piano teacher, whom she had not seen for years, called to see if she wanted to meet in downtown Boston with some young people who were starting a bookstore. That chance call made her reflect on the importance of saying yes to posibilities as an older person. "I could have said no and just sat there; then this incredible life with Dan would not have happened." She and Dan, in addition to raising nine children, worked together in their various bookstores as well as in other projects for justice and peace. In the late forties, they met the Crowleys and became West Coast leaders in the Christian Family Movement. They were perhaps the first people to advocate for a national peace academy in the U.S. But the key aspect in her own transformation toward self-esteem was the love that Dan and she shared. "I was loved in a way that I would hope every human being could be loved. I really mean that Dan brought me a gift of love." She spoke of it as a love that did not constrain, but rather opened one to inner personal realms and to the world. "In that kind of love, you know you are not alone." She also noted that an important aspect of their successful relationship was the ability to share with each other and yet to allow space for independence.

It is also in the context of an extraordinary marriage and sustaining family life that Rose has been able to bear significant sufferings. A son-in-law was murdered on a good-works trip to Latin
America. Her own son, John, died of AIDS a few years ago. The
process of his illness and dying had a deep effect on the whole
family, she says. For parents brought up with the sexual strictures
of Catholicism, acceptance of a gay son was not easy. But she and
Dan accepted John and invited him to bring his gay friends into
their home. She and others cared for John during his illness, and
she has since become active in AIDS work in Oakland. When she
spoke about John, she looked at a summery tree just outside the
window. "Trees are important to me," she said, "as that tree was
losing its leaves in October, John was dying. In March, as it began
to sprout new leaves, that's when John died into new life."

Statements like that characterize Lucey's Christian religiousness
that in good part was shaped in the context of her family. She and
Dan, in their bookstores, were always pushing at the edges of new
reformist thelogy for changing the Catholic Church. And their
home was a meeting place for reformist clergy and laity. But at a
deeper level, the experienced love of husband and children was the
core of her prophetic thrust for church and societal renewal. She is
angry at the church for its formalism, legalism, and authoritarian
rule. For her this constitutes a hypocrisy of power that keeps the
gospel message from being lived in ways that she experienced it in
family life. Rose Lucey thinks that the authoritarian church, with
its rote and seemingly artificial observances, caused nearly all of
her children to walk away from it. It is somewhat ironical that a
good family life can turn the young away from the church, if they
envision it as the opposite of what they experienced at home.

Lin Ludy's Ohio childhood was characterized by many losses.
She doesn't remember her father who drowned in a storm when
she was four. Financial exigencies demanded that her mother work
as a school teacher in another town distant from the home of the
aunt who took care of Lin. When her mother visited, the child
recalled her vivid personality in the extended family environment
of her aunt's home. But during the nine months of the school year,
she was largely deprived of her mother's presence. "At an early
age, I had to learn about letting go, about not clinging to what I

wanted," she says. Ludy finds that letting go graciously in face of the losses of elderhood is an important quality of healthy aging.

Active involvement in the church has marked Ludy's life from an early age. But in her early Presbyterian upbringing, she didn't know how to relate to God as father, not having experienced fathering in her early years. "Fortunately," she says, "I married a man who was a very good father to our four children." Observing his relation to their children, she came to appreciate God as a caring father. Her reflections on family experience in relation to a person's sense of God, whether positive or negative, has received considerable scholarly attention in our psychologically oriented age. Shortly after graduating from the University of Michigan, she and Bert married and settled into the traveling life of the Department of State's foreign service where he was a financial officer. Most of his work centered on Latin America. "We were both raised to be helpers," she says, pointing to their foreign service duties as having a strong helping component. She looks back on their home life and work as successful because "we were undertaking a job, doing it for others, finding personal satisfaction in it, and enjoying ourselves along the way."

Ludy didn't want to paint an idyllic picture. As in all marriages, there were ups and downs. "Bert and I fought a lot and made up a lot." They have had to struggle through serious illnesses together, but a combination of laughter and prayer got her through the crises. For Ludy, being married fifty years is "more than a success; it's a gift, a grace." She is happy with her four children because of who they are: "caring people, who do that in a very natural way." Her daughters led her into an appreciation of feminism and equality for women. This became a special concern for Ludy in light of the unequal opportunities of her own hardworking mother. Her growing feminist consciousness revived her frustration at seeing wives as mere appendages to foreign-service officers. "The government like the church got two for the price of one: an officer and a hostess."

She appreciates the fact that her marriage allowed more leeway to break with the pattern of the subservient woman. She indulged her independent streak by directing the public activities expected of a foreign-service officer's wife to church-related situations, which was not customary. As the desire to pursue her religious interests increased, Ludy went to a seminary at age fifty-five. At first, she wanted only to deepen her knowledge of theology, but because of what she refers to as a mystical experience, she felt called to ordination. After the disappointment of being told that there were no churches available for a person of her age, she realized that the powerful call she had was not to be a pastor in the usual sense, but to be a minister for spiritual development. It was then that she discovered the Shalem Institute in Washington, D.C., that trained spiritual directors. "When I got into the spiritual-direction program there, I realized that it was what I sought and had already been doing. It's nice as an older person to look back and say 'yes, this happened, and I didn't understand what was going on then, but now I can.'"

During a long life, Lin Ludy has continued to exercise the lesson learned in childhood of needing to let go and to trust that the future would be right for her. This attitude is characterized by her learning to become a clown. She and her husband have performed as clowns in church liturgies and elsewhere. When the clown puts on white face and bright colors, she explained, the clowning person dies to her usual self. "The clown can let go of the old self with its conventions and expectations and open up to the new. More of us need to incorporate the message and style of the clown as we age."

Michael Erlanger, businessman and poet, is an outstanding example of the power of family influence to both harm and to foster human development. He was born in New York City to well-to-do parents who had inherited a textile company from immigrant forebears. His memory of childhood was that of a lonely boy taken care of by governesses, while his parents pursued their outside interests: his mother in theater, his father with the family business. His mother was frequently depressed in a dysfunctional family situation. Michael was sent away to school at age twelve where he discovered anti-Semitism as the only Jew in an exclusive institution. It was a rigid school with no room for creativity. During his six years there, the sense of loneliness and alienation, begun in his family milieu, intensified. During these first two decades of life, he remembers one aunt as the only person "who really cared about me."

At the University of North Carolina, he majored in English "and loved it." This immersion in literature tapped into a deep dimension of his soul, but he wasn't yet able to honor the artistic penchant in himself. "In college, I drank too much, drove too much, and got in with the wrong crowd," he says. After two years in Chapel Hill, he drifted through other schools without much motivation. At Ohio State he majored in animal husbandry, again evoking his deep love of animals, especially horses. But after a stint in the army during World War II, he largely closed off his artistic side to enter the family textile business as the only sensible way to get ahead. It was an important turning point for him. "I realized that I wouldn't get anywhere as the literary person I was. I adapted to the business world and became more conservative."

His marriage to Mary Erlanger would eventually lead him to a second great turning point in his life. The daughter of a Kansas minister, Mary experienced a stable and loving family situation. In addition to raising two children, she has had a career in journalism and much later in counseling, receiving her doctorate from the University of Georgia at age sixty-five. Michael became the chief officer of the family business, driving himself in the business world despite two heart attacks in the early sixties. His literary inclination was never completely suppressed as he managed to publish two novels during these years.

But what was to be a major change in his life came in 1980 when he underwent a quadruple heart-bypass operation. He ended up in a coma for nine days, "dead three times, resuscitated three times." When he woke up from the coma, his family was at his bedside. "All of a sudden for the first time in my life," he says, "I realized I was loved because of me, and not because of anything I could do or give. I was just loved because I was me. And I realized I loved them because they were they, and there were no strings attached to the love." This was very new for him, because "I was brought up with strings attached to everything."

After this surgery, he and Mary became involved in dream groups that further unleashed his creativity and brought new insights about his childhood. He was able via dream work to understand and make peace with incidents of sexual abuse and violence in childhood. During his retirement years, he has published poetry, become an accomplished painter, and has written a play that has been produced. Mary and Michael Erlanger attribute much of their creativity in later life to the friendship, trust, and respect that their marriage has generated. For Michael especially, the relationship has been a catalyst for becoming the person he was meant to be, untapping the creative potential that had been suppressed by the wounds of childhood. Looking back on his life, he says: "If I had it to do over again, I'd devote more of it to raising and working with animals."

Becoming One's Own Person

As we saw in the case of Michael Erlanger, one's family of origin and one's marital family can profoundly influence transitions in the aging process. The following three women portray different modes of finding their true selves and callings in the give-and-take of marital situations.

In some ways, Elise Boulding, who emigrated from Norway when she was three, was destined to be a peace organizer and advocate. Her mother was a pacifist who marched in demonstrations and wrote plays about peace themes. Elise grew up hearing about the horrors of gassing and trench slaughter in the First World War. Just as children later had a fear of nuclear war, so she was frightened as a child by fantasies of being gassed. She had also constructed a safe haven for herself, imagining that she would flee to the mountains of Norway to hide from gas attacks. But during her senior year in college, Norway was invaded by the Germans. She had lost her safe refuge from war. This was an early turning point for her, as she realized in a profound way that there was to be no safe place. "I understood then that the only way we were going to have safe places would be to create them." She also came to see, partly through the influence of Norman Thomas who spoke on campus, that fashioning communities safe for life was closely connected with overcoming social injustices.

Elise, the eldest of three sisters, spent her earliest years in a stable family in a lower middle-class section of Hillside, New Jersey. She remembers her father as a warm, affectionate parent who focused much attention on his children. Her mother, though less affectionate ("I recall being on her lap only once"), was close to Elise "in every other way." Her mother developed something of a martyr complex, she says, but Elise felt that her father did not really appreciate her mother's situation. Elise became aware early of inequities in male-female relations. But her parents were very supportive of her education, eager for her to succeed, "which I mostly did." Elise Boulding's religious life, an important aspect of her later career, was nurtured in the context of her father's Scandanavian piety. Although her mother didn't believe in God, her father was deeply religious. His father had expected him to become a Lutheran pastor and gave him a family Bible from which her father read aloud on special occasions.

When Elise graduated from Rutgers, she went to work for a publishing house in New York, but she didn't like the environment, because she felt she was losing her values. She moved on to Syracuse University for graduate work where she met her husband, Kenneth, at a Friends' meeting. In keeping with her peace and nonviolence perspective, she had begun to attend Quaker meetings while at Douglass College of Rutgers. Kenneth Boulding was already a well-known economist and Quaker minister when they were introduced in the lunch line after the service. When she heard him talk during the service, she remembered him saying something about loving one's wife and children. "Oh dear," she said to herself, "he must be married." It turned out to be a happy misapprehension, and they were engaged in eighteen days.

For the next two decades, Boulding combined intense family dedication, raising five children, with community building through the Society of Friends. She does not think of her years in the home as unconnected with wider social purposes. "Childrearing," she says, "meant that the home was the center for wider community action and peace work. I was intimately rooted in family life and in my parenting role." But gradually she began to see that she was living too much in the shadow of a famous husband. He traveled widely for public speaking. As she tired of "standing outside of Kenneth's circle of admirers," Elise thought that she was sacrificing her own sense of identity. She began to feel frustration at having to carry so much of the childrearing responsibilities.

A crucial turning point for her came in the mid-fifties when they were living in Palo Alto. She was feeling depressed about the state of the world. "I seem to remember deciding that I would live as long as I needed to see my youngest child to independence, and that was it." Their house guest at the time was a Dutch historian who had just written an award-winning book about imaging the future. Boulding found that with some language study she could read the book in Dutch, and she decided to translate it into English. "Up to that point in life," she says, "I knew I was an intelligent person and a reasonable companion for Kenneth. But I had a feeling of awe for the high-powered intellects continually surrounding me." The process of translating the book required that she read more history and philosophy. "I realized that I, too, was an intellectual." This awareness motivated her to return to school for a doctorate in sociology and to shape a very signficant career on her own, outside of the shadow of her economist husband. She developed ideas that would be in strong contrast to those of her husband on such topics as the reasons for world poverty. "He was my teacher in the beginning because I didn't know enough," she says, "but eventually when it came to interpreting events, we went in opposite directions. I've been living in creative conflict with Kenneth Boulding for many decades."

Just as Elise Boulding had to struggle through familial issues to find her personal potential in the realms of academia and peace work, June Singer had an upward climb toward success as a Jungian analyst. Singer is well known for her writings, especially since the publication of her widely read primer to Jungian psychology, *Boundaries of the Soul*. Her father, a "solemn man," had less influence on her than her journalist mother who was "innovative and exciting." In an odd way, her mother contributed to her writing career by helping her in a writing contest in the sixth grade. June won the award, but she felt like a fraud. "I think that for many years after that I did my writing to prove that I could do it on my own."

Later when she wanted to become a physician, she heard the culturally conditioned negatives from her father: "You mean a nurse, don't you, dear?" When she said no to nursing, she found that the "only other respectable thing a girl could do was teach." She took a degree in education, even though she didn't want to become a teacher. "But at least it got me through college." She was also to be helped later as a Jungian therapist because she ended up majoring in literature and art. When Singer reflects on people of special influence in her early life, she remembers Uncle George, a professed atheist, who lived in the north woods of Wisconsin with a wolf as a pet. As an impressionable girl, she was thoroughly convinced by her uncle that atheism and communism "were the way to go." She would eventually question these dictates, but what is more significant about Uncle George was his lesson on being oneself. She learned that she could be different, that she could tap into what she truly wanted to be in spite of conventional mores.

The endeavor to become herself according to inner impulses is more clearly seen in the course of her marital life to a rabbi-psychologist. "I was very much in the background almost all the way through the marriage. I felt very insecure," she says. Her husband became interested in psychology, doing a doctorate at Northwestern, and later he enrolled at the Jung Institute in Zurich. After recovering from a debilitating illness in her thirties, Singer was told by her husband that in Zurich she was not to attend the Jung Institute, although she had previously enrolled in a psychology master's program at Northwestern. But Singer was learning to listen to her unconscious. "If the unconscious says you should enter the training program, my husband had nothing to say. You don't argue with the unconscious at the Jung Institute." Most of her career attainments as analyst and author came well into midlife.

Singer speaks of Esther Harding, a pioneer Jungian analyst, as a most important catalyst for her own development. Harding "took her under her wing" and helped her to explore the connection between her femininity and her own inwardness. Singer's accomplishments in Chicago were remarkable. She was one of the leading founders of the Jung Institute of Chicago and became something of a mother figure for analysts in the area. "I was a goddess when things went well, but a devouring mother when they didn't," she says. In spite of her attainments, she was discouraged from pursuing a doctorate in psychology by educators at Northwestern. Again, she followed her inner voice and completed a doctoral degree, although she was denied financial aid at the university because of her age and gender.

Against the various forms of discouragement in family life, Singer has tried to be faithful to her inner calling. She speaks of trying to respect a certain destiny or endowment within us that many people stifle or allow society to crush. "We have a kind of direction," she says, "that we're supposed to go in. Like a tomato plant; it's supposed to produce tomatoes. It isn't going to produce pears or peaches. We have certain seeds in us, like divine sparks that reside in the human spirit. Our task is to liberate them." June Singer has had to face intense losses in the course of attempting to live according to her inner potential. She had to deal with shock and loneliness when her husband died suddenly. Her greatest loss was the death of a daughter, her only child. "I learned to cope with despair and aloneness," she says. The greatest turning points of her life happened in the context of those losses. She came to creative solutions concerning these deaths through her own inner work, finding unconscious resources to support self-acceptance and "going it alone."

To evolve out of a family of origin and through marital families to become one's own person takes many forms. For Norma Levitt this process had a good deal to do with learning to listen to her own intuitions about people and money matters. She remembers her childhood as free and privileged in the home of a lawyer father and a mother who taught school until Norma was born. Home life for her and her brother was stable with reliable parents. They were affectionate with her but not overtly with each other. Norma recalls herself as a model child conforming to the expectations of her parents, just as her rather formal mother (who always dressed up when her father came home) adapted to the conventions of an upper middle-class matron. Only later in life would Norma learn that the conformist pattern set for women in her childhood would need to be broken.

Married at twenty-one, she had to fashion new ways, very different from those of her mother, to balance child care with an intense desire for involvements outside the home. She had experienced wider interests from childhood when at the age of ten she was excused from school to do a project with the League of Nations. As a young mother with three children in a space of four years, she had to shape new modes of child care while she continued to involve herself in religious and political activities. Moreover, her husband's work in the sugar industry meant travel for the family as they lived in different parts of the country. During World War II, he was frequently away from home. With full responsibility for her children, she realized that she "couldn't just contine to search for her own will and way." She speaks of these years as a time of tension between childrearing responsibilities and significant involvements in organizations.

Many of these activities had to do with Reformed Judaism and with the United Nations. Coming from a relatively secular home, she had little knowledge of her own religious tradition until she began to study it seriously as a young wife. She eventually organized and led Jewish study groups in comparative religions, and she wrote new liturgies and prayers that have been published nationally. She has held leading roles in Jewish women's groups. Other interests have been interreligious and international, such as planning an environmental sabbath which was adopted by the U.N. in conjunction with Earth Day. Norma Levitt has discovered that becoming her own person is closely linked with being able to express her beliefs and convictions through her work.

Another important dimension of discovering her own potential relates to financial problems that struck Norma's family in recent years. After selling his own business, her husband lost a great deal of money through dealings with unscrupulous persons. Levitt speaks of the last decade as a traumatic time, not only because of the financial losses, but also because of illnesses and accidents. She has had a third hip surgery and her husband has suffered various ailments. At one point she had to take over the family finances, a turning-point experience in her life. She has had to reassess a simpler confidence in her husband's abilities. "I wouldn't choose to go through all this again, but I learned a lot," she says. "For a long time, I was very fearful and angry. Now I see my husband more realistically. I've stopped being the little girl who transferred her wonderful view of daddy to her husband, who would take care of everything." Her socialization taught her to leave finances to men. Now she wishes that she had managed her own accounts from the beginning. "I think little girls in this country should get household and financial training."

In her mid-seventies, Norma Levitt looks back on a continuing search to become the full person of which she is capable. In part this journey of self-discovery has been in reaction to the ways of women inherited from her mother. In part it has also been responding to new challenges. "The effort that it takes to express who I am has been there all the time," she says. "It's often hard to make that effort, but I can't think of not making it." She speaks of preparing for old age not in a formal sense, but by doing at each stage of life whatever expresses her deeper self. In her earlier years, it was harder to find that authenticity of person, because she was too concerned about what others thought of her. Now her vision of self and others is clearer.

Summary Reflections

We have looked briefly at elders reflecting on the importance of their family lives, both in childhood and as adults. Some had to overcome the odds of social and economic hardship. When we think about the negative aspects of Ross Gritts's early life—orphanage, prejudice, and addiction—we are reminded of possible pitfalls in our own youth. With a few changed circumstances, we might have taken a different route in life. We might also be able, like Gritts, to remember one or other family member who encouraged the fulfillment of a crucial dimension of our character that we would cultivate only much later. Despite the experience of poverty and racial prejudice in childhood, Gertrude Wilks was able to build on the heritage of a strong mother and father, even in the face of many adversities in her own married life. What are the traits of our families of origin that have sustained us in difficult times?

Other elders experienced difficult family situations in their formative years or in their own marriages. Perhaps like Lillian Rabinowitz, our thoughts of childhood and of our later marriages evoke painful memories. Yet other events in her life elicited deeper personal resources within. Some of us have had similar problematic family lives. We might reflect on the happenings and people who acted as substitute families for our own growth toward richer elderhood. Clara Crook reminds us that even in difficult marital situations, we manage to learn something very important about ourselves. How many readers can relate to such discoveries about themselves in similar conditions? Perhaps, like Virginia Davis, we have lived too long with an irremediable family situation. Have we like her learned to integrate such mistakes into a wider context of creativity, letting go of long-held fears for a more hopeful life? Gregory Bergman's childhood tells us that even illness and alienation can be integrated into a pattern of creativity. Had he not personally experienced injustices as a boy, he might not have become the later advocate for a more just society. How have our own illnesses and encounters with injustice shaped the future direction of our lives?

Still others were blessed by family milieus to be able to find their true potential. Certainly this would be true of Patty Crowley whose marriage was positive both in terms of its inner life and also in light of her long collaboration with her husband in the CFM. Yet her family life continued to grow in new ways after her spouse's death. We might ask ourselves whether our family lives have been too static, too bounded by the limited concerns of the nuclear family. How ready are we in elderhood to extend our families to include people and causes that we hadn't embraced earlier? Rose Lucey offers another instance of a good marriage that blossomed not only in offspring but also in vital social commitments. It can be helpful to reflect on how our closest relationships helped or hindered our expansion into a creative elderhood.

Yet even in the latter examples of good relationships, family memories are not without pain. Michael Erlanger's experience of unconditional love from his family at the time of surgery caused him to understand by contrast his unloving circumstances in childhood. Lin Ludy's fruitful marriage contrasted with her fragile environment in childhood when she had to live away from her only parent. Ludy and Erlanger had to learn, early and late, to let go of idealized expectations and make their peace with things as they are. How well have we come to terms with our clinging to false expectations of how things should have been concerning our families of origin and our marital relationships?

In different ways, the last three elders in this chapter highlight the ambiguous tensions of family commitment and the discovery of their own vocations in life. All three had to balance family nurturance with a struggle to develop careers outside the home. Elise Boulding emerges from the shadow of her famous husband to pursue her own dedication to scholarship and peace work. June Singer follows the directives of her unconscious, overcoming obstacles to becoming a Jungian analyst. And Norma Levitt rises beyond her early family conditioning to develop her talent as a religious leader. These three impel us to reflect on the polarities in our own value systems as we try to balance the realm of intimacy with worldly enterprises. They also invite us to ponder the sacrifices and the "trade-offs" in our choice of involvements. What contributes most to the unfolding of our fullest potential, both for self-development and outward service?

Yet whatever the blend of negatives and positives in our family histories, integrating these experiences into our becoming identities as elders is very important. There is no one way to become more whole. Surely, experiences of authentic love at various points in our journeys are crucial for each of us. And we can take courage in seeing the resiliency and multifaceted coping skills that creative elders reveal in expanding their lives. Perhaps the most significant aspect of these stories is the varied process of integrating family histories into making sense of ourselves in old age. It is important to do the work of reweaving the inherited tapestry to understand ourselves. In the next chapter, we continue to explore this process more directly in terms of working lives and major turning points.

CHAPTER 2

Learning from Work and from Turning Points

We spend a large portion of our lives at work, whether it be working at home or at an outside job. Many studies confirm the close relationship, especially for men, between self-esteem and some measure of success in the world of work. With the substantial increase of women in careers outside the home, it is likely that their professional and occupational lives will impact significantly on their personal self-respect. Women who have lived more traditional lives as homemakers and mothers, often joined to volunteer activities in the community, also need to take stock of all those years as constituting their working lives. Our task, then, as elders becomes one of making sense of our work choices and endeavors. Our work has helped to shape us into the persons we have become. The creative elders in this book explore the benefits and debits of their jobs and other activities. They watch for turning points in life that may have redirected their careers. And above all, these older persons want to understand how their work experiences and their turning points have prepared them for valuable contributions in later life.

Balancing Home and Career

The older women participants in this project were often fore-runners of the contemporary phenomenon of working women. Of course, women have always worked very hard in the home as well as outside. Nor do we mean to disparage women who have lived mainly as wives and mothers. Their contributions to the welfare of families and children are inestimable. But the following women who joined home and outside work in various combinations through the years give us lively examples for reflection. They are early models for a growing cohort of working women. Some of them worked outside the home nearly all their lives; others linked traditional roles with partial outside activities and eventually moved into second careers. Yet all of them had to stand against the tide of convention, which was less willing to accept the place of women in occupations and professions.

Charlee Lambert's passage into creative elderhood exemplifies the difficult tension experienced by women of her generation to balance a troubled marriage, childrearing, and an outside career. A specialist in elder abuse and other problems of older people, Lambert has also written over twenty plays of an educational nature, focusing on social problems and health issues. She has had to learn how to write grant proposals, operate agencies for the elderly on soft money, and stay a step ahead of local politicians in Georgia. She married early to a man who later developed problems with which she couldn't cope. She raised six children in a marriage of forty-two years that ended in divorce. Although she had to make a living on her own after the break, her involvements outside the home began years before, moving from volunteer work toward a more specialized career in aging.

As her children grew toward adulthood, she schooled herself for a career in the field of aging. Since she had majored in theater in college, she was able to use that knowledge in shaping a second career. For Lambert, an important turning point happened in the early seventies. On a retreat in Michigan, she helped organize a worship service on "rediscovering our lives." This event led to her returning to college against the wishes of her husband. He saw this move as the end of their marriage, because "she was out of [his] control, and was defining herself as a unique individual," she says. Lambert blames the mentality of the fifties in large part for restricting women's options in the world. In the thirties and forties, women were needed in the labor force, either for economic reasons during the Depression or for patriotic reasons during World War II. "We were taught to be useful in that earlier time," she says. "I took a course in automobile mechanics; after the war, we were confined to the kitchen. I wish I hadn't let myself be hyped so completely into the family-children syndrome of the Eisenhower years . . . because I knew better."

Lambert wrote and directed a series of short plays on elder abuse for the education of older people and professionals in aging. She talks about taking these shows on the road to various corners of Georgia and beyond. Gradually she became well known as a communicator and organizer in the aging field. She sees herself "as a kind of hub or clearing house for getting older people the help they need." Sometimes this can be information about health care or legal assistance or hospice arrangements; other times it can involve specific aid in cases of elder abuse. From her concrete experiences with frail older people, she has deepened her knowledge about the financial, emotional, psychological, and physical dimensions of elder abuse, a topic little discussed in public until recently.

Reflecting back on her long, rocky marriage and her ventures into a career, Charlee Lambert says: "Never be dependent on one person only." She further explains that we shouldn't expect one person to fulfill all our needs. "He fulfilled my play and provider needs, but he couldn't be there for my deeper emotional needs; they were too scary for him." She balances her assessment of the long marriage by insisting that she learned many things as the wife of a corporate climber in the automotive world, things that would prove very useful in her own career endeavors. "It's never all black and white; you learn a lot about people by playing hostess for a corporate official," she says, "but I wish I had spent more time on my needs rather than his career." Although raising teenagers in the late sixties "was grounds enough for divorce," Lambert also marvels at the way her grown children tend to repeat different styles of family-work modeling in their own lives. The older ones seem to replicate the earlier years of the marriage when things were better in the home. The younger children seem to have taken on some of the traits Charlee Lambert developed in her more career-oriented period. "One of my daughters has a corporate executive husband who is away a good deal; she has learned to compensate her needs in other ways," she says.

Barbara Payne-Stancil became an accomplished gerontologist and the founder of the gerontology center at Georgia State University. But her road to a successful career ran through the very difficult terrain of being married to a troubled husband for thirty years. Her first marriage began by eloping at seventeen, an action that alienated her from her parents for some time. Payne-Stancil remembers the trauma of her parents refusing to let her back into the house to collect her clothing and possessions. Barbara learned about the "trials of loving people" and the pain of being rejected by those who loved her. The rift with her parents would eventually be healed, but her struggle to pursue an education in a household with two children and a manic husband persisted. His moods could be explosive and turn physically abusive or they could be moderate, even benevolent. Part of the constant stress was living with his unpredictability, especially later in the marriage when he turned to alcohol. Payne-Stancil reflects on the questionable set of convictions that kept her going during all those years: that faith and love would overcome deep-seated problems, that one just stuck it out despite incompatibilities. When she spoke to a minister about divorce, she told him that such a break would be like death. But the minister responded that "death comes in other ways, too." She realized that he referred to the demise of her self-worth in a destructive relationship.

But Barbara Payne-Stancil enjoyed other resources that compensated for family difficulties in her pursuit of an impressive career. From childhood, her mother had surrounded her with books and encouraged the bright youngster to excel in school. Her involvement in the Methodist Church became a powerful source of support for her continuing education and for her life during the hard times. Both of her grandfathers were well-known Methodist preachers and church leaders in Georgia. The first decade of her working life was devoted to the church where she served as director of adult education in north Georgia. But her strongest resource was the unique combination of qualities in her personality: determination, intelligence, and organization. She fostered a great desire for education by organizing her college and graduate work around family responsibilites. She had a hard time persuading a men's college to give her a degree, and she held out against faculty who thought she was too old for a doctorate.

An important turning point that influenced her career was a brief but very positive marriage to Ray Payne, a social psychologist at the University of Georgia. "Living with Ray before his sudden death," she says, "was a two and a half year seminar in personal and professional creativeness for me." He helped her shape important sociological studies in aging that were to bear fruit after his death. But in conjunction with such intellectual stimulation, "Ray helped me heal myself," she says. "He taught me not to put myself down in light of the first marriage. I thought it was my fault, that I had failed God." He helped her to see the circumstances of that first marriage differently, and more importantly, he assisted her to like herself. Although his death was a great shock, Barbara Payne-Stancil says that she grew in unforeseen ways as a publishing scholar and as a person in the years that followed that relationship. At seventy, she retired from her professorship and is now involved in still another phase of marriage and career. Her present husband is a state politician. "I'm taking up a new direction on public policy in aging," she says. Now the state legislature has become the focal point of her energy.

At seventy-seven Vera O'Keefe walks with a cane to the medical placement office she started in Atlanta nearly three decades ago. She sees herself as a conservative Catholic on the political right. A career focus has been important to her since her youth in New York City, where she experienced her mother's economic hardships after the early death of her father. She remembers her mother's hard work for meager wages. "She chose to clean public schools so that she could keep the same hours we children had," she says. "She could be home with and for us." For years O'Keefe worked as a licensed practical nurse, "attending to some wonderful older people who taught me a lot about life." She shared her income with her mother and siblings. She married "too quickly" in 1943 when young men and women had little chance to get to know one another; her new husband was soon off to war.

O'Keefe's reflections on her working life reveal a two-sided motivational pattern. From one perspective, it was a way, after her one son was raised, to escape the confines of an unhappy marriage. She sees her husband, though relatively successful in his work life, as an emotionally damaged person in part because of traumas suffered in war. Out of his insecurities, she says, he needed to dominate, even to denigrate. "I would have gone insane if I hadn't gotten out of that context." Work became an important mode of psychological survival and a way of not succumbing to resentment. But O'Keefe's medical-placement business seems to be driven by much more positive motives. "I love the interchange with people," she says. In the workplace she is free to be herself, to make her own mistakes, to set and achieve goals. But she underlines the motif of delight, of fun in her work. "I do it for love more than money," she says. "When people respond to me, I'm uplifted, I'm connected. . . . You know, I give to you and you give to me."

One gets the impression that, despite her religious and political conservatism, she can be surprisingly self-critical and willing to grow to new levels of maturity. Showing no sense of victimization, she says she probably should have divorced her husband long ago. She points to mistakes she made in raising her only son. But she has learned that she can't change other people. "I can hardly change myself," she says. But she keeps open to such change in herself through psychological and spiritual readings. For example, the writings of Norman Vincent Peale have been influential for her. She also continues her involvement with self-help groups. "They are helping me find out how to be less codependent," she says. Her combination of family problems and work involvements has taught her to be more patient and understanding in later life. But her work life outside the home has become the context for her expansive spirit in later life.

Just as it doesn't take extraordinary intuition to detect an extroverted type personality in Vera O'Keefe, Lillian Schacht-Lavine comes across as a true introvert in the Jungian typology. This may seem strange for a woman who in her youth wanted to be an actress and gave up that pursuit for a long, stable marriage. After acting, her second love was flying airplanes; for a brief period, she became a flight attendant for Eastern. Later in life, when her three children were older and more independent, she returned to her early inclinations, but in a different way. In middle age she turned the yen for acting inward, returning to school to achieve a doctorate in communication arts, especially in psychodrama. Her flying became inward and imaginative, as she explored new territories of dream and myth. She enjoys individual counseling with others as well as teaching classes on finding one's inner world.

But her own needs motivated this late-life career. "I'm a classic Jungian example," she says. "Home and children, a good marriage . . . all these satisfied my emotional needs as a young woman. But at thirty-nine I longed to investigate another side of myself: the mental, imaginative, inward self. I wanted to find out about myself at a deeper, individual level." She also speaks of this turn as finding out that she had a brain and could use it. Or she talks about it as moving from being chiefly a family caregiver to becoming a seeker after her own truth. She didn't need to make this move for financial reasons. It was just not enough for her to be wife and mother. "I needed to succeed in something I chose outside the family," she says. "I was searching for my own self-worth outside of domestic conventions." Her goals are not money or fame. "My goal is to be a wise old woman and share that with others," she says. Lavine criticizes society's age-old way of restricting women to roles of serving others, defining themselves almost totally by external standards. She points to Eastern spiritualities that counsel us to serve and explore ourselves in later life as the right road to wisdom and as a preparation for death.

By her own account, Lillian Lavine was fortunate to have a supportive marriage "between two strong people who loved each other and really strove to make things work out." She finds that her interests outside the home made life easier for her husband, who had to be away on business for long stretches. He was relieved of the burden of worrying about her as an abandoned and bored woman confined to the house, harboring resentments about his worldly life. As he came closer to retirement, her interests sparked banked fires in him. In recent years, he has been able to express his nurturing, domestic side through art and gardening. He has also become involved in coordinating a senior eduction program. Mutual respect and letting each other be free are the qualities she says have contributed to a marriage that supported different career lines. "We remain individuals together."

Balancing career and family on the way to a creative elderhood manifests no single pattern. Some persons have accomplished such a journey out of difficult marital situations; others in cooperative husband-wife relations. Sometimes important turning points mark the path in visible ways, such as Lambert's retreat experience in Michigan or Lavine's powerful awareness in midlife that a whole side of herself remained unexplored. In other cases, new paths open up subtly, as with O'Keefe, without detectable shifts of direction. Ella Mazel offers still another example of an elder who has managed to combine a business out of her home with a successful family life.

Yet with Mazel, even more dramatically than with Lavine, certain psychological events occurred in her life that indirectly but powerfully affected her family relations and her work as an editor and designer of books. A shy and silent child, she was nurtured in a hardworking, intellectual family of Jewish immigrants from Eastern Europe. She describes her family as Socialists and agnostics who were not emotionally demonstrative, but who gave her much "backbone" and a sense of independence. "I was raised to take care of myself, not to depend on a man," she says. "It was understood that I would go to work after schooling and contribute to the family. If I got married, fine. If I didn't, fine. I was the only girl I knew who had that attitude."

Ella and Bernie Mazel married in 1942; from the start she collaborated with him in his book-publishing ventures. In 1948 with the arrival of the first of four children, she continued her editorial and book-designing work at home, a task she continues to this day. The great mental trauma of her life was the sudden death of her brother, Harry, when she was thirty-one. "The death of my brother changed my attitude toward life and death," she says. Ella describes this major turning point as a profound realization that "life is an accident; death is an accident. The things you worry about and plan for are less likely to happen than the things you never worry about." Although Mazel's tradition is Jewish, this insight and what follows from it is a core Buddhist awareness about the impermanence and transience of life. Her application of the insight to her own life also echoes the disciplines of Buddhism. "So I've had that philosophy," she says, ". . . really, it's a very good way to live because you're less likely to be disappointed if you don't count on things to be a certain way. You can't count on anything." Again, we hear the voice of the Buddha warning us to stop clinging to false expectations if we would free ourselves for peaceful living.

But just as in Buddhism, simple awareness of something doesn't of itself change a person. One must walk the path through moral and meditative experiences to change interiorly toward living with wisdom. So, too, for Ella Mazel, the shock of Harry's death eventually impelled her into a four-year journey of psychoanalysis. She went into analysis "totally inhibited" and suffering from chronic depression. In analysis she learned in a very personal way how many decisions are governed by unconscious forces within us. "I don't exactly know how or why it worked," she says, but her analyst was guiding her toward self-knowledge and healing. "Treatment with him was different than just talking to any old good listener," she adds. "I came out a different person. I was freed up. Anyone who got to know me only after analysis would find it hard to believe what I was like before." She speaks of that change impacting on every aspect of her life: wife, colleague, mother, book-specialist, mother-in-law, friend, and grandmother.

Combining work and home life needed compromises and wasn't without problems for Mazel. "I just had to work on projects that interested my mind," she says. "I just couldn't be a full-time mother." She admits that she was helped with family chores by paid domestics and by the support of her husband. But she had to confront the displeasure of her youngest daughter who wanted her mother's attention as soon as she got home from school. "Just one minute," she would tell the girl, who walked away angry because of the delay in attention. Ella would explain to her daughter that we needed to do work that was important and enjoyable to us. Later the same daughter became a feminist and has come to understand her mother's need to "follow my life." Mazel has not only accomplished much in publishing from producing a nationally successful college directory to her present editing of the diaries and letters of Anne Morrow Lindbergh. "I always have to have a project," she says. But following her desire, she claims, has also had a positive effect on family life. She reports that recently her whole family, including grandchildren, spent a week together, "and we all had a great time."

Following the Long Career

Some elders can look back on careers that flow from childhood influences, but eventually take new directions within the same river-bed, as it were. Turning points may not be dramatic in such lives, but they are significant, resembling boulders in a stream that divert the flow in unexpected ways. Eugene P. Odum is an internationally recognized ecologist, member of the National Academy of Science, and founder of the Institute of Ecology at the University of Georgia. Moving into his ninth decade, he can remember the early influences that led him into academia. His father had a distinquished career as a sociologist in the early part of this century, and authored a widely recognized book on southern regionalism. In his youthful days, Eugene Odum did not aspire to be a professor, although he was interested in natural science from childhood. He loved the woods and spent much time outdoors with special fascination for ornithology. His father encouraged him to pursue his interests in science, even though Eugene was uncomfortable with the narrow focus of biology at the time. It seemed isolated from the wider network of ecosystems. An early turning point for Odum happened during the thirties when he was completing a doctorate at the University of Illinois. There a new approach to community ecology opened his eyes to the broad study of biosystems.

After a stint as a naturalist in land preservation in New York State, Odum began his long career at the University of Georgia in 1940. He was impressed by the higher quality of students after the Second World War, but he remained frustrated by the tight confines of academic biology. "They laughed at me when I talked about ecology in the biology department," he says. He recalls a colleague saying to him: "We didn't mean to hurt your feelings, but what is ecology?" That event led Odum to write his landmark 1953 book on ecosystems, a text that became widely used in subsequent years. Another turning point occurred in the late fifties when he was on research leave in England. He thought the department was committed to hiring someone in an ecologically related field. When he returned, he found that the new faculty person was a specialist in an entirely different area. Disappointment because of these two "put-downs," as Odum calls them, led to a major career turning point. Odum became convinced that the only way to preserve and develop ecology amid academic turf wars was to found an institute for environmental studies at the university. His success in this venture is a testament to his distinction as a scholar and his impressive leadership abilities in raising funds and building an interdisciplinary faculty in ecology.

Odum presents an excellent example of an elder whose career has kept expanding in ever-wider circles. He pioneered ecosystem ecology under the phrase "integrative science." From the start, he viewed science in a holistic and global way. "We have to change the way we think about things," he says, explaining that we must grasp the interfacing between human needs and environmental values. He compares the relationship between earth and humanity to a host and its parasite, the latter dependent on its host for resources. "In nature, a parasite does not usually destroy its host. Hosts and parasites develop reciprocal relations insuring that both survive," he says. He insists that without healthy natural systems to support human industrial, urban, and agricultural activities, there can be no healthy economy nor a high-level quality of life. He stresses that we should learn to look long-term and prepare to live in a world of limited resources. Contrary to the naive view of competitive nature, red in tooth and claw, he underscores the cooperative dimensions of natural evolution. Sometimes referred to as "the father of modern ecology," he received the Crafoord Prize from the Royal Swedish Academy, an award regarded as equivalent to the Nobel Prize.

Since his retirement in 1984, Odum has extended his career into broader public circles. "I now see myself as a missionary preaching ecology to anyone who will listen," he says. He understands the role of senior scientist as sharing what he has learned from research with other academic fields and especially with society at large. "My classroom is a lot bigger and more important now because I am trying to teach the world," he says. In the style of a southern preacher, this sophisticated scientist uses familiar biblical language about moving from dominion toward stewardship to illumine unfamiliar ecological ideas. His writing has shifted toward popular books, exemplified by his latest work, a completely nontechnical layman's guide tentatively called "Our Big House: Understanding Ecology." Another aspect of Odum's work today brings full circle the sociological analysis of Southern regions done by his father in the thirties. The son in his elderhood moves beyond sociological exploration to study ecosystems in the South, such as marshes and wetlands, challenged by demographic and commercial problems.

One of Eugene Odum's driving insights is applicable not only to ecology but also to one's career in elderhood: "An ecosystem is greater than the sum of its parts." This statement means envisioning one's life whole, to understand how the often ambiguous events fit together into a pattern, a living mosaic. It is from such an insight that an elder can collect skills and wisdom from his or her past to mentor a wider public.

One of the most eminent scholars in the field of aging, Bernice Neugarten reflects on her own long career at the University of Chicago and Northwestern University. Her life is in important ways an example of the unpredictability and diversity that she wrote about in her lifespan psychology of aging. Her father, fleeing from a persecution of Jews in Lithuania (he witnessed his own father killed at the hands of a drunken soldier), ventured away from ethnic enclaves in America, ending up in the small town of Norfolk, Nebraska. This salesman and wool merchant encouraged his precociously bright daughter to pursue her education. "When I was eleven," she says, "my school superintendent told me that I should go to the University of Chicago." At the end of high school, she remembered his counsel and by a stroke of fortune was able to board with a friend of the family in Chicago and accompany his daughter to the university. This unpredictable happening was preceded by another. It was understood by the five Jewish families of Norfolk that Bernice would marry Leo, a Jewish youth who attended the University of Nebraska, where she planned to go. But he was killed suddenly in an auto accident when she was sixteen. This tragedy forced her to reexamine the future.

Most of her life and academic career has been spent in the Hyde Park area of the University of Chicago. It was there that she met her husband and raised two children, while launching the new field of adult development and aging. Again, a chance occurence propelled her into a very significant career. In 1952 she was asked to take over a course on maturity and old age, then a unique course in American universities. "I was equally well prepared to teach a course on childhood or adolescence," she says, "and if somebody asked me to teach one of those courses, my subsequent career would have been different." Yet the unpredictability of life also entails opportunity or possibility. Neugarten was among the early scholars who understood the "demographic imperative" of longer lifespans in the second half of the century and the impact this would have in personal, family, and public arenas.

The sense of unpredictability also undergirds one of Neugarten's scholarly contributions in aging having to do with diversity. Her research led her to criticize popular theories of predictable life-stages. Although Neugarten agrees that societies establish certain age-appropriate time lines over the life cycle, the aging sequence toward maturity in individuals remains very diverse. Her findings also contradict earlier assumptions that personality is formed in childhood and remains largely the same throughout life. "Yet I look around today," she says, "and see so many older, vigorous people doing all kinds of things they would never have predicted earlier." Neugarten's work on personality changes and diverse patterns in aging underscores new options for people as they alter directions within a career or shift toward new callings in later life.

Like Eugene Odum, Bernice Neugarten has received numerous honors for her contributions to the psychological, sociological, and public-policy areas of aging. But for these scholars, the plaudits accompanying a stellar career, while pleasant, are not what counts in the long run. Both of these elders find deeper meaning in how their careers helped others and continue to influence society. Odum directs this altruism toward wider education of the pubic about ecology; Neugarten displays her altruism in the great gratification she takes in having mentored so many students in the field of aging. "I enjoyed getting a national teaching award in 1975," she says, "but my real gratification is in my students. That's where my heart is. Every student was important to me. They had to write the best dissertation they were capable of." Surely, she enjoyed the scholarly achievements of a career that has spanned a half century. But the most enduring benefits of her life's work, on her own account, "was being invested in other people. The best thing was the inter-personal ties, feeling invested in other persons' welfare . . . not just witnessing it, but actively fostering wholeness in another individual," she says.

Like Neugarten, Martin Marty's life began in a small Nebraska town and eventually expanded into a remarkable career at the University of Chicago. His maternal grandfather fled conscription into the Franco-Prussian War and migrated to the Midwest. Again, we see the theme of moving to America to avoid political oppression and to seek a freer life. Marty's description of his parents character-izes in important ways aspects of his own personality and lays the groundwork for his career as a leading church historian. With only eight years of formal schooling, his mother was well-read, retentive, and "quite a feminist." As a historian, Marty reveals a capacious memory for details and events; he also stands on the liberal wing of Protestant intellectuals. His mother brought the play element into the family. "During the Depression," he says, "she provided lots of beer, wine, and cards." Anyone who knows "Marty," even in a professional way, recognizes his humor and the warm twinkle in his eyes.

His father's side of the family was Swiss-German, and by his description "solid, stolid, squat, sober, and straight." His father gave up the option for a large farm and chose a college education, becoming a Lutheran school teacher, organist, and kindly discipli-narian. He was Martin's classroom teacher for four years. In addi-tion to his father's friendliness, Martin inherited a strong sense of religious tradition and a trustworthiness or constancy reflected in his long career as a prolific, respected writer seeking to interface Christian history and public events. Marty has also held in creative tension his conservative Missouri Synod Lutheran heritage with the best developments of modern scholarship and ecumenical Christi-anity. Marty's relationship with his brother and sister, both teach-ers, portrays an extraordinary pattern of close friendship and continuity. For fifty years the three have written letters to one another every two weeks. It is not surprising that Marty prefers to envision his career in terms of continuity and expansion rather than abrupt turning points.

But two happenings qualify as important branching points in his life. When he was about to graduate from seminary, he had been scheduled to serve as a Lutheran minister in London. But his imagi-native humor would boomerang and kill the trip to England. Marty and a classmate invented a Christian theologian, producing a schol-arly paper, replete with footnotes, on this fictive character. He also wrote a fake book review on a work of the fictional thinker for the seminary newspaper. When word of this farce seeped upward to the sober Lutheran faculty and administration, they canceled his London sojourn and assigned him instead as an assistant to a sea-soned pastor near Chicago. Written into his call to this parish was the stipulation that every assistant pastor had to do doctoral work, something Marty had no thought of doing. Even after receiving his Ph.D., he wanted to continue as a pastor. For seven years he helped start a new suburban church near Chicago, and he began to write for *The Christian Century,* which launched his publishing career. When he was invited to teach at the new Lutheran School of Theology in Chicago in 1963, he again resisted in favor of the pastorate. He told his congregation about his call to teach and his reluctance to embrace it. But his congregants urged him to accept the post. Thus began the outstanding career in teaching, publishing, and public commentary of the man who might easily qualify as the contemporary dean of Protestant historians.

A more profound turning point in a career marked mostly by continuity was the death in 1981 of his wife of nearly three decades. Her death by cancer impacted on his personal vision of life and also on his work as a historian. During her final year, Marty spent much time taking care of her at home. He had many chances to speak with her and read to her. "I learned to push tomorrow out of my way," he says, "and live for today. Intensity not duration has been our family motto." When he gives advice for aging well, he draws on this experience, insisting on living with intensity today. "The future does not exist yet for us to be able to control it," he says. "Energy has to go into the day." In an even deeper way, his first wife's death underlines a key polarity in his personal and professional life. This is the polarity between perilous contingency and trust in God and in others. "I trust with the full awareness that the rug gets pulled out from under, that cells get malignant," he says. "I experience plenitude, contingency, and transience. I think about it all the time." He knows that the precariousness of life can undercut the trust. But he adds that wounds and blessings are webbed together. How one wrestles with the polarity is what counts. "Meaning," he says, "happens because there's never a day that's just blessing, and there's never a day that's just wound."

As an historian, he realizes the relativity of human events and judgments. He doesn't aspire to make definitive statements; what he calls "the tonal character" of his work matters more. In part this means bringing his world of scholarship into dialogue with public history in the making, with the intense needs of the present. It pleases Marty when his students go into the pastorate with a commitment to social action. But the lines of force for him also move back from public dedication to the world of scholarship. Whatever way he chooses to turn in the back-and-forth rhythm of his career, he talks about operating from a center core of personality. For Marty this has been a core shaped by powerful continuity of family, friends, and religion tempered in a world of transience and unpredictability.

From 1978 to 1987 John McDonald was an American ambassador to the United Nations, appointed twice by both Presidents Carter and Reagan. Most people would have been satisfied after such a prominent culmination of a long career in the foreign service to retire into a life of private pleasures. But McDonald went on to direct the Iowa Peace Institute and more recently the Institute for Multi-Track Diplomacy, where he remains involved in global issues of conflict resolution. Thinking back on his life, he attributes his career success in part to a secure family background with strong ties to his parents. His father was a career cavalry officer who met his mother in the European theater during World War I. She had gone overseas with the YMCA to assist the troops. He remembers his mother as a feminist who ran her own business as a stenographer in New York City. Later she went back to school in Hawaii to obtain a master's degree. But his father was his model for imitation. John wanted to become the military general "his father should have been but wasn't."

Although McDonald's working life seems continuous from law school to foreign service to ambassadorship, an important turning point occurred when he was eight years old. He was hospitalized for two years with a bone disease which in effect terminated his plans for a military career. When a diplomat spoke to his class in high school, he decided to pursue a similar life. A second turning point happened much later when he gradually realized that his adversarial training in law school was not the right road to resolve conflict. After a year at the National War College, "where you learn much more about making war than peace," he says, "I was assigned to the United Nations as an ambassador on global issues." At the U.N., he became aware that a win-lose ideology doesn't work in multilateral contexts. If he wanted to achieve a goal, it was vital to give up the competitive formula of the prosecutor and "bring others into the cooperative process," he says. "I had to give up the philosophy of win-lose and try to negotiate a consensus." As a U.N. official, he organized a number of agencies such as a volunteer group modeled on the Peace Corps, disaster-relief operations, and an environmental program. In some ways, McDonald was prepared for his life's work from childhood by being exposed to racially and ethnically different people as his father's military position meant frequent moving for the family. But his main skill was mastering the art of making a bureaucracy work "for what I wanted," he says. "If you can master bureaucracy, you can do all sorts of things."

McDonald's career teaches us important lessons about fostering our work well into elderhood. His first rule is "to be as happy as possible in the present job." He found that many of his colleagues were either looking backward or forward, ending up dissatisfied with their present work, and not able to give it the energy it deserved. McDonald sees a close link between job satisfaction and aging well. "My father taught me early in life," he says, "that if you don't like what you're doing, stop it and do something else. If you can't tell work from play, you'll have a happy life into old age." He understands some of the constraints that keep people in frustrating work, but he thinks far too many people let the process of dissatisfaction build too long. "I'll never retire," he says, "even though I'm officially retired. Retirement is the wrong state of mind. People I know who retire to play golf usually end up in the graveyard within a year."

The ambassador followed his own advice by taking on the directorship of the Iowa Peace Institute. The purpose of the institute is to promote alternatives to violence through conflict management, global education, international development, and world trade. McDonald insists on focusing these general goals into hands-on, doable projects in Iowa and beyond. A final career message of this elder statesman for aging well is similar to that made by President Jimmy Carter when discussing his own nonretirement. It is crucial to be involved in causes that benefit others. McDonald's continuing career links closely with his answer to what gives his life its deepest meaning: "Helping other people," he says. "If I can bring peace to others and resolve conflicts, my life becomes more worthwhile and happier as a byproduct of such involvement."

Life-Shifting Turning Points

In the examples above, we see important turning points in careers that move in a continuous direction. All four people in the last section set out on vocational paths early in life and made important changes along the way as new experiences led to novel insights. In elderhood these persons teach us from their example how to integrate the past in ways that provide launching pads for creative work in old age. The people in this section portray more dramatic changes that affect not only their work lives but also their deeper self-identities. In some ways, their life-changing experiences resemble those of the women in the first section of the chapter who underwent divorces. Yet the "divorces" of the first two persons below are in some ways more radical than marital breakups, because the institution to which they pledged their lives called for a total dedication to the service of God in professional religious life. The first two sketches present elders who altered their commitment to the Catholic ministry in dramatic ways. The extraordinary changes in the thinking of Catholic religious professionals since the Vatican Council of the sixties prepared the ground for such unusual life-changes. The last case presents a somewhat analogous turn in the life of a famous "Protestant nun."

John Duryea, a warm and gentle man, presented a very attractive image of idealism as a young priest in the days before Vatican II. He grew up in a stable, professional family with a long relationship to Stanford University. His grandfather had been the first chemistry professor at Stanford, and John would become Catholic chaplain at the university. Both of his parents were converts to Catholicism, and were careful to raise their son with knowledge of and respect for the church. Duryea wavered between choosing a career as a geological scientist or as a priest. The world of nature has been very important to him since his first trip to the Sierras at the age of eight. Only his Aunt Minna opposed his entrance into the seminary. "It would be such a waste," she said, after his first year at Stanford. Once he got used to the less mature environment of the seminary, he settled into the preordained path toward the diocesan priesthood. His first apprenticeship in a parish went well, but then came a stint in New York with an authoritarian, "mean old buzzard, who was prejudiced toward blacks and wanted to get Jews to come for bingo," he says. This experience of the dark side of the official church undercut his euphoria about the ministry. But his next assignment in an Oakland parish restored his confidence as a priest, even though he "was just carrying out ministry within the rigid structures of a legalistic church." He had not yet developed the theological knowledge to be able to question church strictures on such issues as birth control and divorce that caused suffering to many parishioners.

Most of his priestly ministry would be spent on university campuses, first at San Jose State and then at Stanford. The kindly accessibility of his personality made him a successful community builder at San Jose, although he was an "abysmal failure" as a fund-raiser. A decade in the sixties and early seventies as a Stanford campus minister was the high point of his priestly career within the official church. He developed a broader community around the new liturgy and became involved in civil rights and antiwar issues. During this time of great hope for change in the church, he became freer within himself, bolstered in part by the theology of Vatican II which presented a far more open vision of the church than the legalistic model he had assimilated in seminary days. "I began to find," he says, "that I didn't have to discover an authoritative source to justify what I believed in. I knew something was right from my inner experience and my reflections on the gospel." This inward liberation led to what he characterizes as the main contribution of his ministry: "helping people to get freed up or unstuck in their religious ideas, so that their whole personal development could proceed healthfully."

But his greater inner freedom brought on a major crisis in his relationship to the Catholic Church. In 1974 his friendship with Eve, a widowed artist with two daughters, was intensifying toward love and commitment. Duryea sees himself as a man who hates conflict and thus tries to avoid it. "The fear of conflict," he says, "often kept me from confronting problems, and especially disputes with authority figures like bishops. I was quite skilled in avoiding collisions without compromising principles, but it didn't always work." He and Eve were becoming more isolated and lonely. He finally had to face the break with his bishop and declare that he intended to marry. Duryea speaks of his meeting with the bishop and the prospect of leaving the clergy as "terrifying. I have never felt that sort of fear since," he says.

Leaving the clergy for Duryea meant not only a new "career" of being husband and stepfather for the first time in his mid-fifties, but also the financial struggle of helping to support a family with a modest-paying job in a bookstore. Yet Duryea moved into family life without cutting off his priestly ministry. Over the years, he has led a small, alternative community that meets for worship and mutual support. He continues to say Mass and perform weddings for those who relate to his Angelo Roncalli Community, named after the reformist Pope John XXIII. As a man in his seventies, he looks back at these sharp changes in his life-course as learning experiences. "I have changed in becoming much more open to new ideas," he says, "capable of assimilating them without feeling threatened. And I am satisfied with fewer friends and fewer events." He has also learned to stay open to "whatever comes." Family life has taught him to be more conscious of his feelings in close relations with others. "I've learned more about love," he says, "and I'm using love in the sense of caring, being fused to another person through caring. I can see how absolutely barren life would be without love." Another constant in his life has been love for the mountains and for natural science. He sees himself as a competent mountain guide and naturalist. Not only does he experience an intense relationship with nature on his hikes, but he also believes that a richer contact with nature would help people age with more peace. "It would be much easier to accept dying," he says, "if you are in touch with nature in its constant change, death, and rebirth."

At sixty-nine, Margaret Ellen Traxler can look back on a career marked by intense turning points. This Catholic nun has been referred to as a woman of two eras, one a time of traditional Catholicism and another of prophetic outspokenness within the church. She grew up one of five sisters in a closely knit rural family in Henderson, Minnesota. Her nurse mother and country doctor father worked together in birthing babies and bringing health care to a far-flung farm community. On his deathbed, her father turned to her mother and said: "Oh, Mama, haven't we had fun!" Her grandparents lived and died as part of her extended family, providing deep roots through storytelling and care for their granddaughters. The influence of an observant Catholic family and a

Catholic high school helped to determine Traxler's choice to enter the School Sisters of Notre Dame in 1941.

The life of sisterhoods in the forties tended to be bound by rigid rules and a cold sprituality that tried to submerge the individuality of the nuns. It was a time of complete obedience to superiors (dissent was judged irreligious) and isolation from one's family of origin. Traxler says that she was able to make friends in spite of this discouraging atmosphere for relationships, but "it was a hard life," she adds, "mainly because of the irrationality." Pastors who knew little or nothing about education became school superintendents, and women superiors constituted a "gerontocracy" with scant understanding of the younger nuns. "So we had to pretend to play their game," she says. But within the classroom she was free to communicate, whereas outside of class communication was stifled. Traxler admits that she adapted to the discipline and found her teaching work fulfilling until the sixties when change in church and society would profoundly challenge her self-image and philosophy of life.

An early turning point in her career happened when she was a student at Georgetown University and wandered through some of Washington's districts of abject poverty. This was an awakening toward social justice that she would build on a few years later in Selma, Alabama, during the civil-rights marches. A newpaper photo from that period shows Traxler in full nun's habit standing in a line that was confronted by state troopers. The Selma experience also alerted her to the interconnection of human-rights issues, especially pertaining to women. She saw women working bravely for civil rights alongside of men, but "I also saw how they weren't included in the decision-making of male leaders. And they still aren't," she says. These experiences eventually led her to found the Institute of Women Today in a poor neighborhood of Chicago. The institute endeavors to help poor women and children, many of whom are minority people. A ministry among women in prison is also an important part of the institute's work.

Civil rights and feminist issues would converge in a remarkably public way in Traxler's life as a nun. She would apply the insights derived from these movements to the Catholic Church, especially as these affected the status of women. Since the Vatican Council of the sixties, religious orders of women have undergone major changes toward greater self-determination and choice of ministries. Traxler, as founder of the National Coalition of American Nuns, spearheaded the progressive wing of that reform effort. In 1984 Traxler collided with the male hierarchy of the church in a dramatic public event. She was a cosigner of an open letter to the hierarchy on permitting open discussion about the ethics of abortion among Catholics. When the statement appeared in The New York Times, Rome's reaction was quick and severe. The priest and nun signers were ordered to recant or face expulsion from their orders. Traxler and other Sisters refused to accept this decree, calling for dialogue in the church.

After conciliatory discussion with leaders of the orders involved, the Vatican backed down on its strongest sanctions. But the voice of collective dissent was effective in ways that would have been impossible in Traxler's early career as a nun. She talks about herself as having passed a threshold at the time of organizing NCAN to be a group that would speak out on women's issues. "Since I passed that threshold," she says, "I wanted to speak the truth as I see it. Aging people must speak their truth, realizing, however, that we can be deceived. So we need to be self-critical, too. But what have we got to lose in standing publicly for our convictions?" Since the Second Vatican Council, Traxler's career has moved her into a polarized stance with the official church. Gone are the days of simple obedience. She sees the present pope as the misguided defender of a dying patriarchal system that does not reflect the best gospel values. Yet she works within the church as a nun committed to social justice. This balancing act is more understandable if we listen to her distinguish between institutional and gospel values. "My attitude toward the institutional church has totally changed," she says. "In ways I see it as a cesspool of patriarchy. But I'm still committed to the ways of Jesus. After all, religion should be doing good for people."

To think of old people as agents for social change was largely a foreign idea in gerontology until Margaret E. (Maggie) Kuhn founded the Gray Panthers after her sixty-fifth birthday in 1970. Like Margaret Traxler, Maggie Kuhn, referred to as a compassionate revolutionary, has stood against ageism and for purposeful living in elderhood. Like Traxler, she has operated within and outside of church organizations. In subtle ways she was prepared from childhood for her work in later life. "My mother and I were close friends all our lives," she says. "We loved each other until the end." Kuhn's Panthers stress the cooperation of young and old in all projects. Kuhn's compassion for suffering started early in life. Her brother's schizophrenia kept him in and out of hospitals. She took care of him at home for many years, as she would later care for her mother. "She was severely handicapped by arthritis," Kuhn says, "as I am. But it was a bond that drew us closer."

Careers have quiet turning points that are sometimes recognized only later in life. Kuhn points to her Aunt Pauline as a powerful influence through her twin commitments to the early women's movement and her work in Sunday school developments. Kuhn herself prepared to be a teacher until an unusual incident altered the course of her career. In her first class, as a teacher in training, an eraser fight broke out while she was trying to use a new technique to stimulate an otherwise dull grammar lesson. Kuhn tried to stop the confusion by throwing an eraser just as the regular teacher entered. After this incident, her father suggested that she rethink teaching with its discipline problems and decide on another course. She redirected her career toward staff work with such church-related organizations as the YWCA, the Alliance of Unitarian Women, and for many years the Presbyterian office for church and society. Still another turning point in her life was the breaking of an engagement to marry a physician. "I realized that he wanted a 'good wife' who would quietly center her life on him," she says. Years later he saw her on the Johnny Carson show and called to say that her work was inappropriate and socially radical. "I felt saved," she says. "If I had married him, life would have been so different. Now I'm having a glorious old age."

The turning point that cast Kuhn into national and international prominence happened when she faced mandatory retirement after forty-three years of working for social change. Her long career of involvement in labor causes, civil rights, and women's issues came to a head when she "got very angry" at being forced to retire at sixty-five from her post at the National Council of Churches. With five of her retired colleagues she began what would become the Gray Panthers, an organization of young and old working together to eradicate ageism and promote peace and social justice. Since 1970 she has been able to apply the skills and knowledge learned in structured organizations to new models of work. "In my old age," she says, "the limits of structures have been removed. I'm free to move outside of institutions and take risks, to test new patterns of activity, to break new ground by teamwork." Working as a collaborative team is very important to Maggie Kuhn: "I believe that it is with a team that we affirm our humanness."

Kuhn opposes the mentality of retirement as it is generally understood in our culture. Too often it reduces the old to the status of what she calls "wrinkled babies" who are treated with paternalism. Key to her thinking is living with purpose, cultivating goals after people retire from their jobs. "Then you don't retire from life," she says. "I think having a goal that is attainable and challenging is a marvelous way to keep energizing yourself." She stresses the freedom of the old to speak out for important causes, try new roles, and take risks. Kuhn makes these novel career options more specific. The old, she thinks, should test new lifestyles of cooperative living in small groups. They can reach out to build new coalitions among racial and class divisions, since age is a universalizing experience. The old should be watchdogs of public bodies, she says, guardians of the public interest. They can be advocates for consumers' rights, for nursing-home patients, and for the elderly in general. As stockholders, the old can become monitors of corporate power and responsibility. For Kuhn, the new careers of the old should reject ageist paternalism and become purposeful endeavors. The old, in her vision, can be liberators, enablers, and energizers.

Summary Reflections

In the last two chapters, we have examined the lives of older people in terms of their families of origin, their adult families, and the turning points of their careers. Two underlying questions drove our inquiry. What have these people learned from their histories and what can we derive from their stories for our own healthy aging? Each of us will differ in applying lessons of elder wisdom from these stories.

From the first section of this chapter, we are confronted with questions about balancing commitments to family and to careers. This question is becoming especially acute for women whose traditional role has been in the home. Perhaps some, like Charlee Lambert, had to take up a career partly from personal desire and partly from necessity. What were the turning points that motivated us to make similar moves? It may be that some had to struggle with difficult marital situations while these shifts were occurring. Some women may, like Ella Mazel, have encountered less difficulty in blending family and profession. But even in such a continuous path, important life events could become branching points for new directions. For Mazel and for Lillian Schact-Lavine inner, psychological changes through therapy strengthened them in their career moves. How many of us in middle age may have realized that home involvement was not enough to fulfill our needs? Or like Vera O'Keefe, we may have worked outside the home partly because it was uplifting and partly because it assuaged a problematic home environment. Barbara Payne-Stancil's experiences point to still another pattern. During a distinguished career, she was helped greatly by a good second marriage to engage her work with a more positive outlook. Many women reading this book may have dedicated themselves to childrearing, homemaking, and volunteer activities. By comparison and contrast with the elders described, what were important turning points in such a life pattern? Men might ask themselves not only about turning points in their work lives, but also how well they balanced family and relational aspects with their commitment to jobs. How do men understand the personal gains and losses of their major life-involvements?

In the second part of the chapter, we observe that seemingly small events bring about important career directions. Eugene Odum starts a major ecological institute because of misunderstandings in the biology department. Bernice Neugarten opens up a new field of developmental aging after she is asked to substitute-teach a course. Martin Marty launches a significant professorial career after chance events in seminary and parish bring him to the University of Chicago. We might ask ourselves what subtle and seemingly chance happenings in our lives drew us into certain lines of work. There usually are deeper lessons learned from turning points in one area of life that affect another. The death of Marty's first wife teaches him about wounds and blessings in life. As a professional, he learns to intensify his ability to live in the present. What might have been similar happenings in our broader lives that impacted on the way we approach our work? John McDonald recalls in later life his father's dictum about not retiring from meaningful commitments if one would age well. How many of our turning points, like McDonald's, can be seen from the vantage point of older age to be building positively toward richer enterprises in elderhood?

Turning points usually imply some continuity with the past, but for some this continuity is realized only after intense personal upheaval. John Duryea exemplifies such a combination of preservation and turmoil in his break with the official Catholic priesthood. Although she stays in her religious order, Margaret Traxler undergoes profound changes both personally and in her ministry because of confrontations with a patriarchal church. Both of them approach their elderhood as deeply changed people. Although shifts in our lives may not have been as public as those of Duryea and Traxler, we can ask ourselves about our own changes at a more profound level. What were the turning points in our lives that bring us to elderhood with a new heart and a new mind? How would we describe that alteration of vision and feeling in ourselves? Have we learned with Maggie Kuhn to live with purpose? Difficult turning points in her life such as family illnesses, a decision not to marry, and the blow of mandatory retirement are absorbed as creative lessons that shape her late-life achievements in aging. As we look back on our own turning points, we would do well to ask with Kuhn: What do we want to do with the rest of our lives?

But in an overall way, chapters 1 and 2 tell us something important, namely, that aging well means exploring our life histories with all their pain and promise. To know the way forward in old age, we must understand where we have been. Moreover, by starting with this review of life-histories, we will appreciate more fully that the themes for aging well in the following chapters arise from real experiences of the old and not from abstract theories imposed on them.

◆ ◆ ◆

CHAPTER 3

Empowering Your Elder Self

In the last two chapters, we have explored the family and work lives of elders who typify the creative people in this book. We stress these beginnings and turning points to emphasize how we are all rooted in personal and family histories. It is important to keep this rootedness in mind as we move into chapters that focus more directly on themes for aging well. These topics about creative elderhood are not abstract ideas conceived in an ivory tower. Rather, they emanate from elders who are reflecting on their complex experiences over a long life. Moreover, realizing that the following chapters are immersed in concrete stories helps us appreciate how the themes must be differently applied. Each of us has a unique genetic component and a specialized story, personal and social. The following collective insights about aging well will apply differently to any specific reader. There is no one way to live our later years with benefit. Many paths with varied configurations open before us. Now that we have looked at the general terrain of lifespans, let us each become cartographers for our individual journeys, choosing roads that lead to a more creative elderhood.

This chapter centers on empowering the elder self. This means concentrating on themes that focus on energizing the individual, on searching for sources of potential strength within us as elders. The subheadings are given as imperatives to indicate that they are calls to serious reflection and action.

Eliminate Ageist Stereotypes

Ageism means discriminating against a person because he or she is old. It may also be combined with other forms of discrimination such as racism or sexism, but in our culture discrimination based on age has a life and intensity of its own. Subtle or overt ageism carries the message that older people are, as Maggie Kuhn puts it, useless, sexless, and mindless. And being perceived as old begins quite early in a society driven by productivity and competitiveness, qualities associated with youthful vigor. The world of major corporations exemplifies this attitude. There one can be considered old at fifty-five. Since people are living well beyond that mark, a large sector of the population is subject to ageist attitudes. Two important problems are connected with ageist stereotypes. First, they often influence us in quiet ways. We are subliminally conditioned to think of ourselves as out of the loop when the media, advertising, politics, education, and many other zones of public life feature youthful activity. But the second problem with ageism is more poisonous to our self-identities: We gradually believe the stereotypes, incorporate them, and act them out.

These negative attitudes toward being old resist correction because they go deeper than the youth-driven character of modern societies. Being old has also to do with decline and death, topics we take up in chapter 6. The young and middle-aged tend to fear and avoid these prospects as long as possible. As a way of denying their own eventual aging and decline, some people mock the old as a pseudospecies unlike themselves. It is important to realize the depth of our resistance to aging, so that we do not naively assume that the underlying fear will evaporate through a strong public-relations campaign. But when we grasp the power of ageism, we will be in a better position to lessen its control over our minds.

Desmond Tutu, Anglican archbishop of Cape Town, appreciates the power of ageist stereotypes. He talks about the respected place of elders in traditional African life. The old were considered repositories of wisdom for the community, and they exercised important roles in tribal society. But in modern society, he notes, "old people are often made to feel like appendages, nuisances, or barely tolerable creatures." Older than Tutu by nearly two decades, Clara Crook has had more time to experience ageism in her life. She thinks that our educational system needs to be changed to assist the young to appreciate old age without the negative baggage attached to it. "I propose a program that starts in kindergarten," she says, "to throw out the notion that only young is beautiful, that being old means emotional and mental deprivation, that it portrays a woman as an old bag on the edge of poverty. To hell with the damn shopping discounts! The stereotypes present a picture of sad dependency."

Crook also believes that many midlife children help to perpetuate ageist views of their parents, since they haven't viewed aging as a normal lifespan process. She gives a telling example of this attitude in reference to grandparenting for her own children. "I love grandparenting," she says, "but the down side is that I'm perceived as a grandmother only. What happens to the rest of me? My son doesn't seem to be aware that I'm a whole person outside of grandmother." Here Crook captures a key element in ageism beyond its directly negative perceptions. It also confines the old person to limited roles rather than viewing the old as total personalities with many needs, desires, and potentials. Mary Erlanger emphasizes the value of teaching people about the process of aging to appreciate how people age in different ways and manifest a varying range of human proclivities and choices. She points out that a significant method of overcoming ageism consists in finding and demonstrating various role models for older age.

The people interviewed for this book are examples of such models who defy the misrepresentations of ageism. Listen to a few of these voices on how they deal with the term "old." Evelyn Ho, a Chinese-American elder and social activist for aging issues, sees older persons unwittingly fostering the stereotypes that injure them. "Once their children are raised," she says, "they just stay home and become passive; men put away the tools of their work lives and settle in front of the tube." Active in community affairs, she doesn't see herself as conforming to the harmful image of a dependent old lady. "Be involved," she counsels, "and bring some sunshine to others, especially those who are shut-ins." Claire Randall, former president of the National Council of Churches, talks about the women of her generation who fell into the trap of basing their whole lives on their children. Often such persons lack a reason for being once their children leave home. She notes that the churches have given women opportunites for active involvements they might not have otherwise had. But she says of herself: "I never think in terms of being old. I continue to be deeply involved with Church Women United. We're always looking for new ways of living with today's challenges."

"I don't like old people who act old," says Lillian Lavine. Her friends tend to be younger people who aren't preoccupied with aches and pains. "I like vital people," she says, "and I try to maintain a vital mind." Susan Carlton-Smith is an artist and a book illustrator. For her, persons who reveal ageist stereotypes probably lack imagination, a quality she shows in abundance through her unusual artistic creations assembled from unlikely items found in nature. Her nature sculptures depict a world of imaginative surprises. "I don't mind getting old," she says. "I feel exactly like I felt all my life. I find so much in the world of nature that is new and exciting for me." Maggie Kuhn has probably stated the case against ageism as powerfully as anyone. In an earlier dialogue (in *Maggie Kuhn on Aging*, edited by Dieter Hessel, p. 14) she sounds the clarion for a new image of the old: "We are not 'senior citizens' or 'golden-agers.' We are the elders, the experienced ones; we are maturing, growing adults responsible for the survival of our society. We are not wrinkled babies, succumbing to the trivial, purposeless waste of our years and our time."

Seek Balance in Health and Things

This book focuses mainly on the psychological, social, and spiritual aspects of aging, but empowering the self requires at least a brief discussion on preserving health and dealing with money. When asked to talk about how to age well, a number of elders referred to the importance of physical well-being and a degree of financial security. But nearly everyone who expanded on maintaining health stressed taking responsibility for one's own physical welfare. The tone of their remarks decried passivity, a too prevalent attitude of turning one's health care over to professionals. Of course, all agree that medical experts can help in many situations. Helen DeChatelet, a former midwestern school teacher, emphasized this spirit of self-initiative in health care: "Stay away from too darn much medicine and running helplessly to doctors who prescribe too many treatments and things like that." But this advice against passivity is balanced by holistic advice for staying well. In addition to having a few good friends and a wise counselor, she tells the old to seek intellectual stimulation. She "reads and ponders" and watches "educational stuff" on TV, participates in study groups and listens to classical music. This woman in her mid-eighties also does volunteer work with a support group for caregivers of the aged and counsels the very elderly.

Key words for health maintenance among these creative elders are initiative and balance. In part, this consists of the familiar advice about regular exercise, eating right, weight control, and pacing oneself in terms of activity and rest. But equally important for total health are the psychospiritual components. Janet Kalven, an educator and leader in a women's community, the Grail movement, has survived two surgeries for colon cancer and has undergone a colostomy. She underscores the importance of one's attitude: "If your attitude is to make a big deal of illness and center your life around it, then you go one way. But you don't have to do that. It's important not to make a whole career out of your physical problems." Joanne Stevenson, a leader in developing a senior center in her community, emphasizes the importance of preserving health in old age, but she adds immediately that health is connected with "being able to do things and not sit back and be taken care of." To be well, she insists, seniors need to be interested in something bigger than themselves.

Lin Ludy reminds us of the value of touching for health and healing among the elderly. "Just putting your hand on a shoulder or arm or knee communicates beyond words." This draws the other into a healing circle of concern. Ludy sums up the interplay between physical health in later years and spiritual dimensions by the striking figure of filling a vacuum. "I don't hear as well as I used to," she says, "and I don't see as well. I sometimes have pains walking. But if I dwell on these, they become the center of my life instead of something else filling the center. Nature abhors a vacuum. Something is going to go into that space of diminishment."

She thinks this is why older people resort to alcohol and drugs or become TV addicts. "But if I can let go of perfect health gracefully," she says, "I open up a space for something bigger that I call the 'holy' to enter that void. Instead of losing something through my bodily diminishments, I open up my deeper self to empowerment."

It is interesting to note that when asked about the most important aspects for aging well, only six of over one hundred participants talked about money or possessions. And most of the six mentioned it somewhat in passing. This in no way negates the importance of financial security in old age. It could be that since these elders were not directly asked about finances, they did not advert to the topic, or perhaps they took for granted that a basic financial safety net was presupposed. Moreover, the participants are themselves not in the lower socioeconomic class. Apprehension about one's economic fate surfaced more readily in connection with reflections about major illness and long-term care.

Earl Brewer, a retired professor and an expert on aging, advocates financial preparation for later life through a plan for regular savings, enhanced by various investments, to add to pension and social security support. Peter Kelley, a professional agent for artists in New York, thinks back on his own physical and emotional illnesses when he says: "Being financially secure is a big relief. Aging is a major problem for people without money." The well-known actor E. G. Marshall also brings up the signficance of health insurance, a pension plan, and "money to live with." In general, two overall themes arise related to material things and a good old age. First, the advice is to enjoy things but not to make them the goal of life. Elders talk about seeking relationships and experiences over material things. The point here is to balance the scale more heavily on the side of humanistic values and goals than on that of money and possessions. Secondly, in line with the latter perspective, the movie actor Eli Wallach urges older people to simplify their lives, cutting away less important exploits with their attendant worries so that an elder can concentrate energy on significant endeavors.

Activate Your Resources for Inner Creativity

Middle and older age are prime times for exploring our inner sources of creativity. After the struggle of establishing a basic identity, a career path, and intimate relationships in our younger years, we are poised for the inward journey. This consists in making experiential contact with our deeper reality and in developing our unique gifts and ideals. It does not mean withdrawal from the world or from personal responsibilities. But the inward journey is a crucial quest for discovering who we really are and what we can become in later life. Our hyperactive, externally oriented culture frequently denies or blocks this contemplative process with tragic results for both mental and physical well-being. In a roundabout way, the relatively new interest in Asian techniques for inner growth and holistic health has rekindled awareness of forgotten Western modes of reflection and meditation. Archbishop Desmond Tutu, a man intensely involved in South Africa's social change, speaks of the contemplative life as a key value for the aging process. "As we grow older, we slow down," he says, "and we ought not be ashamed of that; it's part of the right pattern. We should have more time to grow inwardly and intercede for others." We notice in these remarks the interfacing of inner development and outward care for others.

Zalman Schachter-Shalomi, a rabbi and professor of Jewish mysticism, talks about the inward journey as part of the "eldering process." In his work with groups of elders, he sees both the negative side of "deafening oneself to the screams of the unlived life" and the positive aspects of cultivating the contemplative road. He presents a graphic image of how many people deny inward work in our culture. "I look ahead and see the angel of death dancing there," he says, "waiting for me." In this situation, most people shut down, "go into a knee-jerk response, and their future becomes opaque out of fear. They back into the future," he says, "instead of walking straight ahead." When people back into the future, they see a past often full of failures that they don't want to view. "This puts people into a box," he says, "no future, no past, and a shriveled present. I call this the psychic field that mimics Alzheimer's."

Schachter-Shalomi by contrast advocates a contemplative approach to positive aging toward creativity. Contemplation opens up our intuitive potentials; it "formats more portions of the brain," says Schachter-Shalomi, "than we have been able to up until now." But, he hastens to add, this use of computer language may be misleading. The creative process is qualitative, not quantitative; it is more a matter of being than doing. Of course, there is no sharp distinction between being and doing. Rather it's more like a rainbow of possibilities with being and doing blending into each other. In this rainbow of potentials, he says, "there's a kind of doing that's more on the being side; it may have to do with mentoring, with shaping, with life craft, with appreciation." But opening contemplative spaces for inner growth in later life is especially hard in an externally driven and youth-oriented culture. When people are willing to shatter the hold of the culture, what he calls the "fifty-five shift" can occur. But it is important to add that developing a contemplative direction in life doesn't happen by merely wishing it or conceptualizing about it. Schachter-Shalomi's entrance into the contemplative mode resulted from prayer, meditation, and other contemplative arts experienced in Jewish spirituality, especially its mysticism. "You need labs to learn this stuff," he says, "not just the forebrain." These "labs" can be found in traditional religions as well as in modern psychological movements.

Elderly therapists like Elizabeth Howes and June Singer have spent their careers teaching people to mine inner resources. In her eighties, Howes reflects on her own task in old age: "My growth is most important for me. I want to become more centered, integrated, loving. My purpose for living is to become the most I can become. And I certainly haven't accomplished all that." Howes adds, however, that becoming more centered and loving through the inner work of exploring the unconscious entails encountering everything within, including one's darkness and hate. Howes has blended images from the Judeo-Christian tradition with her Jungian therapeutic approach. She speaks of becoming centered by prayer to go inward, but prayer takes on a psychotherapeutic cast: "Prayer means I reorient my whole attitude, whether I'm open or closed, committed or indifferent."

The movement toward personal wholeness, she remarks, consists in maintaining a polarity between light and dark within. "The tree of knowledge of good and evil is at the center of each of us," she says, referring to the Eden myth. "Therefore, we have choice as we move from the expulsion to the journey back to wholeness." Singer echoes this theme when she says: "I think if we don't look at ourselves and see the darkness in ourselves, we'll forever project the darkness outside." She regards it as her task to help people see their own darkness and to recognize that all are capable of evil given enough provocation. Eli Wallach puts a positive twist on encountering our negativities in later life. With an actor's sense of the human condition, he says: "Old people should get angry. You've got to have hates. You can't say it's all beyond me and sit in an institution like a vegetable. It's healthy to have strong feelings against rude people or rock music if you don't like it." Wallach insists on the importance of keeping one's imagination and emotions alive for psychosomatic well-being as an elder .

Cultivate Your Self-Reliance

To become more self-reliant or independent is an aspect of developing inner resources. Creative elders emphasize this trait for aging well. It doesn't mean rugged individualism that ignores communal responsibility or that refuses help from another in appropriate situations. That would be an undesirable extreme as would its opposite, excessive dependence. In our culture, however, attitudes toward the old, based on ageist stereotypes, encourage passivity and dependence. Mabel Broom is 106 years old. After her husband died in 1927, she has made her own way in the world. While holding various jobs, she helped raise a granddaughter. When asked why she thinks she has lived so long, she responds that she loves life and wants to live. But she also adds that she "feels free in herself. My doctors told me I had a lot of inner strength. I can depend on myself." Of course, there is no one ingredient for assuring a sense of self-reliance in later life. People are complex in their own makeup and in their cultural conditioning. But a number of self-reliant elders underscore freedom from multiple fears as a crucial part of being independent. "Don't be afraid," says Mabel Broom. "I have confidence in myself; I've a good mind and I wake up every morning with a song in my heart. I have a feeling of goodness and liking in my inner self."

Mary Erlanger links the experience of losses, whether actual or anticipated, in old age to fears that stymie self-reliance. She lists physical, relational, occupational, and status losses that foster a spirit of dependence among elders. Yet Erlanger points out that old age, even with its losses, can free people to confide in themselves. "They don't have to meet the same expectations, fulfill the same roles," she says. She believes that older persons can be helped to open up, to move beyond their fears toward self-reliant living and even risk-taking. "People in later life can break rigid patterns," she says, "but most don't do it. Without a therapeutic environment for change, they are paralyzed by old fears." As an elder, Erlanger finds herself much more inner directed and less concerned about what others think. Nonagenarian Simon Greenberg, who oversees the daily care of his frail wife and then goes off to his office at Jewish Theological Seminary, puts a unique twist on the relation between fear and lack of self-reliance. "I have greater fear of not trying than of failing," he says. This could be the motto of the self-reliant risktaker in late life.

Still another way of expressing self-reliance or independence among older people can be seen in resistance to social convention. Joseph Fichter stood against conventional attitudes both within the Catholic Church and in his wider community. This Jesuit priest-sociologist conducted a study of opinions among American Catholics on birth control and other issues. His superiors were told by the Vatican that he shouldn't be engaged in such research. To publish his work, Fichter had to stand up to authorities who did not want to challenge conventional teaching. Earlier in his long career, he became a prime target of the White Citizens Councils in New Orleans for his work to change race relations. Many Catholics served on the councils, and they complained strongly to his superiors that he was involved with "those people," the blacks. His study of patterns of police arrests in the early 1950s upset the police and caused the FBI to interrogate the president of his university about him. When Fichter looks back at these events, his only regret is that he didn't take even more aggressive stands for his convictions. "I'm much wiser now," he says in his eighties, "and I'd take bolder positions to maintain my beliefs and my research."

To become an independent elder, one who speaks in his or her own voice, calls for a resilient spirit. Archbishop Tutu speaks of "being amazed by the resiliency of older people." I. E. "Ike" Saporta, an octogenarian architect, developed his resiliency from early life. Born to a wealthy Jewish family in Greece, he tells the story of his tenacity from the womb. He was the youngest of seven children and came along "by mistake" when his mother was thirty-nine. "She tried jumping off tables and chairs," he says, "to get rid of me when she was pregnant. I had to hold on for dear life, you see." After a remarkable career as a student in Germany and an architect in Greece, he joined the resistance, first against a right-wing dictatorship in Greece and then against the Nazi invasion. He was eventually captured by the S.S., but managed a breathtaking escape to the mountains by a clever use of his ability to speak German. Saporta's example of self-reliance may be more dramatic than the journalistic stances of Claude Sitton as editor of a Raleigh newspaper. But taking an independent stand against convention won him a Pulitzer in 1983. "Well, I questioned what some North Carolinians held most dearly," he says, "including Senator Helms and basketball. Then I got in trouble with the Jewish community for likening the situation of Palestinians to that of blacks in Mississippi."

Creative elders urge older persons to be as self-reliant and independent as possible. This amounts to preserving the ability to speak in one's true voice in elderhood rather than conforming to external programming. Charlee Lambert stresses the pitfalls of allowing ourselves to become overly dependent on one person. A combination of health problems and financial constraints make it very difficult for some seniors to avoid the trap of dependence on a single individual. But the consequences can sometimes be devastating when the caretaker indulges in physical or psychological abuse. Lambert also knows from personal experience the precarious financial position that an older woman can experience through late-life divorce. Since divorces among the elderly have been increasing in recent years, financial dependence on a spouse has led to crisis situations for many women. Prior reflection and planning are most important for an elderhood that will enjoy a reasonable degree of psychological and material independence.

Anne Zimmerman, a nurse and long-time leader in professional nursing organizations, keynotes the value of self-reliance in later years. After an unsuccessful marriage early in life, she realized the importance of maintaining as much independence as possible about major personal decisions to be able to manage one's life. "If you can do that over a lifetime," she says, "you are not so overwhelmed by decisions you have to make as an old person." When she received her license to fly airplanes in the days Amelia Earhart, Mary Thoits was well on her way toward a life of self-reliance. Thoits, who conducts educational programs for the elderly in California, stresses the importance of taking responsibility for one's own life. "Too many people let life control them," she says. "We are responsible for our own lives. If I don't like something that is happening to me, I can make changes. Also being in control means that you stop blaming others." Beyond practical issues concerning self-reliance is the broader perspective of elderhood as a time for developing one's true voice, one's authentic individuality. Edna McCallion, a religious and social activist, sums up the holistic benefit of a life of self-reliance and independence: ". . . to age well, you've got to keep realizing who you are as an individual, and be able to live and express yourself as that unique individual."

Increase Your Self-Acceptance and Self-Esteem

A remarkably large number of the persons interviewed find greater self-appreciation in later life. Sometimes this is expressed as feeling more confident or less inhibited by external obligations and fears of what others think. Dorothy Kearney, a retired librarian and spiritual counselor, talks about how she is different as an elder: "I feel more confident. I'm not afraid of people. I don't care what color they are or what background." Harriet King, an Atlanta homemaker, echoes this common sentiment, saying that the biggest change in her as an older person is greater self-acceptance and self-liking. King's statement underscores a key element in fostering self-esteem: that it result from a keener sense of self-acceptance. Miriam Blaustein, a community activist in San Francisco, talks about learning to accept her limitations, as a series of small strokes have impaired her vision. Yet self-acceptance in an older person means letting go of false expectations about perfect health or personal fame or other perfectionistic images of how things should be. "If I can let go of these things gracefully," Lin Ludy says, "I can accept myself as I am."

Such a person has a much better chance for enhancing self-esteem. Ludy says that she accepts herself much better now than when she was younger. "In the early years, you don't have a lot of self-acceptance. This lack of acceptance lasts a long time, to judge by the people I've seen in spiritual direction. People need psychological and spiritual help with that." She finds that a deepening of her contemplative life and letting go gracefully are like "two parts of yin and yang." The letting go that fosters self-acceptance and leads to self-esteem does not mean becoming passive or giving up.

Rather the letting go of false expectations, engendered by an individual or by society, becomes a source of energy for one's self-liking. In the Taoist image of yin and yang, the yin moment of release makes possible the yang moment of new strength. Our excessively yang Western culture leads to diseases of mind and body. Its lack of balance is hard enough on the young and disastrous for the old.

The yang or active phase in the life rhythm of the old also brings self-esteem as a byproduct "of the joy of working to alleviate social illness," says Lillian Rabinowitz. In this she is repeating the wisdom of Aristotle who held that happiness could not be pursued for itself, but only as a byproduct of doing something worthwhile. Rabinowitz remembers how "terrible" her self-esteem was in early middle age. The difference has been her work on behalf of the aging in health clinics and residential-care facilities. "This is the most enjoyable time of my life," she says, despite her physical limitations brought on by a number of surgeries. She experiences greater self-esteem, she says, "because the future is still open and exciting for me." Vera O'Keefe reveals a similar perspective on self-esteem. "The most important thing," she says, "is to find your own identity and enjoy doing what you want to do. Don't try to please others, but do what you want." O'Keefe is aware of her activist proclivities and finds a heightened self-concept by interacting with people in her medical-placement work.

Yin and yang moments combine in the way Anthony Soto, a married Catholic priest and sociologist, talks about his own self-acceptance and self-esteem. "I have had to learn to stop trying to control and determine everything that happens in my life." Since childhood and during much of his long career in the Franciscan order, he strove to prove himself as a Mexican-American and to control the world around him. Because of a good marriage and new work experiences, he has learned to abandon the intensely yang training he had imbibed in a "Germanically structured" religious life. His success both as a pastor and later as the founder of a job-training program contributed to his sense of self-esteem. But what mainly changed Soto's intense striving to prove himself was finding love through a middle-age marriage. "This has really changed my life," he says, "to fall in love at age fifty for the first time in your life, something prohibited in my past, this thoroughly overturned everything I had stood for." He feels much more positive about himself as an elder, both because of the gift of marital love and also for his career accomplishments. "I am not less than anybody else," he says.

The theme of serenity seems to capture the mood of many creative elders when it comes to self-esteem. Janet Ferguson, whose career has been that of "caring for those entrusted to me," pinpoints this sense of serenity: "I feel much more comfortable with myself now than I did at an early age. I am more accepting of myself and more at peace." Ferguson, who portrays the Quaker quality of meditative activism, also underscores a note common to others, that is, a greater tolerance that accompanies self-acceptance. "I have become much less critical of others," she says, "as I have become more accepting of myself." Luella Sibbald, a Jungian therapist, wishes that she could have had the confidence in herself experienced in her eighties when she was younger. "If I had the boldness and self-security I feel now," she says, "I would have followed my longing to become an actress."

The joining of serenity and self-esteem is directly linked to a deeper sense of wisdom. Mary Erlanger finds wisdom and self-esteem combined in later life because she is much more inner directed. "As an older person, I have a lot more self-esteem," she says. "I'm much less concerned about what other people think about what I do or say. I'm much more inner directed, more confident in my own intuition . . . I feel wiser." Coining the helpful phrase "a distilled sense of wisdom," Bernice Neugarten helps us understand the linkage between self esteem and serenity. This scholar in the field of aging has had a long time to observe the ingredients of self-esteem in older people and now in herself. She explains this distilled sense of wisdom: "It means that having lived long, you know things you couldn't have known when younger. That's a source of comfort and of self-respect. It's a distillation. I think many reflective elders have developed it. All life experiences leave their traces, so you're different as you grow older. With that wisdom comes a sense of serenity. It's what I want to bring more and more into my life as an old person."

Learn to Laugh at and with Yourself

In recent years, more attention focuses on the relation between humor and health of mind and body. Norman Cousin's remarkable book about how laughter at comedy movies helped him recover from a serious illness sparked new public interest in humor and well-being. A number of contemporary therapies emphasize the value of rediscovering the inner child with its sense of play and fantasy. Many creative elders speak of humor and playfulness as vital ingredients for aging well. Gregory Bergman says that his wife once told him that he never grew up. Although Bergman continues to write articles about serious social issues, a turn of phrase, a smile, or the glint in his eyes reveal an abiding, warm inner child. "I still have that," he says, "that intrapsychic kid at the circus." The inner child can help us cope with stress and physical disabilities. Partly crippled by polio, Gerda Blumenthal, a former professor of French literature, reflects on how sad it is that so many people ignore or suppress their inner child. "We need to revive that inner child," she says. "It is not dead, it's just buried under our terrible seriousness." She reminds us that play is very serious, as in playing a musical instrument. If we play with intensity, giving ourselves to the enjoyment, we are able to live in the present. Other elders stress the importance of embracing the gift of the present moment. When we are enjoying our work become play right now, we are not trapped in the past or future.

Eli Wallach, after a lifetime on stage and in films, emphasizes the value of tapping into the inner child and into our imaginativeness in general. He continues to act in theater, sometimes with his actress wife. During the interview in his New York apartment, we could hear the voices of his wife and daughter in another room practicing lines for an upcoming performance. It was clearly a household full of imagination. "You've got to keep imagination and emotion alive as an old person," Wallach says, "because inside of everyone is the child. He's still there in me. I mean, when I look in the mirror, I ask who that old guy is. That's not me. I'm still the young man, still pulsating, still wanting."

Humor comes in many forms. A few people have special comedic gifts for making others laugh. Such persons possess a unique sense of the incongruous or the ironic, and they develop techniques for communicating humor to audiences. But even without such special talents, most of us have the potential for laughing with and at ourselves. To laugh at ourselves implies a kind of friendly mockery at the pretensions that we assume about our importance. Such self-laughter is not a put-down that lessens our basic self-esteem.

Rather, it is a kind of centering process, a truing of the wheel, that keeps us focused on authentic values. Laughing with ourselves manifests self-enjoyment in spite of the vicissitudes that life visits on us. With such laughter we become our own best friends. We see both kinds of humor in creative elders. Desmond Tutu, Nobel Prize winner and world-renowned civil-rights leader, hopes that as he ages, he will not take himself too seriously. "I very much want to retain my ability to laugh," he says, "to appreciate the humor as well as the pain of life."

Clara Crook demonstrates a sense of humor as she reflects on the condition of being old in American society. She rejects the culture's tendency to reduce the old to dependency when she says: "I don't buy the golden years business, that cutsey-wootsey business of darling grandparents baby-sitting the kids of their yuppie offspring." By eliciting a smile in the hearer, she makes the point that elders have other important things to do in the world, and that they need to be taken seriously as full persons. Frances Pauley, whose social activism continues into her eighties, began the first public-health clinic in Decatur, Georgia, in the 1930s. When the poor parents of black and white children began bringing their youngsters to the clinic for basic health examinations, she was told that the segregation laws of the state were being broken. With a smile in her eyes and on her lips as she tells it, she remembers the intrinsic humor of her solution to the lawbreaking. "We managed that pretty well," she says laughing. In the middle of the hallway, her staff constructed an arch without a door, but with no signs for segregating the races. When the grand jury came to investigate, she said: "See, this is the dividing line. They went away happy and we had them ask the county commissioner for more money, which we got." Sixty year later, Pauley enjoys telling this story as she helps prepare dinner at a shelter for the homeless in Atlanta.

Pauley injects humor into each tale she tells whether it's about coaxing reluctant ministers to give donations to school lunch programs or using her wiles to keep sheriffs from throwing her out of town as a perceived troublemaker in civil-rights disputes. "A sense of humor is great," she says, "but how do you get it if you don't have it?" Of course, she knows there is no easy answer to this query. But she does add a bit of advice: "Stop feeling sorry for yourself, and find things to do that make you happy. What I enjoy will be very different from what you enjoy. Do things because you like to, not because it's a duty. Real freedom and humor come from within." One would judge Janet Kalven to be a serious person, devoted as she is to social causes. But when we listen to her talk about two cancer surgeries and a colostomy, we hear again the empowering words of not taking oneself too seriously. We sense her ability to laugh with herself, to stand alongside herself, as it were, letting her inner friend minimize her fear.

In spite of physical difficulties, older age can become a time to sluff off the overseriousness of youth and unleash the joyful possibilites of our suppressed inner child. In the three examples below, we find elders who have learned to tap into that child. In all three cases, however, laughter and joyousness in old age result from a deepened self-identity and self-esteem. In Arthur Stark, a famous labor arbitrator, we see this link between increased self-esteem and the ability to enjoy art and culture. "When I was young," he says, "I was always introduced as Louie Stark's son." His father was a well-known labor journalist. "Now people know me for what I am and do. I have this feeling, yes, this is really me; it's not just 'son of.'" From this vantage point, even as he continues his arbitration work, he enjoys music, theater, art, sports, and reading. We hear the voice of the inner child when he reflects on what he would do otherwise if he lived his life over again. "I'd spend more time with music, playing it, not just listening. As a kid, I studied a few years at Julliard. I'd also expand my life in the direction of painting and drawing." His wife, Dorothy, an artist and sculptor, has influenced this side of his personality.

The link between increased self-esteem in later life and the ability to play stands out in Rose Lucey. We have already seen how her journey brought her from the self-depreciating "Guinea-Wop kid" in Boston to become a senior of many accomplishments. As a key example of her elderly playfulness, she has already prepared a celebratory funeral service for herself. "I want it to be a huge party to thank everyone." This attitude deserves our reflection. How many people can even face the reality of their dying, much less conceive of it as a time for grateful celebration among family and friends? Why aren't more of us capable of this outlook? Perhaps an answer has to do with the interplay between self-esteem, gratitude, and playfulness, even in the face of death. Perhaps this is what Bernice

Neugarten meant when she spoke of death as a life-goal to be approached in serenity. Our negative perspectives on death also derive from an excessively youth-oriented culture that tries to limit play to the strenuous enjoyments of the young.

"Laughter is the gift of God's healing," says Lin Ludy. She talks about herself as a solemn child reared in the Presbyterian Church. God was someone to serve in seriousness, not the laughing entity to whom Meister Eckhart would later introduce her, when she read this medieval mystic. Humor and playfulness was to come later through her married life to Bert. "He has this wonderful way of using puns that can break open a situation," she says. Again, Ludy, using theological language, makes the point about self-love and the ability to celebrate. Too many religious groups, she says, present the commandment to love with the wrong emphasis by insisting on love of neighbor first. But the commandment, she insists, tells us to love our neighbor as ourselves. "This means you have to learn to love yourself first; do that and the love of your neighbor will come," she says. "When neighborly love flows from loving God and loving yourself, it's a wonderful triad."

Ludy's involvement with her husband in clowning activity has heightened her awareness of the importance of play. They have both studied clowning and have performed in church and in other social gatherings. "If I had life to do over," she says, "I would find more time for laughter." She sees it as regaining from childhood our lost sense of surprise and celebration. Ludy urges us to celebrate many life-events that we take for granted. "We limit our celebration to births, marriages, anniversaries, and graduations" she says, "while we should extend it to all sorts of things." She counsels us to celebrate winter snow and the coming of spring, as well as very ordinary things like the cat climbing on a lap, searching around, then settling down. "Celebration doesn't always mean balloons and noisemakers," she says. "It can be an inner reaction of joy, pleasure, and delight when you recognize: 'This is nice.'"

Develop Purpose and Interests

To empower the elder self, each person needs to develop goals, purpose, and interests. One of the premises of this book is that too many people shut down in late middle age, depriving themselves of full human development and denying others the benefit of their skills and insights. Rabbi Greenberg underscores this predicament when he says: "Most people get weary of life very early. They dread retirement. I've long been convinced that the greatest enemy of life is boredom. Unless people know what to do with themselves, they get bored." But to know what to do with oneself involves having worthwhile goals and interests. This section on developing interests broadens the scope of self-empowerment. In one way, it still focuses on the individual self, and yet it also removes the self from excessive self-absorption. After describing her serious physical illnesses and disabilities, Maggie Kuhn draws away from self-absorption, saying: "An agenda is more important than my physical problems. There's a certain healing in that. I see healing in having purpose." Kuhn insists that we empower the individual self by drawing it into wider purposes. "I believe strongly," she says, "that too many people live privatized, individualized existences. They relate mainly to their families. And when their families die or are in disarray, they have nothing. There has to be greater outreach, wider expansion of the self. It's the way to healing and growth."

Creative elders express a sense of purpose in many ways, often in keeping with a lifetime of experiences in various careers. Such is the case of Herbert Karp, a geriatric neurologist in Atlanta. At seventy-two, he is planning to go to Israel, pursuing multiple interests, some of which relate to research on strokes and dementia. One has the sense that Karp is exploring his own capacities in his eighth decade as much as he is studying neurology. "It's dangerous," he says. "I'm testing myself. I don't know how well I can still learn." He will be participating in an intensive Hebrew language program, "knowing that one of the aspects of cognitive function most sensitive to aging is acquiring a new language." He is also involved in an Israeli laboratory for molecular genetics, hoping to uncover fruitful research that can be applied to Alzheimer's disease. Still another goal in the Israel soujourn involves working in a long-term facility that treats late-life degenerative diseases. "It's important to have an intense commitment to something for healthy aging," he says.

William d'Antonio, long-time director of the American Sociological Association, demonstrates interests that align with his career as a teacher and administrator. But in d'Antonio we note an honest statement of ambivalence about aging experienced by many. His voice combines regret at losses associated with aging and a clear determination to pursue new goals. "I must say that I'm not graciously growing older," he says. "When my knees hurt after handball, I resent it. My eyes are getting worse and my sex drive is diminished. That's no fun." Yet in the next breath, d'Antonio talks about his excitement at the prospect of teaching in Russia and doing more research on religion and contemporary society, his academic specialty. He proposes to combine teaching and other professional experiences to focus on helping graduate students learn how to teach and not concentrate uniquely on research. "I'd like to generate something of national value on this," he says, "and I want to work on resolving the hate-inspired violence on college campuses." For him, keeping interests alive is vital for wise aging. He sums up this purpose with a moral motive: "We have a moral obligation to do something with our lives. You save yourself by helping to save others. Maybe that's what God and love and religion are all about."

Now that she has put behind her the heavy burdens of presiding over the National Council of Churches, Claire Randall finds new freedom to pursue her interests with Church Women United. Part of her present purpose is to foster new ways for women to make satisfying contributions outside the home. "There are so many things that need doing," she says, pointing to nonprofits and volunteer organizations that languish for lack of people who have time to devote. Randall realizes that many working women today have less time for such groups, but "when these women retire," she says, "they will be skilled and trained. You don't have to be young to keep an organization alive. You can build it on retired women." Winona Sample exemplifies such a woman. After her retirement from the California Office of Child Development, she continues to serve on various boards and has become more active in American Indian and women's issues. "Outside interests are crucial," she says. "To age well, people need to find things they love to do. They should never retire from that."

For Charlee Lambert, creativity in later life coincides with having a number of interests and needing to produce something. This production can be anything that gives pleasure from flower arranging to working on social causes. "You need to feel that you're making some contribution to society," she says. Lambert continues to work into her later life as a consultant on many aging issues, including elder abuse. She works in part to support herself and her very elderly mother who lives with her. But when she talks about retirement, Lambert insists that it should be "retirement to something else that has meaning for you, not retirement into the stereotypes of a diminished old age." She looks forward to writing a book about elder abuse and adding to her twenty-two plays written to help organizations in their educational processes.

"You have to have strong interests in life," says Janet Kalven, "something you are trying to accomplish. I'm eighty and people are always amazed when I tell them how old I am." Kalven has been inducted into the Ohio Hall of Fame. Her citation reads: "Janet Kalven has combined her deep religious commitment with her educator's insight into a lifetime of advocacy for women." Yet this honor is not a reason for living on her laurels. Kalven moves toward new goals, such as finishing a book and preparing the next national conference for a network of women's groups. We can also learn from Kalven the value of being part of a stimulating movement such as the Grail, which explores new life options in feminism, ecology, interracialism, and international bonding among women. Kalven's unflagging sense of purpose in old age becomes energized by her close relationship with such a community. We will return to this topic in chapter 5 for a further discussion of the importance of communities beyond the family to help us maintain and create new interests and goals.

Summary Reflections

In this chapter, we have seen that creative elders find self-empowerment in a number of ways. They reject negative stereotypes about aging and they take steps toward holistic, mind-body health. They try to simplify their material lives. We would do well to ask ourselves how much we propagate or fall victim to ageist stereotypes. Are we among those whom Archbishop Tutu says see the old as appendages, as dependent burdens in society? Think about the images of the elderly that are presented by the media, by the comments of our own friends, and even by well-intentioned proposals for a national health plan. If we give it a little thought, we will realize how many of those images are negative. Can we

challenge our cultural attitudes by rejecting the stereotypes for ourselves and seeking to be the role models that Erlanger wanted and
that Crook urged to be included in schooling the young? Part of
our task is to remain imaginative, according to Carlton-Smith,
about how we image ourselves and present ourselves to society.
This means seeing ourselves as elders of the tribe, not wrinkled
babies, in the imagery of Maggie Kuhn. On the issue of health, a
key theme among these elders is two-sided: not making a career
out of our physical shortcomings and taking responsibility for our
own health. We might ask ourselves how well we combine the lesson
of Helen DeChatelet who advises us to take initiative for maintaining our own health in a balanced way. Eli Wallach reminds us
to simplify our lives in older age so that we can focus our energies
in satisfactory ways.

The fast pace of modern life fills our days with external concerns.
It is hard to develop habits of inwardness, to open up contemplative
spaces. Yet creative elders underscore the importance cultivating
inner resources for aging well. Elders like Tutu and Schacter-
Shalomi urge us to move away from incessant doing to discover the
quiet inner world of spiritual strength. Psychologists like Howes
and Singer deliver the same message in the language of developing
our inner and unconscious realms with their light and darkness. We
will have more to say about this theme in chapter 7. But we might
ask here how much time we set aside for thoughtful reading, prayer,
and contemplation, personal journal work, music, art, theatre and
films that can stimulate our inner resources. Are we trying in later
years, as Wallach suggests, to keep our imaginative and emotional
life alive?

The theme of self-reliance recurs often among creative elders.
They talk about it in different ways. Mary Thoits and Anne Zimmerman speak of taking control of one's life. Charlee Lambert
warns against depending too much on one person. Joseph Fichter
shows self-reliance in terms of standing up for important causes.
And Edna McCallion refers to it as expressing oneself as the unique
individual that one is. Yet the centenarian Mabel Broom puts her
finger on the key reason why we shy away from self-reliance,
namely, our various fears. The exploration of our fears, their origins
and diverse manifestions, can be a very beneficial inward project
for aging well. Mary Erlanger advises us to find a therapeutic envi-

ronment to engage our fears and to support steps beyond our fears. How well do we take charge of our own lives? How much do we live diminished existences dictated largely by social expectations or by one or another person? When we live by delegated powers, our own voice, in Tillie Olsen's sense of our full potential, is silenced.

The movement away from our limiting fears toward self-reliance is linked in the minds of creative elders to fostering self-acceptance and self-esteem. A number of interviewees spoke about being more self-confident and self-accepting in later life. They worry less about what others say or think about them. They like themselves more than they did as younger persons. Lin Ludy may have underlined a main cause of fuller self-acceptance in such elders when she talked about letting go of false expectations and demands placed on ourselves. We might ask ourselves how well we cope with certain "shoulds" and "oughts" that we carry unexamined through the years. Some of these obligations and rituals place excessive burdens on our self-acceptance. Anthony Soto and Lillian Rabinowitz remind us that self-esteem is often a byproduct of worthwhile involvements that help others. This point relates directly to the issue of maintaining purpose in elderhood as discussed below. Thus self-acceptance and self-esteem have their roots in Ludy's inward letting go and also in continuing to make contributions to our communities. Such self-acceptance leads to a spirit of serenity, based on the "distilled wisdom" mentioned by Bernice Neugarten. This serenity is not a sad resignation for such elders. Rather it is an attitude of mind and heart that approaches life peacefully. How well do we face each day with similar serenity?

The empowered elder self has developed a richer sense of humor that enjoys the ironies of life. Gregory Bergman refers to the "intrapsychic kid" that refuses to let him grow up completely. Eli Wallach looks in the mirror and sees his inner child behind the visage of an old man. These inner children bring out resources of play and laughter that give resiliency and spice to elderhood. Gerda Blumenthal tells us to reflect on turning our work into play in the now of everyday, because serious play is a lively work like music-making. Desmond Tutu knows that older age brings certain diminishments, but he encourages us to appreciate the humor of our situation as well as the pain. For each of us the expression of our inner child will differ. But wherever we are in the aging process, we can stop regularly to enjoy life's incongruities and celebrate the particular moment. An ability to celebrate, even amid difficulties, seems to mark the lifestyle of creative elders. Lin Ludy counsels us to celebrate even routine happenings around us; Rose Lucey wants her friends to have a party when she dies. What keeps us from sharing this attitude?

Finally, we hear from these elders the message of sustaining purpose in order to empower the aging self. During our working years of youth and middle age, our days are structured and driven by the goals of making a living. When people retire from their jobs, they often lack the externally structured incentives to be productive. Many end up lacking a strong reason to get out of bed in the morning and, if they can afford it, they drift along somewhat passively in leisure activities. In this situation, the risk of disempowering the elder self is great. The issue of renewing and sustaining purpose for older persons is among the most crucial in the whole eldering process. Planning for new options and goals after traditional retirement must begin as early as middle age and even earlier. Herbert Karp tells us we need an intense commitment to something worthwhile. We see Claire Randall, long after her retirement, finding purpose with Church Women United. William d'Antonio talks about cultivating moral purpose through his projects for bettering higher education. As we age, what steps are we taking, either individually or in planning groups, to explore lives of purpose for ourselves in later years? Winona Sample reminds us that people should never retire from what they love to do. In the next chapter, we see how these elders expand the rings of self-development, both within the context of their own histories and outward toward new possibilities.

CHAPTER 4

Expanding Your Elder Self

Most people do not think of older age as a time for important self-expansion. On the contrary, we remember being told in our youth that elders had their lives behind them. The general stereotype of the years after retirement from one's job depicted withdrawal, physical frailty, becoming more dependent, and slipping by inevitable steps into a second childhood. The thought of an expanding personality was reserved for youth who had their lives ahead of them. The sad thing about such stereotypes is that old people conform to them all too easily. Society's message about what it means to be old in a negative sense impacts us consciously and subliminally. The media are full of stories about long-term care, Alzheimer's, medications for the old, dwindling social security, and lonely elders on park benches or in single-room-occupancy hotels. These are, of course, real issues to be faced, but the overall picture forms a fearsome prospect of what it means to get old. Our vision of old age becomes colored by the negativities of aging, and all too often it results in a self-fulfilling prophecy.

In this chapter, we continue to show how later life can be a time for expanding the elder self, a time for exciting development in many directions. Slowing down itself can be turned into focusing on doing things that are more valuable and enjoyable for both personal and social development. Being free of certain job and family responsibilities can allow us to launch into new experiences in later life. We can learn to turn the quantity exploits of younger years into quality endeavors, thus contradicting prevalent social stereotypes. The creative elders in this book provide models for revisioning the patterns of elderhood. In the following pages, we learn from them about positive modes of reminiscing, lifelong education, turning the unpredictable into new possibilities, increasing our inner and outer freedom, and embracing later life with gratitude.

Integrate Your Past into Your Present

The past is not just water under the bridge. That is much too physical an image for the place of reminiscing in later life. As human animals we have the marvelous capacity to remember and express many of the experiences of our earlier years. Whether these memories are painful or pleasant, they are all-important for shaping who we are as older persons. We tend to critique some old people for living in the past, telling us the same old stories in a vain attempt to return to another time. Although such living in the past can become the negative side of reminiscing, it also demonstrates our longing to enjoy the past or to try to reconcile and heal past hurts. The constructive way to deal with memories is to explore them, to recollect them for the sake of our present and future life. We are all that we have been, and we need to know that past for all that we can become. Today a number of valuable techniques exist for life-review or autobiographical writing to aid individuals and groups mine the resources of the past and integrate them into the present. If an elder can realize in life-review work that he or she has already developed important coping skills and insights about life, that person has a better chance to experience worth and power as an elder.

Integrating one's past into the present implies a healthy tension between social or family ideals of the self and a person's attempt to discover the ever-developing actual or more authentic self. Working with journal groups exploring autobiography may bring out guilts and resentments. Unhelpful self-images, instilled by social roles and family expectations, surface for reexamination. Gradually, an individual comes to distinguish more clearly the true dimensions of self-identity. This permits one to find continuities with the past without becoming enslaved by it. Working with memories can help a person trace the ways by which ethnic and family backgrounds shaped values and gave meaning to life. Again, just as with formulating an adequate self-identity, the older adult may have to challenge inherited values in order to shape new guidelines for future living. Persons who can use the past to plan for the future may also experience less depression, a frequent condition of elders who are unable to establish new purposes in old age. Furthermore, working with memories gives greater confidence in one's cognitive capacities and stimulates mental activity. In light of much public concern about dementias, older people are urged, both in reference to physical and mental faculties, "to use it or lose it." Finally, reminiscing about and recording one's stories contributes to one's extended family. Younger members appreciate knowing more about their forebears, while older persons learn to view their own parents and relations with greater empathy.

Zalman Schacter-Shalomi calls this kind of work "life-harvesting." This means going back in memory to retrieve and relish accomplishments of the past. "When one can go over the past, one can harvest the good memories," he says. The sense of harvest has to do with collecting crops that can nourish the older individual. It is not merely an arbitrary game that one can choose to play. Harvesting crops is crucial for life; it is a matter of nutrition or starvation. So, too, on a humanistic or spiritual level, dealing with memories nourishes the psyche to digest the past and have the strength to move into the future. Schachter-Shalomi reminds us that there are "sorrowful mysteries" in the big file of the past that say, "don't touch because all you're going to find is anxiety, fear, and pain." But if we look at what seems to be a failure with the help of a counselor, we discover often enough that "the failure is the carrot that God hung in front of my nose to get mileage out of me," he says. In his unique language, Schachter-Shalomi tells us that "the fallout of my failures are my successes." If we are willing to face our difficult memories, those that deeply engage our feelings, we learn valuable lessons for future relationships and choices.

This process is referred to as the healing of memories, especially when an earlier experience caused us intense hurt. Or it may be that the reawakening of a memory reminds us of pain that we have caused another. *Wild Strawberries,* a film by Ingmar Bergman, powerfully depicts the healing of memories as an elderly Swedish doctor and his daughter drive to Stockholm where he is to receive a major award for his medical work. The events of the journey awaken unpleasant memories in the old man about his neglect and abusiveness in earlier relationships. His daughter also confronts him about these issues, as he undergoes a cathartic experience of remorse and forgiveness. Gregory Bergman talks about the importance of staying connected with his roots. By the rhythm of going back in time and coming forward to present situations, he stays in touch with something bigger than himself. One is not so immersed in the moment that he loses perspective about the broader pattern of life and how the whole bears on events at hand.

Continuity with one's past brings happiness in old age, says Earl Brewer, who in his postretirement years as a professor carries forward sociological projects that have been maturing for a long time. In this sense, the university is an unusual institution that offers an emeritus person support facilities for his or her interests. Many occupations and professions, however, do not provide networks of continuance after retirement. When a retiree is suddenly cut off from years of involvement with a company, his or her self-identity can be profoundly challenged. The memory stream of who one was in a particular ambiance is cut off with potentially negative outcomes in terms of self-esteem and life direction. What Gerda Blumenthal calls the tapestry of a life is torn. She associates continuity of past and present with the act of weaving. None of the threads of the weaving are absolutely determined. "I think we weave our life with the threads that are given us, which are contingent," she says. "If I were given different threads—lighter, darker, thicker, thinner—what would I have come up with? It would have been a different pattern, but it would still be unmistakably mine."

Reminiscing helps us view the whole tapestry of our lives. Sometimes the process will trigger the memory of a key turning-point event subliminally remembered into late life. Janet Ferguson recalls such an happening when she was a young student in London, away from the close tutelage of her family. Up to that point in her life, her mother, who lived vicariouly through her, made most of her important decisions. Ferguson describes the scene of repeatedly returning to the window of a travel agency for three days before she could muster the courage to book an excursion on her own without consulting her mother. Finally, she made the reservation. "That afternoon I returned to my digs at the YWCA so excited, so elated, that I sat in my chair laughing, truly aquiver with my new-found freedom," she says. "Lifelong restrictions had fallen away, and I felt like a bird soaring out of its cage, testing its wings." Reminiscing may also elicit more complex memories like those of Harriet King who remembers the day in 1986 when her husband was diagnosed with Alzheimer's. King, who has cared for her husband at home since that time, recalls their half-century marriage and how that event altered the strands in her life tapestry. Looking back without rancor but with some nostalgia, she talks about her early desire to go to medical school, which got sidetracked by marriage and family responsibilities. "If I knew then what I know now," she says, "I would have gone on in the field of medicine."

The process of working with memories also permits us to see changes in the tapestry of ourselves over the span of a long life. This is a valuable dimension of Schachter-Shalomi's "life-harvesting." "I'm still young at heart, still a romantic, an optimist," says Virginia Davis, "and I still believe there are more good guys than bad guys." But she has become more aware of changes in her personality. "I think more deeply. I'm less impulsive, except when it comes to having fun. I'm less sure of my advice when it comes to helping those close to me. I'm less patient with the trappings of modern society: recorded messages, loud music, trivial talk, banality, and greed. I love more deeply." Katherine Forsyth, a nun and educator, reflects on some personal similarities and differences during her seventy years in a religious order. Throughout her life, people have come to her for counseling on their problems. For a long time she felt guilty about the resentment this fostered in her companions. "I don't feel guilty about that any more," she says, "about people liking me and coming to me with things they want to talk about." As an older person, she also expresses openly feelings such as sadness over the closing of her college, feelings that she would have suppressed as a young nun.

Creative elders warn us, however, against focusing too much on the past. They retrieve aspects of their past for the sake of the present. June Singer is clear on this point: "I don't believe in looking back and saying 'if only.' I believe that's an exercise in futility. I did what I did, good, bad, and indifferent; here's where I am at this moment and I have to go forward from here and not worry about regrets over the past." She also tells us what "going forward" means. "It comes to seeing the future as tomorrow, the next day. If you get your three score and ten, the rest is gravy, more gift. Each day is given to you. If you do something of value with it, it's a day well spent." Clara Crook echoes these sentiments with a special reality-testing from her hip surgery. "I have always set goals for myself," she says, "and I still do. But I no longer have long-range goals for myself. That's hard because I won't see my grand-daughter graduate from college or get married, nor will I see the fruition of a lot of my work. But I have a future. I have tomorrow and want to live it in a quality way. I used to say this stuff, but now I really believe it since my hip surgery."

Creative elders do not get lost in the past or the future. They use reminiscences for the sake of the present, and they don't postpone today for expectations that may never be realized. It was striking to hear someone like E. G. Marshall, the movie actor, put so little emphasis on his celebrity career. Rather, he spoke about some of his new theatrical engagements. He wasn't interested in dwelling on screen or theater successes of the past. That was over and done. "I live in the present and don't dwell on the past," he says. Celestine Sibley is a well-known feature writer at the *Atlanta Constitution* who uses her memories of people and places for engaging pieces in her frequent columns. Of all the writers in the paper, she would most likely be the one to harvest remembrances of earlier times and old friends. But when she was asked about how to age well, she referred to her mother who lived actively in the present: "My mother, who was 83 when she died, never had an idle day in her life. She read a lot, she gardened, and she liked to have company and cook." One gets the impression that Sibley herself would want to imitate such an elderhood immersed in pleasurable activities of each day. Musing on her own eventual retirement from the news-paper, she says: "Although I can't afford it yet, I think retirement has a certain charm if you have the money to travel, put a roof on your house, and plant flowers without begging."

One can postpone life by living in the future as well as living in the past. Both memory and anticipation, a kind of "memory" pro-jected forward in time, tend to distract us from what is immediately to be enjoyed. Harriet King says that it is nice to have something to look forward to, but she cautions us not to live in the future but in the day at hand. What she says about young people in terms of living ahead of themselves pertains to the old, especially those who have never broken the habit of living as prisoners of the future. "Young people don't realize how quickly time goes by and how fast they lose opportunites. If there's anything you want to do, you better do it now or soon," says King. We have all known elders who seem unable to live in the present, who drift regularly into the past for a real or perceived comfort. Others lean into the future in their fantasies about what their friends and children ought to be doing for them. Either way, life in the present is diminished. Such elders easily become victims of reverie and resentment as today is held hostage to yesterday or tomorrow. Gerda Blumenthal sums up the wisdom of living in the present by telling us that we unify all of our aging periods—youth, middle age, and elderhood—when we embrace the present. "It is very important for aging well," she says, "to live your life as fully as possible in the present. Then you wipe out certain distinctions between the stages of youth, middle age, and old age. You are who and what you are, and you give yourself completely to the challenges with which life confronts you every day, instead of living artificially."

Continue Educating Yourself

A constant theme among creative elders for expanding the self in later life focuses on intellectual stimulation and fostering curiosity. Let us look first at an elder who stays intellectually alive through his art. Lamar Dodd is a highly respected artist and for half a century has been a leader in the art department at the University of Georgia. Although his paintings depict many objects and themes over such a long career, two sets of work are especially interesting in light of curiosity and intellectual vitality. One group of paintings portrays space flights in Florida over a twenty-five-year period. In different degrees of abstraction, these works demonstrate an imaginative mind struggling to capture what Dodd calls "the truth of things" in space flight. A second series of paintings came to be when his first wife underwent heart surgery. After that operation, the surgeon invited him to paint the drama of open-heart surgery in process. The ensuing works grasp the intensity, color, and meaning of this life-and-death intervention. "Challenges help," says Dodd, "to keep me intellectually alive in my work, in touch with new creative potential." An impressive challenge for the elder Dodd has been that of continuing to paint after two strokes left his painting arm partially paralyzed. Yet his artistic curiosity and his drive to get at the meaning of things have combined to produce new paintings done by supporting the disabled hand with his normal one.

Fostering curiosity and lifelong education is a twofold process. In part creative elders educate themselves as individuals, and in part this learning takes place through interaction with others. We see this pattern in Miriam Blaustein who, with limited eyesight, finds excitement in reading about Jewish myths and ethnic stories. Yet she also develops herself by active involvement in neighborhood civic improvements and by working with children's day-care centers. Similarly, Katherine Forsyth in her eighties takes a new course or two a year at her order's college, and until three years ago taught a course. Now she tutors students in math and mentors them in other ways. "Lifelong learning is a crucial aspect of aging well," she says. Beatrice Schiffman, who has been working directly with elder centers for two decades, associates constant inquiry with fostering better health in older people. "I think you have to keep learning all your life," she says, "because learning keeps your mind stimulated whether its through reading, taking courses, or personal involvement in arts and crafts. If you can bury yourself in such things, you don't get preoccupied with the state of your health."

As a former newspaper editor, we would expect Claude Sitton to encourage keeping up with current events. "Read widely and stay abreast of public affairs," he says. Some elders continue their education through travels connected with Elderhostel. Others attend the growing number of senior universities or "universities of the third age," as these movements are known in Europe and elsewhere. "Too many old people think they know all they need to know," says Lin Ludy. She talks about how important it is to maintain a sense of curiosity and look for surprises in life. Ike Saporta surprised himself and his doctors when ten years ago he developed colon cancer which spread to his lymph nodes. He was given a 50 percent chance to survive for six months. But when he became cured of the illness, his own physician attributed healing in large part to his intense love of life and beauty. Saporta, an architect, is also an artist whose drawings hang in his living room. His home is open to young musicians who can be heard practicing in the music room. "The quest for knowledge and the love of beauty," he says, "are more important than material wealth." Saporta, who has seen his financial fortunes rise and fall at various times in his life, speaks from personal experience. Something about the look in his eyes and the smile on his face convinces one that these sentiments are genuine.

"To prepare well for old age, read a lot and ponder what you read," says Helen DeChatelet. This elder school teacher exemplifies her own advice by attending seminars and workshops, participating in study groups, "watching educational stuff on TV, and listening to classical music." But DeChatelet also keeps learning by counseling other elders. "It's important to have a good counselor," she says, "someone to talk with, someone who will accept you as you are no matter what you say." Looking back, she regrets that she didn't appreciate this counselor role earlier. When her father wanted to talk about his aging, she would change the subject or refuse to listen. "I feel bad about that now," she says. But at the time she did not have the wisdom she possesses today, she claims, a wisdom that comes from more adequately facing reality.

Willis Hurst, a cardiologist and educator, underscores and refines the link between lifelong education and wisdom mentioned by DeChatelet. Hurst, author of a widely used textbook on heart medicine and former personal physician for President Lyndon Johnson, stresses the element of curiosity for sustaining one's education. His mother, a school teacher, emphasized intellectual curiosity and learning from his earliest years. "It's tragic that the young," he says, "have their initiative and curiosity blunted by family, environment, and society." We might add that our educational system, through rote learning and regimentation, also suppresses the inquiring spirit of the young.

Hurst adds an important interpretation of educating ourselves toward wisdom in later life when he describes the "wisdom loop." Wisdom comes from facing many problems in life, thinking them through, and coming to decisions on a course of action. But the key point for becoming wise is "to become extraordinarily sensitive to the results, that is, the impact of your earlier thoughts, decisions, and actions on other people." Wise persons learn from the repetition of the process and fold back what they've learned into decision-making for the next situation. "It's a loop," he says. "There can be no wise person without the loop." He emphasizes the importance of cultivating a spirit of learning in himself as a teacher and in his students. For Hurst part of this spirit consists in staying interested in a wide range of issues beyond one's area of specialization and in shaping around himself a community of inquiry.

Hurst's idea of the loop toward wisdom can be seen in other elders who teach and learn at the same time. Jimmy Carter has launched his Atlanta Project to enlist volunteers from different strata in the city to assist the needy in a variety of ways. This program is expanding into areas of housing, education, physical education, and a number of other realms. But Carter is not only teaching and encouraging people to share their skills, care, and time. He is also learning through public discussion and criticism of Atlanta Project's undertakings. When Carter talks about his initial insights about the new endeavor, he refers to his own concrete learning experiences through visiting the poor in housing projects and in a neonatal unit where he saw underweight and drug-afflicted newborns. He admits that as president and governor, he had not understood in such tangible ways the plight of the poor. The former president becomes a constant learner in order to lead his new project.

Eugene Odum continues to do some teaching and writing in ecology, but he is also engaged in new ways of educating himself. Odum, sometimes referred to as the father of modern ecology, now strives to reach a wider, more popular audience through his lectures and publications. He continues to direct a technical study of the Georgia landscape to aid in establishing an infrastructure for land-use planning. But he is also having to learn new communication skills to address the general public in order to achieve his late-life goal of being "a missionary preaching ecology to anyone who will listen." The title of his latest manuscript, "Our Big House: Understanding Ecology," reflects his elder vocation to reach the widest possible audience. He describes human life systems as parasites on our host, the earth. To keep "the parasite from killing the host" is a new way of thinking for most people, he claims. Odum works to find the best modes of mass communication to propagate ecology. He educates himself in new ways of popularizing his environmental messages.

Welcome Possibilities, Even Surprises

Very few people in our culture associate older age with new possibilities. In subtle and overt ways, we connect aging with limited options, with lessening energies, and with withdrawal from the new and exciting. Advertising, movies, as well as the print and visual media, inculcate an image of the old in rocking chairs watching the world go by. Life is behind them. The best they can do is enjoy a little leisure and attend to their aches and pains. But creative elders reject this ruling image of old age, both in their thinking and actions.

Schachter-Shalomi, who conducts workshops on the eldering process, awakens people to a different way of looking at later life. "People don't know how much choice they have," he says. "I want to show them that they have an embarrassment of riches." Old persons actually have more time to welcome new possibilities; earlier their lives were more constrained by keeping jobs and raising families. Home, school, and workplace laid down a limited track for their activities. Now they are confronted with Maggie Kuhn's question: What do you want to do with the rest of your life? "When they begin to see how much choice they have, they start getting anxious," says Schachter-Shalomi. They begin asking what other people do. In some ways this anxiety indicates a fear of trying something new, but it also manifests a lack of role models. "Hardly anyone knows the role of an elder anymore," he says. The elders in this book offer us such models, if we look closely at their attitudes and actions in old age.

To prepare themselves for embracing new options, people need to face and work through the fears and anxieties that arise. Michael Erlanger, who paints, writes poetry, and works on dreams after a long career in the business world, understands these fears when faced with new possibilities in later life. "Most people are closed because they are frightened," he says. "They could break these patterns in older age, but most don't because they are too rigidly fixed in old ways." Mabel Broom at 106 teaches a similar lesson about moving beyond one's fears in order to stay open to possibilities. "Don't be afraid," she says. "Welcome the things that come to you. That's the way I try to live, with a song in my heart and trust in God. But I'm not sanctimonious. I'll say 'damn' if I don't like something." It is probably true that many persons in later life are discouraged by their fears from greeting new possibilities. They talk about being set in their ways, and they try to avoid the experience of vulnerability that comes with facing novel experiences. But many other elders would be able to overcome their fear of the new if they had good counseling and some form of group support. They can take courage from elders who model such venturesomeness of spirit.

Edwin Hayden, an evangelical minister and religious editor, has a unique way of describing his philosophy of staying open to things. He likens his journey in later life to a motorist who sees the world through different panels of glass. "The side windows let him see his neighbor," he says, "while the rear-view mirror shows him where he's been. The wise driver, even at the end of his trip, will look mostly through the windshield, which shows the road ahead. Keep looking forward to things in life." Hayden does not give this advice lightly. For many years he had to make the best possibilities out of his wife's struggle with Parkinson's disease. In a book that he wrote about these experiences, Hayden advises us not to equate the difficult with the impossible. He talks about the things that he and his wife continued to do after they became hard. He discusses enjoying what they still had together as special gifts rather than bemoaning what was lost. Such an illness is certainly not an option one would choose. But adapting to it helped him live out his own advice to others: "Learn something you don't know and do something you haven't done." He had to learn about untapped depths in their relationship, and he learned to do difficult new things like pushing her wheelchair while not succumbing to guilt and embarrassment. An unforeseen benefit of coping with his wife's illness was becoming cured from his own hypochondria. He saw doctors frequently until his mid-forties, about the time she became sick. Involvement in her care cured him of being a hypochondriac.

As an example of staying open to possibilities, Bertram Gross's remarkably varied life stands out. "My mother wanted me to be a professional writer," he says, "but my father just wanted me to be a human being." His journey to those goals over eighty years brought him to many unexpected milestones. He turned to professional wrestling in the mid-thirties when, with an advanced degree in literature, he couldn't find a job. Eventually he got work as a reporter for a magazine where he learned a good deal about politics. He even became a Communist for a while during the late thirties. Again his life changed when a friend became head of the U.S. Housing Authority in 1938 and offered him a job in Washington. In the late forties, he became executive secretary for the Council of Economic Advisers and expanded his experience of economic policy in Korea and Israel. His many publications helped him become a professor in various universities. "I like change," he says. "I'm something of a butterfly, going from one thing to another. But I like challenge, new interests, new worlds to conquer. I keep six books going at the same time." One of his latest challenges has been to write a set of politically critical lyrics for a rap group. Even after a heart attack in 1979 and bypass surgery more recently, he is writing a book on Gandhi and another on human rights. "Being old and sick is marvelous," he says, "and I'm a holy terror with the doctors."

In his late seventies, Douglas Cook complains about having less energy and needs a nap in the afternoon. But he talks about "accessing possibilities" for aging well. This retired minister sees many options for older people: "If you're retired and have independence," he says, "you can choose what you want to do, where you want to put your energies. You can start something if you want to or you can pick up on what others have done." Cook has no problem with friends who are content with playing golf as elders, but this would not be satisfying for him. Instead he uses his experience of church service in India and the Philippines to work with foreign students at Emory University. He tries to help them with their personal, cultural, and monetary problems. "There are lots of ways of aging well," he says, "but for me making a difference is crucial." In Cook, we see an old man who continues a lifetime of dedication to people in a new way, open to options as they present themselves. He also finds personal satisfaction in fulfilling real needs of others. "You have to take what you have and what you're given," he says, "and go from there."

A similar theme of going on from what one is given stands out in Anne Zimmerman's answer to a question about what she would do if she could live her life over again. She speculated that she would probably not have married. Her husband left her with child shortly after the wedding. But she adds immediately that then she would not have had the daughter who has been such a joy in her life. If she had it to do over, she might have gone on to more schooling. Again, she realizes that if she had taken that road, she would not have started her administrative career with nursing associations that led to national prominence as president of the American Nurses Association. Zimmerman was accessing that amalgam of possibilities and necessities that constitutes every life. As an octogenarian, she continues to welcome possibilities despite a number of skeletal surgeries in recent years. She is active as a minister of care for her church, even though her earlier encounters with a rigid form of Catholicism were not supportive. She also remains involved in groups that are trying to reform the health-care system. A lifetime of staying open to options brings her vicarious pleasures when she thinks about the nursing students she taught at Loyola University in Chicago. "It is such a joy to see people I've contacted as a mentor prosper and develop. I think they got the genesis of that from my course. When I see these people whom I've helped working influentially for justice in health care, it gives me more satisfaction than anything else."

Possibilities come into our lives through hardship and disappointment as well as through kindlier invitations. When we learn to turn these unbidden events into potentials for insight and action, we train ourselves for an elderhood of accessing possibilities. Maggie Kuhn's life as it approaches its ninetieth year gives us personal examples of turning seeming defeat into new vistas. "I've had a glorious life," she says, "but it's had its share of tragedy and loss." One of these was the illness of her brother whom she took care of in her home for twenty years. His long mental illness made her realize the importance of mental health and how little we know about it. Not only did this experience make her more sensitive to mental-health needs, but it seems to have spurred her on in her work with the Gray Panthers. "The day he died," she says, "I got on the plane and said, 'I haven't landed yet.'" Again, she transformed the disappointment of her mandatory retirement at sixty-five into a national movement of elders who explore new ways of remaining involved in important social causes.

Kuhn's openness to possibilities from her personal life relates closely to her accessing of social options. She is writing a book about the intersection of history and biography in her own life. She notes how her own perspective has changed by becoming involved in social movements. "In my lifetime," she says, "I have seen all these movements: labor, civil rights, women's, peace, and environmental. All of these have impacted on my life and called on me to change my thinking and action." She realizes that change is diffiuclt for many people; clinging to the known feels comfortable. But her work with the Gray Panthers, as we see from the testimony of some elders in this book, shows that older people can change and access possibilities. In very important ways, Kuhn's legacy countermands conventional wisdom about the inflexibility of the old. She has inspired a new vision of elderly potential that transcends the perspective of major organizations like the American Association of Retired Persons. In general, the AARP works for the interests of older Americans, but it does not summon them to a radical rethinking of elderhood, a vision that offers the old a new self-understanding in society. Kuhn sounds such a call when she says: "I like to think that we old people with our varied experiences are elders of the tribe. We're not concerned about our own interests, but about the tribe's survival and well-being."

Welcoming possibilities and surprises implies a future for the old. The messages about this topic in contemporary culture are ambiguous. One voice announces that for the elderly the future is behind them. They are has-beens in a society driven by the young and the beautiful. If the old possess wealth, they had better cling to it, because the young will soon take or inherit it. This message pictures the old as facing a beseiged future with defeat assured in a competitive world. Another voice portrays the future in terms of scarcity and decline for the old. The old are urged to focus mainly on issues of health and physical or social security. This is a reduced future, hemmed in by anxieties. Still another voice presents a golden-ager future characterized largely by leisure and consumer activities. Although there are elements worth taking seriously in these modern orchestrations of the future in old age, their overall vision is bleak.

Creative elders stand against these cultural messages and carve out quality futures for themselves.

It would be too lengthy to describe in detail here the many things that elders propose for the time remaining to them. Even in brief the list includes endeavors that contradict the cultural perspectives mentioned above. They talk about reading, lecturing, and writing. They look toward enjoying music and the arts, as well as engaging directly in some form of art or craft. They speak about traveling, visiting friends and family, grandparenting, taking courses, and doing things that bring them more closely into contact with nature. They want to open up more space in their lives for contemplation and other techniques for meditatively integrating their lives. With an almost universal sentiment, they look for ways of serving others and the needs of the planet. Perhaps Charlee Lambert best characterizes the sense of a creative future for the elderly when she says: "I want to stay productive and reflective. The future for me is a time to share and to receive, but above all, the future should be a time of passionate living for us older people." To live toward the future with passion is another way of talking about welcoming possibilities. This is a far cry from the the image of the future for the old as presented in modern society.

Elise Boulding advocates a process of continually creating new futures by acting on what one sees in the present. She counsels older people to remember how they might have envisioned futures when they were younger. Some of what they projected into their futures came to be. "You built up images of the future in earlier life," she says, "and some of what you envisioned came about. This process needs to go on in older age, too." She sees this imaging or visualization process as important for the old. "What it is that you would like the world to be like tomorrow tells you what it is you should do today." Boulding insists that this process is not escapism, but rather social daydreaming on behalf of society. One becomes responsible for bringing the dream into reality. Although the future is unpredictable, it is also in a true sense present in us now. The way we imagine it and work toward it determines in part how it will be. Schachter-Shalomi is also an optimistic futurist about the role of old people. He foresees them acting as arbitrators and mediators in a world that is evolving toward greater communicability. In light of the destructive divisions among and within nations today, his vision of conflict resolution on a grand scale may appear overly optimistic. Yet to link his vision with that of Boulding, the process of dreaming forward positive tendencies and technologies of the present may be a crucial ingredient for bringing them about. Schachter-Shalomi envisions the communications revolution leading to a kind of "global telepathy, a heating up of the planet to such a level of communicability that it will jump the wires into new forms of conflict resolution."

Foster Elder Freedom

One of the best things about being older, say many elders, is an experience of greater freedom. Often this sense of being liberated stems from a lessening of family and job burdens, but just about as frequently it also results from a kind of inner liberation. For those who are open to change at a deeper level, the gradual winnowing process of life helps these elders sluff off psychic and spiritual burdens of the past. Another way of talking about this development is to see it as a dynamic between freedom from and freedom for. In life-review interviews, this pattern repeats itself as persons reflect on their past situations of internal and external restraints. Often these "captivities" from which they experience freedom are also connected to negative self-evaluations or to less firm self-identities in earlier years.

Tillie Olsen talks about this freeing of persons in terms of their being able to communicate their thoughts and feelings from the center of who they really are. It is matter of breaking silences imposed on us by family, society, and by our own fears. "I feel that the passion to communicate, to express oneself, is inherent in human beings," she says, "but circumstances often deny people the opportunity to develop such expression." One of her best-known books, *Silences*, reveals the many ways by which individuals attempt to break their silences to speak or act authentically. "To be able to put things in the context of their whole lives," she says, "to be able to comprehend the patterns of the past and to be able to articulate all this to themselves—that's what I feel has been the domain of the privileged. And that's what I want everyone to have." As an acclaimed writer, Olsen has accomplished this goal in a literary way through her stories and essays. But other people have potentials to realize the freedom to communicate in their own ways. In the aging process toward greater freedom, persons need to cultivate what Olsen calls "that divine spark of resistance, not accepting what is ordained or given to you." She is referring to those life circumstances that gag our true voices and keep us from experiencing the freedom that creative elders know in later life.

Elders express freedom from past confinements in a number of ways. For Miriam Blaustein, who has lived as a social activist from her days in an Israeli kibbutz to her present civic involvements in San Francisco, a deep personal pain has been estrangement from a daughter, her only child. This has also meant estrangement from an only granddaughter whom she doesn't get to see. Through therapy and self-reflection she has learned to let go of much of this pain, even though she doesn't understand why the break occurred. "I'm learning to live my last years without the pain and mourning associated with it," she says, "and I don't build up expectations that the situation will change. But I won't march through the rest of my life with my chin on my chest." When Lillian Rabinowitz says, "I'm a free soul," the statement resonates in the context of much hurt and confinement earlier in life. Her years of active work on behalf of the elderly have given her a fuller sense of her true personality. This in turn has helped to free her from resentments over failed marriages and other family disappointments. Neither Blaustein nor Rabinowitz denies the pain of their memories, but they welcome their release from the intensity of these deep wounds. Rabinowitz also adds an important reflection related to letting go of the unchangeable past: "I'm not as rigid in my moral judgments as I used to be. I'm much more willing to accept what I find out about people, realizing that life is both good and evil."

Gerald Taylor, a Carmelite priest, looks back in elderhood on a long and difficult story of freedom from addiction to alchohol. He remembers a very dysfunctional family with angry and abusive parents. "They fought all the time," he says, recalling that his father took a strap to him and his mother would hit his head against the wall. At first he sided with his mother, but eventually came to befriend his father and understand how he, too, was abused in the relationship. He talks about living in a fantasy world as a child, not doing well in school, until he convinced his parents to put him in a Catholic school. He sees that strong desire to go to a Catholic school in the fourth grade as one of the "God-events" or turning points in his life. Much of his ministry was spent as a navy chaplain which allowed him the privacy to indulge his alcoholic addiction. "Although I went to a lot of parties in the navy," he says, "I was a private drinker; my serious drinking happened after the public partying was done." His closest friends didn't know he had a problem until he began having blackouts. "I would cook a meal and have dinner," he says, "and the next morning I'd see pots and dishes with no memory of having prepared or eaten a meal. Then I knew I was in trouble."

He resolved repeatedly to stop drinking, and would follow the resolution for about three days. "I would pray and make promises to God," he says, "but I wasn't able to do it." In the mid-sixties he went to a recovery meeting, but "was scared to death" and didn't go back for three years. On his way to his ship in Norfolk one morning "with an enormous hangover," he saw a sign "Happiness is a Recovered Alcoholic" with a phone number. He called the number saying that he was a navy chaplain who was sending a fellow officer to the meeting. The recovering alcoholic saw through the ruse, befriended him, and led him to two years of participation in a self-help program. Although he has been sober since then, Taylor recognizes his proclivity to addictive behavior. But his sobriety made possible another turning point in his life, the completion of a master's degree in social work at Rutgers when he left the navy in midlife.

Reflecting on the difficult passages in his journey, Taylor talks both psychologically and spiritually about his freedom from alcoholic addition. "I have come to the realization of who I am," he says, "and I'm satisfied to be who I am." He thinks about the many things that condition and confine us early in life, "all those voices of family, associates, the church . . . we finally have to get free from all these." For him, one of the great graces of getting older is not having to prove himself anymore. "I can be myself," he says, "and I have a craving for truth and honesty, no matter where that may take me." This new sense of freedom has led him to visit his parents' graves to forgive and be forgiven. It has also allowed him to disagree with the Catholic Church on many issues. His honesty with himself has drawn him away from viewing God as the vindictive parent he knew in childhood. "If this is a good, kind, and compassionate God," he says, "then why do I have to worry if I don't agree with the church on some point?" Honesty and freedom are closely linked for a man with Taylor's background. "If my aim is to find out as much truth as I can about myself, God, and the world," he says. "I may have to stand alone sometimes, but it's finally a peaceful place to stand."

The main lines of Peter Kelley's story describe another journey to greater freedom in later life. A singer and actor in his early years, he later became a successful talent agent in New York. Kelley portrays his parents as strict Catholics in a dysfunctional marriage. His relationship to his father was stormy "with lots of lickings with a razor strap. Yet I became a duplication of the old man," he says, "in different ways; I was domineering, controlling." He looks back on his early church experiences as emotionally repressive. He remembers the fear that gripped him when he was told by a priest in the confessional that his masturbation was a mortal sin worthy of hell. "All the youthful sexuality welled up in me like a bomb," he says, "always ready to trigger new fears. I confessed masturbation every day." The parochial-school nuns were a source of emotional support "which I didn't get at home." While his mother supported his musical career, his father opposed it, never going to one of his concerts.

According to his telling of it, Kelley's bondage became his sexual addiction. He married in college and eventually had six children. "But I lived a double life," he says. "I had rationalized myself into a promiscuous kind of sexuality in which there was hardly anything I didn't try. I did such a con job on myself that you can't believe." Years later he began to realize that his conduct was hurting other people and himself. "I began to see that I was a sexual addict in the classic sense and became disgusted with myself." He found that "all the confessions in the world" didn't help with his deep emotional and spiritual problem. Meanwhile his wife was engaged in a long struggle with her own problem.

Kelley's road to freedom from his addiction is marked by both spiritual and psychological moments. He recalls the experience of hearing a voice when he was preparing for a sexual activity. The voice said that he would be helped if he took some spiritual steps on his own. "Since that moment," says Kelley, "I have not had a liaison with another woman." A major psychological turning point for him was a long series of truth-telling sessions with his wife who was working on her own recovery. These painful encounters gradually led to reconciliation and a new level of mutual acceptance in their marriage. For Kelley, psychological and spiritual recovery programs have been "like a new Pentecost," opening up avenues of freedom in later life. He is now involved in the Pastoral Formation Institute, a movement that trains lay people to promote religious life in areas where clergy are not available.

Robert McAfee Brown, a well-known theologian, underlines a point that relates to both of the men above who experienced freedom from forms of servitude. Looking back on a life of extensive publication, teaching at major universities, and involvement in movements for social change, Brown sees his life "as trying to do battle with idols." Idols, in this sense, can be anything that claims absolute rightness or power, whether in areas of politics, social structures, cultural ways, or religious teaching. Taylor and Kelly in their own ways struggled with idols of addiction that held sway over their lives. After a prominent career as author and teacher, Brown has "deabsolutized" his own perspectives in later life. "My theological convictions are much more modest," he says. "I don't want to claim inordinate things. And I'm becoming more able to let things go." He no longer feels guilty if he isn't in the latest demonstration for a chosen cause. He feels freed from taking himself too seriously. "I felt harrassed for many years," he says, "as there never was enough time to do everything, and I'd take on more than I could handle." Freedom from compulsions to save the world single-handedly can led to much greater serenity "and time to enjoy my family."

Katherine Forsyth says that she feels freer and younger in her eighties than she did at fifty. "I was condemning myself for everything then, taking life too seriously, feeling guilty if people praised me," she says. For this elderly nun, the freeing process had to do in part with coming to terms late in life with issues of her own sexuality. "I was educated in that old negative form of Catholic piety," she says, "which held that you weren't holy unless you were suffering or at least half miserable." Overcoming the guilts connected with accepting human love was a gradual, freeing experience for her. Although the context of Dorothy Stark's life has been very different from that of a Catholic nun, there are some interesting similarities. Stark, an artist and sculptor, says that the best thing about being older is her greater sense of personal freedom. "You don't have as much to struggle with." For Stark this remark relates to transcending a negative self-image and overcoming other pressures in family life. An unhappy childhood left her insecure, submissive, withdrawn, and feeling socially unacceptable. "When I was young," she says, "I felt that I was this ugly girl with big feet and foul skin." Her long marriage to Arthur Stark, after both of their initial marriages failed, has been an experience of love freeing her from earlier negativities. "I think my life with Arthur," she says, "has been so good that I feel very comfortable and happy right now."

One of the strongest themes concerning freedom among creative elders is a liberated ability to express themselves. On this point, they confirm Tillie Olsen's vision of breaking silences. What is the best thing about growing old? "The freedom to speak out," says Virginia Davis, "and not care what other people think." "Aging has made me freer and freer," echoes Ella Mazel. In her case, psychoanalysis provided a path for casting off self-limiting burdens of the past. But she also finds that gray hair turns her into a mentor for younger persons. People look up to her for her long experience in life. "I feel much more free to say what I think, do what I want, and not worry about what anybody else thinks." But Page Smith, a well-known American historian, adds an important dimension to the freedom to express oneself. He agrees that as elders "we can speak our minds on matters about which we may have been inhibited earlier." Yet for him this liberated expression should be a freedom to do things with and for other people. He is disturbed by an individualistic exaggeration that links self-expression with narrow needs of the ego. He urges elders to understand their freer expression in a social network. "I think you become a person," he says, "by the way you act in the world and by your capacity to enter sympathetically into the lives of other people."

Even though Page Smith and others remind us to appreciate how much we owe our freedom to supportive communities, the creative elder has internalized his or her freedom in a personal way. He or she is less driven by social convention, because the experiences of a lifetime have gradually brought about an interior liberation. "The real freedom comes from within," says Frances Pauley, who has been a social crusader all her years. And Mabel Broom looks back to more than a century of life to say: "I feel free within myself." It is remarkable testament to the human spirit that our most liberated moments of mind and heart may develop at a time when our physical powers are on the wane. Teilhard de Chardin calls this phenomenon growth through diminishment, while Carl Jung refers to it as the spiritual ascent during the curve of physical descent.

Live with Gratitude

A strong trait among creative elders is a spirit of gratitude toward life. They are able to receive the small and large gifts along the way as blessings that evoke thankfulness. When we listen to their stories, it is easy to understand how these people can be thankful for things that we would consider positive or joyful. But in these lives there have been disappointments, failures, losses, even tragedies. These elders do not deny the pain and hardship of the negative events, but they seem to be able to learn from them or at least to accept them as they turn back toward life. Gregory Bergman suffered greatly at the sudden death of his wife in an auto accident. And he has known his share of illness along the way to his ninth decade. But he has learned to turn the arrow outward, as he says, deflecting the energy that would only intensify his grief into positive actions for others. "Face things straight on," he says. "Don't try to cover over life experiences with denial or euphemisms." He sees himself as a thankful person. "Gratitude is such an important part of life," he says. "I never expected to live so long." Simon Greenberg in his nineties reflects the same sentiment, even though his wife's frail health makes this "the most difficult period of my life." She has been a shut-in for years and he is always on call to oversee her care. But he is glad to have one more day in an already long life. "I'm swimming in a sea of gratitude," he says. "I think gratitude is the basis of character."

Philip Land, an elderly Jesuit who has taught and written extensively in the area of social justice, uses a mantra of gratitude when he faces difficult situations. As a progressive social thinker, he has had conflicts with Vatican authorities. More recently he has had to face serious surgery. In these and less stressful events, Land recites his mantra of gratitude, taken from the Bible: "This is the day the Lord has made, let us rejoice and be glad therein." For Land, tension fades dramatically when he repeats his mantra. He is grateful to be able to continue his writing, but more than that, he gives thanks for living in a small community in Washington dedicated to social change, because it continues to teach him about feminism and new ways of living as a priest. He can say, "I'm scandalized by the patriarchy of my church," while at the same time being gratefully committed to new theological and ethical perspectives in Catholicism.

To age well, says Paul Schweitzer, a former high-school principal, a person must approach life with gratitude. He is particularly grateful to family, children, and friends who were helpful to him over the years. "As you age, you become more grateful for small things," says Joanne Stevenson, who works with senior centers. She points to the "little" things calling for thanks like a beautiful day, flowers, and a friendly person one may encounter unexpectedly. Gratitude is a sign of true maturity, because it connotes a stage of life in which we no longer make excessive demands on others nor do we entertain false expectations about how things should be. The opposite of gratefulness is an attitude of taking everything for granted, of expecting and demanding that the world serve us. It is to be still fixed in the immature dimensions of childhood from which the aging process weans us. Anthony Soto looks back on his life and says: "Gratitude marks my aging. Why have I been so fortunate? Hey, when the summons comes, I'll be ready to go." These elders in their thanksgiving remind us of the words of Dag Hammarskjöld: "For all that has been, thanks; for all that shall be, yes."

Summary Reflections

Creative elders develop themselves by moving back in memory to get a view of their whole tapestry of life, as Gerda Blumenthal says. They gain perspective on themselves in this process of "life-harvesting," according to Schacter-Shalomi, examining successes and failure, hurts and joys to learn from them. In this way, older people can see how they have changed and how they continue to grow. It can be very valuable for us to do reminiscing work through private journal-keeping or in group endeavors. The very process of writing and expressing verbally important memories can be enjoyable and liberating. Seeing where we have been opens us up to new possibilities that we might have missed without such reflection. We discover lines of force in skills, interests, and emotional patterns that can help us make decisions about the best steps to take in the present. June Singer counsels us against an excessive focus on the past, and Harriet King warns about living mainly in the future. In either exaggeration, we miss the present which is the only life we have. Our question becomes: How best to gather up the past for the sake of the present and the proximate future?

Creative aging calls for lifelong learning. Elders repeatedly talk about the importance of intellectual stimulation through many forms of education. We saw Lamar Dodd and Ike Saporta continuing their mental creativity through art. Katherine Forsyth and Helen DeChatelet pursue their education by taking courses and participating in workshops. Elders who spoke about continuing their education, like Jimmy Carter and Eugene Odum, underscored the close connection between learning and teaching as intrinsically complementary activities. We would do well to ask ourselves about our plans and actions for continuing to educate ourselves. Have we abandoned good reading and discussion for more passive pursuits? Do we look for communities of inquiry where we can be motivated to learn more about ourselves and the world? Are we seeking to expand our "wisdom loop," the phrase of Willis Hurst, by building on our experiences with new knowledge?

To see later life as a time for new possibilities challenges stereotypes of old age. As Schacter-Shalomi says, the what and how of accessing new options in elderhood is a still largely unexplored terrain. But more role models are appearing and showing the way. Mary Erlanger and Mabel Broom speak of the fears that keep us from welcoming the new. The gradual overcoming of our fears of trying new possibilities calls for a variety of remedies, some rational, others emotional. Other remedies involve taking concrete steps toward the new. We usually need support from individuals and groups to venture beyond our fears. Yet the role models for accessing opportunities among the elderly are many among the participants in this project. Bertram Gross with his many careers and other accomplishments is characteristic of the others. Welcoming possibilities and even surprises doesn't imply an unrealistic or Pollyanna approach to aging. Anne Zimmerman reminds us about the interplay between limitations and possibilities as we age. And Edwin Hayden, finding creative ways to take care of his sick wife, exemplifies the potentials for drawing mutual benefit from hard circumstances. What are the things that we wanted to do earlier in life but were restrained from accomplishing by our situations? Or what new happenings in our life demand that we reshape our earlier dreams in unforeseen ways? Whatever our circumstances in later life, we can address them, as Charlee Lambert advises, with passion. As an elder, she talks about living in the present with passion toward the future. And Elise Boulding suggests that we image the futures we desire for ourselves and those around us.

Accessing new possibilities in later life means becoming a freer person inwardly and externally. On one level, we have the chance to be freed from negative ways that may have hobbled our human growth in earlier periods. Gerald Taylor and Peter Kelley provide dramatic examples of life-inhibiting captivities in which they found themselves. Dorothy Stark speaks about being freed from childhood negativities that impeded her self-esteem. Katherine Forsyth is free in her eighties from the guilts of earlier years. Robert McAfee Brown looks back on his many involvements as teacher and theologian to detect in himself a freeing from absolutes, from dogmatic visions of how the world should be. It could be a useful exercise, whether in private or in a small group, to ask ourselves what burdensome baggage of the past we are free from in middle age or in elderhood. But freedom from is correlative to freedom for. Are we, with Tillie Olsen, breaking the self- or other-imposed silences that muffled our true voice in the past? In what ways is our elder speaking out an exercise of new freedom? We can let ourselves be challenged by the question of Page Smith: How has our elder freedom been put to work for the welfare of others and of society?

Smith's question brings us to the rim of the third circle after those of empowering and expanding the elder self. In the next chapter, we explore ways in which elders reach out to others and to their wider communities. But we must not neglect a vital ingredient in this whole process, an element that stood out in so many of the elders' reflections, namely, living with a conscious and powerful sense of gratitude. They are thankful for blessings of the past and for each new dawn. This sense of gratitude seems to be a vitally important aspect of aging well. They do not take life for granted. Having a grateful bent of personality seems to spur them on to relish and benefit from elderhood. We would do well to ask ourselves frequently how conscious is our gratefulness for the blessings and the wounds of life. What could be better than to arrive at the last shore of our lives with the spirit of Simon Greenberg, who in his nineties, finds himself awash in a sea of gratitude?

CHAPTER 5

Reaching Out
from the Elder Self

A very strong theme running through the interviews with creative elders has been the importance of reaching out beyond the confines of the individual self. This chapter will focus on the widening rings of this outreach from the family circle to that of the planet. Sally Lilienthal, who directs Ploughshares, a fund for examining the problems and dangers of the nuclear industry, put her finger on the theme of this chapter when she said: "It takes a big will to do it, but the elder needs to become interested in something outside oneself. I think that's the essential thing. The problem is that older people become bored and then grow smaller. They need to get involved with passion." This passion is not limited to social causes. It can range in many directions, such as art, travel, gardening, and other realms. We will explore some of the expanding rings of these concentric circles from personal family to planetary communities in the reflections of creative elders.

Cherish Your Family

Our families of origin as well as the families we later create are usually the networks of our most intense emotions and commitments. The older person will have established deep links, positive and negative, with family members. Adults carry a combination of all those feelings in one proportion or another toward their parents. It is interesting that women among the interviewees were more able to discuss the negative impact of their families of origin than the men. Perhaps this represents a continuation of the women's awareness of relationships and their sensitivity to emotional influence. It may be that men are more inclined to "tough out" the family problematic of their past, or at least to downplay it in favor of perceived positive influences. Four men who achieved high public standing in Georgia stressed the powerful influence of their fathers in shaping the wider social service of their sons.

Ivan Allen Jr., who led the Atlanta community as mayor during its halcyon days of civil rights, speaks reverentially of his father as the most influential person in his life. Sitting in front of a large portrait of the patriarch, the eighty-three-year-old Allen says: "Daddy was my inspiration, a pattern that I tried to follow all through life . . . consciously or unconsciously . . . it's hard to say. But certainly he was in the back of my mind." Allen Sr. was a prominent civic leader and served in the Georgia state senate. Men like Allen show how deeply their families impacted on their own careers. By honoring their inspiring elders in memory, they carry forward into later life the social dedication instilled in them. Jack Etheridge, a lawyer, judge, and leader in mediation, says of his father, who was also a lawyer and the youngest judge in Georgia history: "He's been the idol of my life. I knew from the first day I could recall that I was going to be a lawyer." Etheridge talks about his respect for his father and also about his grief at his relatively early death. Etheridge continues in his later years to be actively involved in wider social issues such as the reform of the judicial and legal systems to serve more fairly not only the business community but the broader public through negotiation and mediation.

Charles Weltner, congressman and chief justice of the Georgia Supreme Court, speaks of trying to imitate his father, a lawyer and first chancellor of the board of regents at the University of Georgia. "He was the main influence on me," Weltner says, "and we always thought of my father as God." Aside from the theological hesitations that a staunch Presbyterian like Weltner might have with such a statement, we see how far into one's life the paternal influence carries. Weltner's courageous stands on racial justice and his work in court reform represent the living forward of his father's legacy of public involvement. Of his father, Joseph Lowery, president of the Southern Christian Leadership Conference, he says: "I have a great deal of respect for him as a man, his integrity and compassion in the midst of strength. He had a very heavy influence on my sense of manhood and selfhood. He gave me a sense of integrity and wanting to serve people as he served them as a businessman." Lowery's Christian ministry from his earlier days of close collaboration with Martin Luther King Jr. to his present leadership of the well-known civil-rights organization carries forward the influence of his father.

The two oldest participants in the project also emphasized how much their families of origin shaped their later lives. Mabel Broom at 106 remembers her father who as a very young man had served the Confederacy in the Civil War and later ran an iron mill in Selma, Alabama. But she attributes her good start in life to two older brothers and a sister. "They taught me to dance, whistle, sing, and they put love in my heart," she says. This sense of family continued after the death of her husband when she helped her daughter raise her own child. What Broom learned from her siblings about living with a positive spirit radiates today in the smaller social environment of a long-term care facility. Cherishing his family is very important in the reminiscences of Broom's nursing-home neighbor, Woolford Baker, who at 101 recalls his decision to leave his family farm in Arkansas to pursue a career in biology. As the first male child, he became the hope of his father for continuing the farm tradition. But when he chose to teach, his father, as Baker recalls with affection, supported him, telling him to be true to what was inside himself. Baker attributes part of his longevity to a sixty-five-year marriage; his wife provided "some of the happiest times a man could know." A repeated statement to his students reflects his appreciation of family life: "I have told my students over and over, if you want to live a good life, get you a good father and mother." Baker's appreciation of the land from his farm boyhood extended into his long career in biology. He became an expert in Southern natural environments and their preservation long before the contemporary ecological movement arose.

To cherish one's family means cultivating bonds of friendship with close relatives to the extent that one can. Sometimes the lines of communication within families have been badly damaged by past neglect or by direct abuse. But one of the best things about being old, says Virginia Davis, is to know that one is "truly loved and cherished" by one's family. Despite her longstanding marital problems, the loving contact of her children blesses her later years. Cultivating close friendships with family members means constant attention to these relationships, just as cultivating a garden implies regular care. Too often we take blood relatives for granted as we might have done in childhood. We look on these relationships as automatically taking care of themselves because "they're family." The truth is that as we grow older, the nurturing of family relations demands the same attention and care as would the development of any friendship. Nothing in this realm is automatic.

Building bonds between family members into our later years takes different forms. For fifty years Martin Marty, his brother, and sister have written to one another every two weeks. It is unfortunate that such letter-writing has virtually disappeared in our electronic age. But the Marty family preserves through letters and other forms of communication the early family cohesion they experienced as children on a Nebraska farm. Ella Mazel uses her skills as a publisher to strengthen and enjoy family ties. She has written and illustrated an extensive family history that reaches back into the Jewish immigrant community in New York and forward into the lives of her grandchildren. She constructed this work in part as a gift to her children so that they would know the many-sided richness of their lineage. The Mazel story also situates the family within the context of national and international happenings as these impinge on changing attitudes and involvements of family members. This sharing of common histories, when joined to the other ways of maintaining personal friendships, promotes a sense of solidarity between old and young in the family. With a note of understatement, Mazel says: "We really get along with each other, old and young."

When asked what gives joy in old age, many participants referred to their children and grandchildren. Bernice Neugarten, who is very well known for her work in the psychology of aging, considers the greatest achievement and joy of her life to be her daughter who has had to cope with muscular dystrophy since childhood. Neugarten speaks with great admiration of her daughter who "never acted like a sick person" and today is a university professor. Other participants who have enjoyed prominent careers with honors and publications also come back to family as a deep pleasure in old age. Robert McAfee Brown and his wife, Sidney, talked about the joy they take in their children and grandchildren, as well as in contacts with other relatives. It is the family that knows certain secret desires of a famous author like Brown. In recent years, his children gave him a cello to his great delight. "It's a side of me that I've neglected most of my life. I played a violin as a kid," says Brown.

One might think that persons who continue to exercise significant roles in the world would list their public accomplishments when asked about what they consider successes in life. But Elise Boulding, whose writing, teaching, and networking in the field of peace and conflict resolution are widely known, says that her greatest success consists "in building a family with five children who are happily married and in having fifteen grandchildren." In a similar way, a social activist like Frances Pauley answers the success question by talking about her family. "I feel close to my children," she says, "and I'm very happy that I could take care of my father at home until he died at ninety-six. And I'm glad I spent the time I did with mother as she was aging." It may very well be the powerful feeling for family that motivates these elders to take on social causes. Rose Lucey, a peace activist, keynotes this point when she says: "I have a great grandson, and I'm not about to sit around and let him grow up in a world that still believes in killing other people."

Lucey's remark helps us to see the link between cherishing one's own family and concern for the human family. The care exerted on one's own family becomes a catalyst for wider issues. Elders provide different insights on this point. Anne Zimmerman, who values her relationship with her daughter, widens her sense of family to include nursing students she has taught. She rejoices in their accomplishments. The same note is struck by Bernice Neugarten whose graduate students have been an extension of her own family. "The deepest academic gratifications for me have been my students," she says. From a different angle, Clara Crook tells us how much she enjoys her grandchildren, but she also reminds us that being grandmother is not her only role. She warns against such confinement, asserting other dimensions of her life as an elder with their own values and needs. Charlee Lambert, whose immediate family extends to five living generations and who has taken her nonagenarian mother into her own home, urges us to build relationships beyond the family. Her work with elder abuse has highlighted the dangers of narrowing one's relationships to family members who may become abusive to frail, dependent elders. We have seen how Maggie Kuhn took into her own home a mentally ill brother and later her aged mother. Her voice, too, strongly advocates going beyond the privatized existence of many elders who have cultivated relations exclusively with their immediate families. "There has to be constant outreach to others," she says. She has witnessed so many people lost in old age, because they did not extend their circle of friends.

Cultivate Friendships

Loneliness can be an acute problem for many elders. Loneliness is not the same as aloneness that can be sought and enjoyed. To be lonely means feeling alienated or rejected or abandoned. Too much of it leads to sadness and even clinical depression. Lonely people may desire sustaining human contacts, but for a variety of reasons be unable to attain them. We all experience it to some extent, and we know that one great antidote to excessive loneliness is a good friend. Many creative elders talk about the importance of fostering new friendships in later life or continuing to develop previous friendships. Old age is also marked by losses of friends through illness, death, or through lifestyle changes like moving away or entering a retirement home. Retirement itself, says Earl Brewer, can distance us from colleagues who formed a friendly support group during our preretirement time. A former college administrator said with quiet intensity that he regretted putting so much energy into his career and not enough into building a circle of friends.

Sexual love between older people should be appreciated over against cultural stereotypes that look upon it as inappropriate or even repulsive. But the linchpin for such love is friendship. Esther Peterson, who held important positions in the federal government, enjoyed a long marriage to her husband Oliver. Peterson's reflections on that marriage stress the importance of a partner being primarily a friend. Looking back on friendships with men, Gerda Blumenthal notes that some of her best relationships were "intensely romantic, unconsummated ones" with men who had the ability to be deep friends. For her, "sex is very tricky. When it comes as the culmination of intimacy, it's glorious," she says, "but when it comes too early, it is more disturbing than illuminating." Sidney Brown, reflecting on a long, mutually enhancing relationship with her husband, echoed the views of Blumenthal and added a new dimension: "Friendship is an area that is very neglected in our culture. It all finally comes down to getting into bed with somebody. But most of what holds us together is not getting into bed with people, but friendship. Long-term friendship and loyalty and caring, and allowing people to grow and change."

Miriam Blaustein, when reflecting on her relatively short marriage and long single life, presents some cautions about late-life intimacy. In the process, she opens up the important subject about the traits of good friendship. "I've had men in my life since Jerry died," she says, "but I never wanted to marry them." Her experience of taking care of a sick husband made her leery of men who wanted to be taken care of. She wanted to avoid that kind of one-sided relationship. In a similar vein, Anne Eaton, who helped found a life-enrichment program for elders, warns against very late marriages. She sees them as unsuccessful, because one party ends up with the heavy task of caring for the other as physical problems compound. "I would have done anything possible for my husband," she says, "but I'll be darned if I'll be anybody else's nurse." With both of these elders, we perceive the need for enough mutuality to sustain a friendship. They seem to be saying that it is virtually impossible to maintain a healthy friendship in late life that is burdened almost from the start with lack of mutual support. Yet there are many subtleties to late-life, special friends. As long as neither partner overburdens the other, romantic relationships have no age limit. It was both encouraging to some and disconcerting to others that Dr. Woolford Baker as a centenarian would be nurturing such a friendship in a retirement community.

Blaustein reminds us that some old people are particularly set in their ways and resistant to change. Such fixity can undermine the possibilty of good friendship which requires a spirit of nonjudgmental accessibility. "If a friend calls in the middle of the night because the cancer is bothering her," she says, "you are available to listen." It is crucial to listen well, she says, for both partners in a friendship, otherwise deep reciprocity and confidence fades from the relationship. One of the parties becomes bored or resentful at the one-way direction of the interchange. Yet it is possible in late life for love to become its best in the form of benevolence. Benevolence means desiring the other's good, what is best for him or her. True benevolence requires more than empathy and good listening. It means accepting the other without condemnatory judgments and it especially implies respect for the autonomous choices of the other. "I have enough good friends," says Miriam Blaustein, "so I'm happy to live alone in my old age."

The topic of friendship engages a key theme of the book, that of breaking our silences, our stymied longing to communicate, to return to the union of human interconnectedness. Tillie Olsen points to still another aspect of friendship among elders, that of a long, shared history. "People with whom you've had a long continuity," she says, "become dearer in late life, especially if the friendship has been profound." Such friendships take many forms. Luella Sibbald has lived with Elizabeth Howes for many years. The friendship of these octogenarian therapists goes back to the mid-forties. "I never married," says Sibbald, "in part because of my negative experience with men from childhood. I just had no respect for them. I've grown out of that, but I remember." She remembers, too, a man she might have married, but after dating her, he told her he was engaged to another. On the question of continuity and discontinuity in friendship, Simon Greenberg asserts that one of the hardest things about growing old is seeing one's friends die. "Almost all of my friends are not accessible anymore," he says. "So many are sick; to see them is very difficult." But at ninety-two he remembers a "miracle" of continuity. During the school year at Jewish Theological Seminary, a young man walked into his office carrying documents that showed him to be the grandson of a first cousin from the same Russian village in which Greenberg was born.

Child psychologist Mary Kunst has followed a somewhat different pattern into elderly friendship. She experienced two violent losses relatively early in life. At fifteen, she learned that her father had been murdered as a bystander in a bank robbery. After a loving marriage of fourteen years, her husband committed suicide during the Second World War. "We were deeply in love," she says, "but I haven't felt guilty about his death. I only blame myself for not understanding his situation better. He had bouts of deep depression and had considered suicide early in life. His mother appeared quite disturbed when I first met her; that meeting felt like a cold hand clutching my heart." After his death, Kunst went into intensive psychiatric analysis for five years, which "was very helpful for me." Kunst, who is childless, directed most of her therapeutic work toward children. "I got a lot of gratification out of that," she says. "It was the next best thing to having children of my own." Her own intense analysis helped her to understand herself better and to be less judgmental, a crucial element in friendship with children or adults. From her many friends, she developed a very close relationship with one woman over a fifty-year span. This friend, too, was to die suddenly in a car accident a few years ago, "after we had celebrated fifty years of knowing each other by driving through Spain," she says.

Kunst emphasizes the importance of friendship for aging well. But she also discusses the interplay of taking responsibility for oneself and yet having one's dependency needs met, preferably early in life. "My mother had a wonderful way of delegating responsibility when we were growing up," she says. "After dinner, we kids sat around a large oval table doing homework. She sat there with her mending. Not an educated woman, she couldn't have helped us with our geometry or whatnot. We were responsible for what we had to do. You know, it wouldn't have occurred to us to tell her a lie about what we had to do." The children had other assigned responsibilities. By taking responsibility for oneself, one doesn't overtax a friendship with excessive dependency needs. People with very strong, unmet dependency needs from childhood have a hard time reaching out to others in a friendship of mutuality. And they have difficulty involving themselves in social causes. Kunst feels that she got her dependency needs taken care of early in life. She believes, however, that it is possible to correct this deprivation to an extent in later life "through a good therapeutic relationship or a good marriage."

As a leading scholar in the field of aging, Bernice Neugarten brought new insight to the understanding of middle and late life. Cultivating friendship is one of the more important patterns for aging well, she says. But she insists on the need for active involvement in building these relationships. Moreover, she notes that friendships must be kept open to change. Again, this reflects Blaustein's point about being adaptable as life-situations alter. Such adaptibility is the opposite of covert or overt demands that the friend continue to respond in old ways. To keep a friendship fresh and growing, says Beatrice Schiffman, requires fresh thinking about the relationship. By thinking, she means not only looking for new ways to enliven the friendship, but also thinking in the sense of keeping one's mind active through new learning and involvements. In this way, a friend has something novel and interesting to contribute to the other. Middle age is an ideal time for fostering friendships that will last into late life. By midlife we have a store of experiences to share from a self-identity that has coalesced.

Sometimes it takes a change in our personal situation to help us appreciate the potential for friendship that surrounds us. Clara Crook says that she has always had significant friends, but until she broke her hip, she didn't realize the wealth of friendliness around her. She talks about it as a very important learning experience: "Because I'm so independent, I don't want any help when I don't need it. But with this hip, somehow barriers came down. There was love and respect coming forth. I guess I've been stiff-arming people—don't bother me with your love. Well, somehow the barriers came down. My friends love me! That was so amazing to me! I think what happened is God looked down and said: 'Hmmm, the independent one. A lot of chutzpah there. She thinks she can make it on her own.' So I fell down and broke a hip."

Friendships are found and developed in a variety of circumstances. Two elderly Catholic religious professionals, a priest and a nun, reflect on friendships in their unusual circumstances. Joseph Fichter has written extensively about the changing situation among priests concerning celibacy. Fichter has been an advocate for a married clergy, although he has found satisfaction in a long celibate commitment. "I really can't say that I've had a big struggle about sex," he says, "but I do have a lot of women friends." Because of his sociological research into the lives of contemporary priests, Fichter is aware of different friendship arrangements between priests and women today in Catholicism. In a semihumorous way, he talks about "long engagements" of priests who stay in the clergy but have intimate relationships with women. This practice, with its quotient of secrecy and duplicity, can cause special stress in relationships.

Katherine Forsyth points out the importance of friendships for single people in general, now that we are living longer. She emphasizes the making and keeping of friends. Catholic nuns have undergone something of a revolution on the matter of close friendships in the last quarter-century. Forsyth remembers well the official discouragements for nuns to have "particular friends," a common admonition before the Second Vatican Council. This teaching was based on a rigid understanding of sexuality and its possible abuse, as well as on a notion of maintaining formal unity in a community. Although Forsyth has changed her views and actions toward close human friendships, she is still of a generation that speaks of Christ as her spouse in ways that sound foreign to many. "I'm very protective of my prayer time alone with my spouse," she says. "Only Katherine can give God Katherine-love. He is loving me, too. I realize now that the love affair is mutual."

Older people make new friends through a variety of involvements. "One of the most important things about our Life Enrichment Center," says Anne Eaton, "is the opportunity it provides for forming new friendships among the old." This Atlanta program enlists the elderly in services for other aged persons, helping to coordinate home visits, meals-on-wheels, and other programs. In the process of doing something for others, elders not only find personal satisfaction, but they also meet new friends. Eaton points out that for many people the ending of their formal working lives means a dwindling of social contacts and a lessening of the potential for forming friendships. "You can't go fishing every day for the rest of your life," she says. At eighty-seven, Helen DeChatelet says she has many friends, because she belongs to different groups and continues to take college courses. She advises the old not to be too solitary, and follows her own advice by participating with other elders in study groups. Such activity encourages reading and other forms of mental stimulation that can enliven friendship.

Hector Leuterio, who came to America from the Philippines after the Second World War, stresses the importance of maintaining friendships in later life. "I've always valued my friends and cultivated new friendships," he says. Leuterio finds that the close-knit Filipino community in San Francisco is a rewarding source for sustaining and making friends. But Leuterio is quick to point out that his friendships cross over ethnic and status boundaries to embrace those from different backgrounds. Since he has dedicated himself to working for the ethnic elderly in California, especially the poor, he is regularly moving across racial and national lines. The expansion of friendship is not only horizontal in its pluralism, but also vertical in the eyes of Anne Zimmerman. "I cherish my intergenerational friends; younger people are helpful and stimulating," she says. When asked how she manages to bridge the age gap, she replies that she is interested in many things. "But what's most important, I'm genuinely interested in the young, in what they are doing and thinking." Zimmerman states that she listens and tries to be accessible to people with problems. A controversial dimension of Maggie Kuhn's Gray Panthers has been their critique of age-segregated living situations in both nonprofit and proprietary retirement communities. Kuhn has criticized these places as segregated playpens and warehouses for the old, because they lack intergenerational living. For Kuhn, this isolation of the elderly not only cuts them off from poltical involvement in wide-ranging community problems, but it also curtails mutually enriching friendships between young and old. It is impressive to note the warmth and attachment of the younger people who live and work with Kuhn in her own home in Philadelphia. In her late eighties, she exemplifies intergenerational friendships.

Develop Intentional Communities

The attempt to extend one's friendships leads naturally toward the formation of "intentional communities." Such communities are small groups in which members deepen their social relations with one another while they pursue common goals. To some extent such small groupings have always existed in fields like art, politics, education, and business. But for elders seeking broader networks than the nuclear family, intentional communities that pursue the goals of spiritual, psychological, and social growth for their members are more pertinent. Sometimes these small groups have a therapeutic focus as in the men's and women's consciousness-raising sessions. Such intentional communites may set a shorter time frame for their collective work than the ongoing communities that we will cite. Moreover, strictly therapeutic groupings tend to have a more limited set of goals, concentrating on the liberation of their members from harmful attitudes and behaviors. In this sense, the various twelve-step programs often become very specialized intentional communities, dealing with addictions and dysfunctions.

A number of creative elders have found sustaining friendships and renewal of life-purpose with intentional communities that focus primarily on common projects. Maggie Kuhn's leadership nucleus in the Gray Panthers would be an example of such a group. This small community is an intergenerational network that operates out of Kuhn's own home. In the process of furthering the organization's goals, members who work together daily become something of an extended family or a "workplace family." Old and young help one another physically, emotionally, and intellectually. In such an expanded "home," Kuhn says that "she keeps learning and reaching out to others. A bond is established among us. It's so enriching to find kindred spirits."

Another example of such a community is the Center for Concern in Washington, D.C. Philip Land finds a very sustaining extended family in this small community of men and women who involve themselves in social justice and feminist issues from a liberal Catholic perspective. The core members of this community enjoy frequent face-to-face relationships as they pursue research, publication, and education. Such a work-based community also becomes a spiritual home as common worship and personal sharing flows from their lives together. Such an intergenerational community of men and women also offers new options for those who, like Land, had previously lived in larger, more amorphous, gender-segregated religious orders. "I draw energy from the younger people who work with me here," Land says, "and this experience of daily, working contacts with men and women has opened me up to the value of optional celibacy for ministers in the Catholic Church."

Intentional communities that cluster around common projects are very supportive for elders. Janet Kalven puts this into the context of her own life when she says: "One of the hardest things for me about aging is the loss of people I've known from the beginning of my life. My brother's death was that kind of grief. But I've known Grail people for over forty years. This is my support community." Although the Grail movement is Kalven's extended family, she has experienced the sometimes wrenching changes that take place in such intentional communities. In its work on social justice, environmental, and women's issues, the Grail has become a more this-worldly, self-critical, and inclusive movement. But these changes in her intentional community keep Kalven open to change at eighty.

"I seem to be learning one new thing a week," she says. "Now I'm learning how to use a computer."

Patty Crowley presents another example of an elder who is actively involved in a supportive small community. This women's group meets frequently in her living room to plan ministries for poor and abused women; they also celebrate liturgies together. Crowley represents a particularly salient example of a person who in elderhood discovered a wider communal family. During her married life, she had been an exemplar for the nuclear family in the Christian Family Movement. Again, Crowley learned to change through involvements with her intergenerational women's community. These changes affected both her life of service and of worship. Her ministry is no longer with middle-class Catholic families but with women at the bottom of society's pecking order, women in shelters and prisons. "I still go to church on Sundays," she says, "but I sometimes don't know why. I guess it's an old sense of obligation. But the liturgies we have in my home are much more meaningful."

Intentional communities are sometimes more oriented toward sustaining friendships than toward service or traditional religious ends. Or the social-cause dimension of the group is indirectly supported by regular face-to-face meetings, usually around a meal or refreshments. Robert and Sidney Brown belong to such a small community whose members have known one another for many years. These tend to be people of similar political and spiritual outlook who have actively supported one another in past social causes and in personal life struggles. Henry Clarence and his wife, Judy, have helped organize another San Francisco Bay area community of long standing, a group more focused on the personal spiritual/psychological growth of its members. This group celebrates around a meal with nontraditional modes of spirituality, and members attempt to sustain one another's spiritual development. In his elder years, Clarence sees himself growing beyond the more external forms of religiousness that preoccupied him earlier. He has involved himself in recent years with Hindu and Buddhist practices. "The meditations and other practices of these movements," he says, "have been very important in helping me develop an interior life and experience the passage through late life graciously." Such personal interior work, according to Clarence, can enrich the intentional community, because "we are essentially spiritual people."

To experience community in small groups has become an important direction among religious people who are dissatisfied with the distance and formality of their larger institutions. Although the small community movement is widespread, it has been particularly intense in Catholic circles since the Second Vatican Council in the sixties. The small community movement has also been envigorated by a similar phenomenon in Latin America called the "ecclesial base community" movement. In the San Jose area, Anthony and Phyllis Soto belong to a community composed largely of Americans of Mexican origin. Before his marriage in 1974, Soto had been pastor of Our Lady of Guadalupe Church where he met his wife Phyllis. "She has been instrumental in directing my life to community," he says. Soto finds that much of his spirituality today radiates from his experience of his small community.

"It's not in opposition to the larger church," he says, "but a needed alternative to the impersonality of the latter." Soto's group meets twice a month in different homes for bread and wine services; often women and children lead the liturgies. But the interaction of community members extends beyond these services. Participants become friends and try to help one another in many realms from counseling to job acquisition. Soto underscores an important relationship between his aging process and this support community. He finds that in later life, his mind opens to the wider mystery of things, allowing him to freely question matters that he had not questioned before. This critical process can be "unnerving" because there are no final answers to life's deepest inquiries. "But if you have a community of like-minded people," says Soto, "you dialogue and find that others have the same search for meaning. It is very strengthening not only to know that others question, but also that they come to similar conclusions."

Another form of intentional community revolves around John Duryea in Palo Alto. In his mid-seventies, Duryea continues to lead a small worship community of sixty to seventy people that began when he left the Catholic clergy to marry in 1976. The mostly Catholic group meets every Sunday at a Lutheran church which has extended hospitality and with whom the group occasionally worships. "Building community has been my lifelong work," Duryea says, "and I really appreciate the small group experience over against the huge church I had before." He likes the variety of choices in preparing the services and the community discussions that follow his sermons. Sometimes members of the community preach. This liturgically centered community provides members with a spiritual home of like-minded persons who stimulate and support one another in a network of friendship. Most of the members are middle-aged people whose children have left home. The group has no organized social outreach but focuses on a spiritual dimension that, according to Duryea, "attunes us to engage in our own social ministries in different areas." This group of relatively older persons exemplifies the yearning in middle age and in elderhood to both deepen one's spirituality and to establish quality, face-to-face friendships within a supportive community.

Embrace the World

One of the tenets about aging well that recurs constantly among creative elders is the importance of committing to something beyond the narrow self. Like a theme in a symphony, the need to reach out in service is heard in many variations. We hear it in the somber notes that tell of negative consequences for older people who can't get outside of their own concerns in a positive way. Gertrude Wilks reflects on her involvement with elders at the senior center in East Palo Alto: "Concerns outside of themselves are crucial for older people. If you don't have that, you will destroy yourself." These wider interests need not be major social causes, according to her. Just sharing with one another the good things that have happened in their past lives or in recent days is enough to link elders at the senior center to sustaining energies derived from community. On the other side of the country in an elegant modern office building overlooking Atlanta, Judge Jack Etheridge sounds the same warning for elders who close in on themselves. "I think the lives of older persons become boring and bitter if they isolate themselves from the wider society and its concerns." For Etheridge it's important to stay socially connected, "even aggressively so."

But Etheridge also insists that embracing larger concerns needs to start at least by midlife, if that attitude is to carry over into old age. He cites an example that has been salient in his own life. When he served in the Georgia legislature in the sixties, he openly advocated the seating of Julian Bond when that black legislator's right to take his elected place was contested. "I had to pay a big price in my career for that choice," he says, "but I'm proud of my stand in the Bond controversy. It set a tone for me about stepping out into risky territory." On the other side of the political spectrum, former Georgia Governor Lester Maddox also emphasizes the value of "being honest with yourself and serving some bigger goal than your own little interests, if you want to age well." While he continues to disagree with such social measures as affirmative action because "it isn't fair," he insists on treating people with respect regardless of race. In his later years, Maddox, who lives in much simpler surroundings than he did as governor, has had to cope with major illnesses. One of the impressive ways by which he reaches out beyond his own health issues is his dedicated care of his invalid wife. "These hardships are challenges that come to us," he says, "and I want to keep giving and serving."

In reaching out toward wider interests, some will serve in ways that bring public notoriety, whereas others will extend themselves in less visible projects closer to home. A person like Maddox represents both modes of serving: the public form in his years as governor, the private mode in the care of his wife in recent years. It is not that one way of altruism is better than another. Rather, what matters is that older persons reach out from where they find themselves in later life. Some elders maintain a wider public orbit in their outreach. President Carter would be an outstanding example of this style through his endeavors at the Carter Center. From there he sponsors health programs in Africa, monitors elections in Central America, launches peace negotiations campaigns, and initiates new volunteer programs for the less privileged in Atlanta. When he indulges his carpentry skills building individual homes with Habitat for Humanity, the cameras make his hammer blows public events. But Carter counsels older people to find altruistic outlets without regard for publicity. "Any senior person who has warranted a secure retirement," he says, "can have a beneficial effect on a young black kid who is inclined to drop out of school. It doesn't have to be a mammoth building project or far away from home." After a little reflection, he comments on a barrier to such involvement: "The problem is that we are often not willing to break out of the tiny, restrictive shell we build around ourselves, looking for homogeneity with people like ourselves."

Other elders continue to operate on the broader public stage, seeing such work as a vital mission in older age. Admiral Gene LaRocque founded the Center for Defense Information after he retired from the navy. This Washington-based organization monitors American military involvements around the world, provides an independent critique of Pentagon activities, and seeks to educate both the public and the politicians. "It's crucial to embrace important issues," LaRocque says. "It's synergistic. The more you do, the more you can do." Yet he is ready to let the center go and turn to other things. "When I'm seventy-five, I'd like to turn this place over to a younger person, because I want to see the organization continue to thrive." But he adds immediately that he is not going to Florida at that point to vegetate. "I've already picked out what I want to do after that," he says. "That is, set up an institution that would educate the public about the importance of Congress and how to improve its status." His plan for such an organization reflects his own conversion in later life to nonviolent modes of resolving problems. "It's the most maligned institution we have," he says of Congress, "and compare it to the high regard we have for the military whose job is to kill people and destroy things." He wants to help Congress "because it is the key institution that makes us great as a peaceloving, democratic country, able to solve problems through negotiation not bullets."

It has been said with some truth that in the aging process we become more of what we were earlier in life. Elders like Carter and LaRocque by reason of personal choices and historical circumstances are positioned as elders to operate on a larger stage. This is also the situation for Joseph Lowery. Although he has retired from his pastorate, he continues to lead the Southern Christian Leadership Conference. "Find a cause," he says, "and devote yourself to it in a holistic way. I mean, don't fragment yourself. I tried to see what I did on Sundays in church connected to what I would do on Monday with SCLC. I wanted to make a difference or at least to give my best shot to making a difference at critical points in the drama of race and poverty." He reminds us that although commitment is important, one needs to enjoy the involvement and have enough of a support community to maintain altruistic vitality in later years. Individuals like Lowery, who have played public roles for many years, also wonder about the effectiveness of their work. "When I see so much poverty and violence in the black community," he says, "I wish I could have been more effective in my ministry." He has been tempted to thinking of the lack of well-being in the lives of many blacks as a personal failure. "But then I realize that the problems are in large measure systemic," he says, "part of a long cultural history that transcends me as an individual." To keep from being discouraged, an older person needs to preserve perspective when he or she engages in social causes. "We need to be thankful," he says, "for whatever we've contributed to making life a little better for others."

Anthony Soto, who had to leave the Catholic clergy when he married, insists that it is very important in later life to feel that one has been and can continue to be productive. "You need to feel like your life has worth and value," he says. "If you don't have that, you're in big trouble." Soto is one of those elders whom Lowery would call holistically and passionately committed to causes. During his clerical period, he worked with farm laborers, then pastored a large Mexican-American church and became a leader in the Cursillo movement to reform Christian living. Soto continues to see himself as a priest outside of clerical structures. Upon leaving the clergy, he earned a doctorate in sociology at the University of California, taught at San Jose State University, and founded a center for employment training that "assisted 54,000 people to find good jobs," he says. Although he has received many awards for his work, Soto does not focus on his own importance in these accomplishments. "A lot of life's successes and failures are luck," he says. "You have to be at the right place at the right time." Perhaps his most valuable advice for older people, drawn from his own experience, is "to stop looking to successful people; rather, find your own gifts and use them. You have gifts that are unexplored and underdeveloped."

Maggie Kuhn is one of those people who had to restructure her life-vision after she experienced mandatory retirement at sixty-five. Although she built on previous experiences in social ministries, she took a risk in starting the new venture of the Gray Panther movement. "In old age," she says, "we should be willing to take risks in reaching out to wider constituencies. After all, we are the elders of the tribe. We must give our wisdom for the survival and well-being of the tribe." She encourages the old to work for worthwhile causes, to reach out to other people in common purpose, and not to cling to the status quo. Kuhn knows that change is difficult for many persons, but in her universe of thought the old should be more open to needed changes. Life has probably brought them more experiences of change than younger people; the old ought to be used to change. Moreover, in risking and reaching out, "there is a bond established with so many kindred spirits, and that's so enriching," she says. Kuhn sees technological and demographic revolutions coming together. She asks the elderly: "What are you going to do with the rest of your life if you retire at sixty and live to be 100?"

Some elders reach out to wider causes on the local level. At eighty, Miriam Blaustein on a typical day will read to children in a nursery school, help a church collect clothing for a homeless shelter, and make a plea before a city library commission to save her local branch. Although she has been temporarily slowed by a mild stroke that gives her double vision, this community activist believes that old people need to participate in the wider circles of life around them. "I don't expect everyone to be an iconoclast and adventurer like me," she says, "but it's vital that the elderly not wait around to be taken care of." Blaustein urges older people to look around their neighborhoods for ways of reaching out. When she first moved into her San Francisco district over twenty years ago, it was another old woman's action that convinced Blaustein that she had indeed moved into a real community. While she was shopping one morning in neighborhood stores, she heard this older lady open a shop door and call out: "I've made wonderful cookies for your coffee break today." When Blaustein heard that, she realized that she had arrived where she belonged, a place where people cared for one another. "And I've been fighting ever since," she says, "to keep it a neighborhood where people develop a sense of community beyond the immediate family."

In Cincinnati, Estelle Bierley at eighty-nine also reaches out to her immediate community as a tutor of kindergarten children and as a lay minister in her retirement facility. "Older people need to feel that they are needed," she says, "that they can be of service. Try to find an area where you can be of service." She prepares liturgies and brings communion to shut-ins. At first people were suspicious of her leading religious activities as a lay person. But gradually she became warmly accepted at the retirement center. "It's a mistake to think that the old can't be adventurers, starting something new," she says. "Invite someone to join you in your work," she adds. "The more people are involved, the more satisfied they are with their lives." As she goes about these activities, Bierley claims that one of the best things about being old is that "women can wear comfortable shoes . . . nobody minds if you're an elder." What we hear in Bierley and Blaustein is a theme about living with commitment to something important beyond oneself. Other elders express this in terms of living with passion or seeking new frontiers of involvement.

But the historian Page Smith reminds us that our contemporary culture militates against such a vision for old people. He decries the huge entertainment industry for the old. "I mean, there's a whole category of people," he says, "who keep old folks entertained. There's tap dancing and ballroom dancing and a hundred other diversions." Smith is not against recreation, but he rejects a current view that the elderly are passive, frail types whose purpose in life is to be entertained. "I think that's terrible," he says, "but if you produce old people who are in a desperate state without inner resources, then I suppose it's commendable to try to distract and entertain them. The problem is that shouldn't be what happens to old people." Smith points to still another pitfall that can keep the elderly from reaching out in new ventures. "We Americans want to plan and control everything," he says, "and when a failure or something painful comes along, we no longer trust that the future will bring us something worthwhile. Instead of waiting in patience for new options, we want to distract ourselves from the discomfort and just keep busy." He sees pain as part of life, not as an experience that should force us into empty diversions or to being overmedicated by doctors. By contrast, Smith wants the old to experience a heightened awareness of nature, the world, and relationships by "entering sympathetically into the lives of other people."

Frances Pauley adds an important dimension to the method of reaching out in service and sharing in others' lives. This consummate social activist tells the story of teaching a wounded war veteran to read English. Many others doubted his capacity to learn. With a few simple books, "borrowed from the Red Cross," Pauley taught him to read. "The real reason he learned to read, I think," she says, "is that a few of us helped him believe in himself, to believe that he could do it." Pauley's point for old people bent on service is to become mentors who give people confidence that they can help themselves. Mary Thoits, who develops educational programs for older people in the Los Angeles area, reflects the same theme in her ideas about altruism. She considers altruism to be very important for the elderly, because it takes them away from exaggerated self-centeredness, which, she says, "can become a sickness." But it takes skillful means to be wisely altruistic. "You think of others and do for them," she says, "but you don't do for others so that it slows their own development. If you hinder their development by doing for them, that's shoddy altruism."

As the elderly reach out to wider human concerns, they encounter a great emerging issue, that of the ecological future of the planet. Thomas Berry, a cultural historian and priest, has achieved international status as an environmental visionary in his later years. As he approaches eighty, Berry writes and lectures about the challenges to every facet of our personal and social lives by what he calls "the postindustrial ecological age of intercommunion based on awareness of the interdependence of all the living and nonliving forces of the planet." By his prophetic insights into the sweep of planetary evolution and the special environmental perils today, he summons older people to take up this cause as a focus for their wisdom. He urges them to foster the ecological movement as their legacy to generations to come. To see the elderly as nonparticipant observers or as self-pleasing consumers is destructive of the old themselves, according to Berry. Their participation in ecological problems is not a matter of choice. "The old participate either as positive contributors or as negative burdens to the community and to the earth," he says. In many instances, the elderly of this generation have experienced a unique transition in the course of this century from a preindustrial society to the beginnings of an ecological or "meta-industrial" period of history. The elderly are in a privileged position to reflect on this lived experience and to assist in shaping sustainable communities in a world of limited resources and splendid beauty.

Earl Brewer, who has been in touch with the earth from his boyhood on a North Carolina farm, has combined his sociological and theological knowledge in ways that are akin to Berry's vision. As a student of futurist literature, Brewer appreciates the great dangers as well as the potentials for a more balanced ecological order. "I have confidence in the future," he says. "I have a faith in the creative goodness of earth and its life forms, including human beings." In a play he has written in recent years, he imagines a conversation between the atmosphere, the lithosphere, and the biosphere. In his call to the elderly, Berry, who knows keenly our planetary ills, echoes Brewer's sense of confidence and hope in the future. "My confidence in a successful outcome rests in the larger dynamics which shaped the earth," Berry says, "and brought forth all living things. This inner providence of the planet is a sustaining and guiding power. It moves by violent upheavals and by silent, delicate processes. Yet I don't doubt its final benevolent nature." Rather than an old age devoted to consumerism and other trivia, these elders summon their peers to find, in the words of Berry, "a more profound sense of personal significance by being a participant in the larger dynamics of the planet Earth and of the universe itself."

A number of other elders seem to grow more appreciative of the natural world as they age. Janet Ferguson notes that throughout her life nature has been a lasting attachment in mountain, forest, sea, and flower. "Only last summer," she says, "I was in a redwood grove in California, and was hushed and awed by the trees, as in a great cathedral." Herbert Karp makes a similar observation about a fuller sense of nature in later years: "I wonder if as we get older, our diminished activity is countered by an ability to perceive more beauty in the natural world around us. I notice that in myself. I've got favorite trees in Atlanta. And as I drive by them, I like to tip my hat to them." The old sailor in Gene LaRocque brings him back to contemplative experiences at sea, to vivid immersion in the rhythms of nature. "The sea is far more beautiful than all the museums," he says, "the sunsets, sunrises, the storms that come and go. The violence of the sea, the tranquillity of the sea. Not only that you see it. You're in it, tossed around, or floating calmly or standing against the wind. It's an adventure you can't get anywhere else."

Ecologists like Thomas Berry and Eugene Odum are calling their fellow elders to turn their special love of nature into the task of preserving the earth. As creative elders embrace wider causes for significant aging, one of the chief legacies they can leave to posterity is a healthier planet. The old know perhaps better than anyone else the toll of human destructiveness. If old people have grown in care and responsibility, they understand what Odum points out as a lesson from the natural world. "We must learn to live long-term in a world of limited resources," he says. "And in spite of its dog-eat-dog appearances, evolution involves a transition from confrontation to cooperation." Against the abusive dominators of earth, the old are summoned to be stewards of cooperation and renewal. John Duryea, a lifelong naturalist, realizes that contact with nature does not automatically make people better. But he believes that a deeper, more spiritual encounter with the natural world can help people age better. "It's easier to accept death if you are in touch with nature," he says, "because nature is constantly in flux, changing, coming and going."

Summary Reflections

As these elders reach out to wider communities, they emphasize improving relationships with one's family whenever possible. Some carry forward in memory the special impact of a particular parent. The first four high-achieving men attribute much of their success to the notable influence of their fathers. A healthy appreciation of the positive influences of our parents and relatives gives us a sense of rootedness in a family tradition. If we take time to honor these gifts from our forebears, we will be more apt to foster better relations with our families. Centenarian Woolford Baker attributes his good life to both his parents and to his long relationship with his wife. We can ask ourselves whether we take time to recollect the many gifts received in the families of our past, and how we might be able to pass along these blessings to younger members of our families.

Virginia Davis reminds us that family relations need cultivation as we would cultivate a garden. Martin Marty through regular letter-writing and Ella Mazel through composing a family history show us concrete ways to cultivate a family's past and present. Most elders place more value on family developments than on the remarkable achievements of their personal careers. Others like Rose Lucey tell us that their family milieus were not confining, but rather opened them up to involvement in wider social causes. Still others like Bernice Neugarten extend their families to include former students. But elders also warn us about excessive confinement in family life. Clara Crook notes the peril of being limited to a narrow grandparenting role, while Charlee Lambert and Maggie Kuhn exhort us to go beyond family concerns in elderhood. The issue here is one of balance. When we take stock of our own family involvements, are we tied into a limited and even stifling vision of life, or are our families vehicles for wider creativity and contribution?

It seems to be coming clearer that friendships beyond one's immediate family may be more important to aging well than would have been true in the past. Today more elderly people live at a distance from their immediate families. The pressures of the modern workplace consume the days of adult children more than in times past. And widowed and single people are living alone to very old age, sometimes with little family support left to them. Therefore, we need to take to heart the admonitions of elders to cultivate friendships for later life. Esther Peterson, Sidney Brown, and Gerda Blumenthal remind us to focus on building friendships within our marriages and in other intimate relationships. Without constant attention to cultivating friendship, marriages can become stale and even abusive. Sex, they tell us, is no substitute for a friendly relationship. And new marriage in late life, say Anne Eaton and Miriam Blaustein, has its own pitfalls of one-sided caretaking. These reflections of older people underscore the importance of giving time and close attention to the status of our friendships.

Creative elders help us in this effort of examining our relationships by exploring from their own experience the traits of good friendship. Miriam Blaustein asks us to ponder our ability to listen, to be nonjudgmental, to want the good of the other, and to foster the friend's own choices. Mary Kunst asks us to examine whether we burden a friendship with our own dependency needs. The other side of such dependency is taking responsibility for ourselves. Beatrice Schiffman inquires about what we bring to a friendship in terms of mutual mental stimulation. She urges us to keep learning and reflecting, lest our friendships fall into boring routines. Bernice

Neugarten challenges us to ponder how open we are to change in friendships, especially those of long duration. Elders tells us that friendships come in many varieties, and that we need to stay open to the circumstances that will foster friendship. They ask us to slow down and seriously consider our priorities about relationships in later life. Old people know how much they suffer from the loss of friends through sickness and death. From this perspective, they summon us to cherish and enhance friendships that will gladden our elderhood.

A number of elders find special support in small intentional communities. There is nothing mysterious about the notion of intentional community. It means that a reasonably compatible group forms around certain goals that may combine social, personal-developmental, religious, or service-oriented purposes. Maggie Kuhn's community coalesces around the goals of the Gray Panthers, whereas Janet Kalven's Grail and Philip Land's Center of Concern concentrate on other missions. These elders are stimulated and sustained by frequent face-to-face relationships with intergenerational communities. Not only do these groupings encourage common goals, but they also broaden the network for friendship in later life. In times of emergency, members of intentional communities band together for mutual assistance. Although Henry Clarence, John Duryea, and Anthony Soto live mainly with their own familes, they can call on a wider network of friends when need requires. Beyond physical needs, the intentional community provides them with intellectual, psychological, and spiritual assistance. In a society that tends to isolate us in older age, we would do well to reflect on the kind of intentional community that best suits our desires. Does such a compatible community already exist in our area? How might we go about finding or creating one?

Conservative former Georgia Governor Lester Maddox summarizes the theme of embracing the world in elderhood when he tells us that to age well we need to serve wider purposes. This is one of the most universal themes among participants in this project. Contemporary technological society exerts two forces on the old. A centrifugal force pushes the elderly to the periphery of life, that is, to isolated leisure functions at the edges of the social fabric. A centripetal energy closes them in to ever-narrowing personal or family concerns. In the words of Gregory Bergman, the old are hurled out of the mainstream of life. The elders in this book stand against the grain of such a society. In small and large ways, they struggle to stay in the stream in order to make their special contributions. Estelle Bierley visits shut-ins and conducts religious services in her retirement community. Jimmy Carter strides the world as a negotiator in troubled situations, and he drives nails for Habitat for Humanity. Frances Pauley gives self-confidence to the homeless, while Joseph Lowery wants to make a difference as president of the SCLC. Miriam Blaustein campaigns to keep her local library open, and Gene LaRocque tries to keep the Pentagon honest through the Center for Defense Information.

In word and action, the message is clear. Elderhood is not a time for retreat from the world and its great needs. These older people may retire from this or that job, but they have no intention of retiring from life. Moreover, they call us to leadership in newer areas such as the ecological crisis. Thomas Berry speaks of the unique vocation of the old to work toward leaving a healthier earth for their children. He says that we must as elders become participants in this larger drama of preserving balanced ecosystems. Eugene Odum dedicates much of his energy in old age to the same cause of becoming stewards for cooperation and renewal among planetary systems. These elders challenge us to embrace the world in creative ways.

Throughout this chapter, we have heard elders talk about moving outward in ever-widening circles from communion with family, friends, and small communities to embrace the great causes of the earth. These multifaceted people tell us that such outreach is vital for aging well. In the words of Gregory Bergman: "A zest for life grows only from the stream of life. I believe in being in the stream of life. Don't allow yourself to be in a side stream for the elderly." But just as Bergman encapsulates the ethos of this chapter, he adumbrates the theme of the next. "The suffering of life has to be embraced and endured," he says, "you can't escape it." Bergman faults contemporary periodicals like *Modern Maturity* for doing a disservice to the elderly because they refuse to look at the "downs of life and integrate these into the stream of life." The next chapter asks the old to lead us into such integration concerning our mortal condition.

• • •

CHAPTER 6

Encountering Personal Mortality

Famous philosophers have told us that reflection on death is the beginning of wisdom. Losses and limits are with us all through life, but in general, older people have had more experience with these intrinsic aspects of being mortal. We do not like to think about death or decline. These unpleasant topics cause some to resent the old for reminding us of our universal fate. But a book that did not explore this dimension of the aging process would be doomed to shallowness. Creative elders show us how to age well by the way they integrate losses and expectations of loss into the fabric of their lives. None of the people interviewed in this project would claim that he or she has fully resolved the anxieties and even the terrors of human decline. But when we listen to them ponder their condition in old age, we get a deeper sense of that ongoing dialogue between life and death residing at the center of each of us. Moreover, much of the excellence of these elders arises from the ways in which they move beyond loss and hardship to take responsibility for their own lives and deaths.

This chapter is about more than death and dying in the usual sense. A wider consideration of death puts it into the context of losses and suffering that form a continuum in human existence. It is both biologically and intellectually true that we die a little every day. But we are more dramatically reminded of this by sudden injuries or chronic illnesses. And these "little deaths" transcend the physical alone, affecting us on the spiritual level of heart and mind. Such, for example, are the losses connected with broken marriages, warring siblings, alienated children, sick partners, and dying friends. In the first part of this chapter, we hear the elders trying to cope with their "small deaths," physical and relational. What do they feel as life's shocks visit them? What have they learned and what can we learn from them? Other sections of the chapter will focus specifically on attitudes toward death, dying, and afterlife.

Learn from Your Small Physical Deaths

Almost everyone responds to the question about the hardest thing in old age by indicating a loss of energy, a slowing down, an inability to do certain things that gave meaning and pleasure earlier in life. Frances Pauley says she can no longer drive at night; Sally Lilienthal no longer drives over the Golden Gate Bridge at night. On the surface, these are small matters, but they point to the beginning of an important social loss. Our adulthood in modern society is marked by a driver's license and the ability to operate a vehicle at will. John Duryea realizes that he can't see or hear as well as he used to, although he is still able to lead hikes into his much-loved Yosemite Mountains. Jan Johnson knows that she "won't be able to join the Marines." Virginia Davis looks in the mirror "and sees the aging process right before your eyes." She experiences physical limitations as the hardest thing about growing old as well as a certain forgetfulness. In a similar vein, Beatrice Schiffman misses the world of work where she was able to enjoy "a sense of purpose by helping other older people." But health limitations no longer permit her to work as before.

But these elders learn to work around their physical limits, and more importantly, the losses themselves impel them to embrace each day with new appreciation. Pauley still makes her way to an in-town shelter for the homeless in Atlanta. Lilienthal is daily at her desk with the Ploughshares Fund that supports projects for a sane nuclear policy. Elise Boulding notes in one expression her sense of energy loss and renewal: "I'm very conscious of diminished energy," she says. "There are times I feel every day of my seventy-five years. But I can still get the adrenalin flowing and give talks, so people have the impression I have more energy than I do. They don't see all the times I have to rest and be quiet. But the odd thing is that I see myself as a young woman, a young person who happens to be seventy-five. That blows my mind." When Janet Ferguson speaks of growing older, she also finds the hardest thing is having to slow down and feeling a waning of energy. But she is quick to add that the best aspect of aging is having more time to order one's life and a deeper serenity of outlook. Her energy decline doesn't appear to interfere with "things I plan to do." These include reading books, taking classes in painting and music, traveling to Alaska, taking up ceramics, doing more volunteer work with women prisoners, learning to use a computer, and writing a history of the Atlanta Friends Meeting.

In addition to a general slowing down, many elders encounter their mortality more acutely in specific physical impairments. For the most part, these health problems occur later in life. Heart problems, strokes, and cancer seem to be the main afflictions coupled with an occasional bone injury through falling. A few have learned to live with disabilities from childhood. Gerda Blumenthal contracted polio as a young girl during her family's harrowing escape from Nazi Germany through the Soviet Union and Latvia. Her right leg has been partially paralyzed since that time. Although she has had a very successful career as a university professor, the legacy of polio has been a constant companion. When she reflects on this disability, she says: "The capacity to accept and not rebel against the givens of life, those things beyond your control, constitutes the better part of wisdom." Blumenthal notes that such coping is more difficult than ordinary problem-solving, because with the latter one has a wider measure of freedom. The polio has taught her to live with less freedom and to relish even more the liberty she possesses. Gregory Bergman also lived with severe physical handicaps during much of his boyhood. From this experience, he has carried a different sense of human frailty into his ninth decade. This active and informed elder, who continues to write for publication, doesn't worry about losing his health as the years go on. One has the sense that he lost it a long time ago and has learned to live with and around physical diminishments. "I'm much more concerned about not having a roof over my head," he says, "of being exploited as an old person than of losing my health." Perhaps elders like Blumenthal and Bergman, who have known serious problems from early years, are more serene at the prospect of less than ideal health in old age. Their expectations have been tempered by experience.

Other elders have lived with health problems since their middle years and have resigned themselves to life's blows without succumbing to them. Arthur Stark, who continues a full schedule as a nationally acclaimed labor arbitrator, has had two coronaries since the seventies. He admits to some apprehension about health, but especially to fears concerning mental health in later years through stroke or Alzheimer's. "You see your friends falling by the wayside," he says, "and I've become something of a eulogist around town for friends who have died. But I don't dwell on health problems or lose sleep over them. My life is becoming more contemplative and less striving. I look forward to doing the things I enjoy until I no longer can." In addition to the psychological traumas of divorce, Jane Dillenberger has had to struggle twice with cancer surgery. Yet, despite these setbacks, her productive life of teaching and publishing in the field of religious art has flourished. Attuned as she is to beauty in the world, Dillenberger felt great reassurance after her first bout with cancer when she saw a rainbow. "It was a powerful experience," she says, "and I knew I would be O.K." Maggie Kuhn offers still another example of someone who has known serious illness from midlife and has gone on to high achevement in old age. She has suffered from cancer, arthritis, and degeneration of sight in both eyes. Like Stark and Dillenberger, she marshals purpose to heal the impact of sickness. "An agenda is more important than my physical problems," she says. "That's how I cope. I salute my bodily disabilities and move on."

When we listen to creative elders talk about the implications of their physical disabilities, we sense that they take these bodily events seriously, but not too seriously. Rather, the heart attack, the cancer, or the stroke become agents for reassessing but not terminating one's involvements and interests. The sickness seems to be a catalyst for focusing energies on developing a neglected side of oneself or for centering on tasks that are particularly meaningful. The illness, like a lighthouse, is both warning signal and beacon, lighting the way to new directions on the journey. Paul Torrance, who has spent much of his academic research exploring human creativity, speaks from his own experience of being disabled by a stroke. "Creativity is the number one thing in aging well," he says. "This means trying alternative ways of doing something and seeking out things you haven't discovered before." For Torrance, creative people cultivate the courage to take risks, not letting physical problems overturn their convictions and goals. He demonstrates these qualities in his physically restricted life in his own home. Although he can no longer drive and moves slowly with a cane, he delights in correspondence with students he has mentored over the years in creativity studies. He also acts as a consultant in research projects on fostering creativity among young people and elders.

Lamar Dodd provides a striking example of Torrance's point about seeking alternative ways of staying creative. Dodd, who helped build the art department at the University of Georgia and who has won many awards for his own paintings, has been partially paralyzed by strokes that affect his right arm. But he has taught himself to draw and paint by holding his right wrist with his strong left hand. The resulting work has both intrinsic beauty and a special intensity, since it mirrors courage and determination in face of adversity. "Challenges have always helped me," he says. "They push me to look deeper for the truth of things. That's what an artist tries to communicate: a passion for the integrity of things, letting the world in and also transforming it according to one's vision." Dodd also notes traits in himself, partly as a result of aging with a disability, that we see in other elders with similar physical problems. "I've become more tolerant of diversity among people with different ideas about religion and politics," he says. "I'm more patient and humble than I used to be. And I realize much more acutely the importance of making the most of each day."

While Lamar Dodd has spent much of his life in artistic pursuits, other elders have shifted away from principally material goals to more aesthetic and interior ones. These changes in life-direction have happened later in life and in part have been connected with the challenge of physical disabilities. Michael Erlanger's nine days in a coma after bypass surgery, "dead and resuscitated three times," mark a watershed in his life. He points out that this event moved him away from the world of business to that of poetry, playwriting, painting, and psychological work on dreams. He had left the treadmill on which others had set him in early life to discover his inner mysteries and to exercise long-suppressed artistic talents. In his own words, he was finally learning "to be appropriate, that's my theme word, what I hope I am, appropriate, learning to attend to what's inside and around me, being open instead of closed with fears."

A similar pattern can be detected in Ike Saporta who regrets that he spent so much energy at an earlier period amassing a fortune that he subsequently lost. He talks about being sucked into the contemporary vortex of competition and profit that curtailed his profound sense of beauty and its expression. Colon cancer that spread to his lymph nodes a decade ago taught him in an existential way about self-healing and about cherishing the aesthetic in himself. "I realized in an experiential way," he says, "that my amazing cure was due in large part to tapping into my love for life and beauty." Like Erlanger, the things that count in life for Saporta have shifted decisively to artistic expression, the cultivation of friendships, and trying to be of service to the wider community.

Whether physical problems remind them of mortality in sudden or gradual ways, creative elders seem to draw wisdom from maladies and move to new levels of insight and involvement. After partially successful bypass surgery, Bertram Gross maintains the feistiness of spirit that characterized his career from his days as a wrestler to those in the high reaches of the federal government. "Being old and sick is marvelous." he says, "I'm a holy terror with the doctors." Gross's attitude is not a Pollyanna disregard for the reality of declining health. Rather, it connotes a certain playfulness and humor in a man who can step back from his ailments and not become their victim. Said another way, he does not identify himself with his physical disabilities. One of the things he loves most in nature is the sky. "I love to sit under the clouds and watch them," he says. This glimpse into his personality seems to correlate with his view of illness and death. He'd rather not have to cope with this dimension of life, but he is able to take the long perspective as one does of clouds passing across the sky. This distancing from physical disabilities permits him to be a lively teacher and to continue to relate to the young in creative ways. He was asked by a rock and rap group to write lyrics for a piece of social criticism to accompany their music. A key theme that Bertram Gross learned through life experience is that there is always progress and regress in social events. "Progress is especially possible when we realize this polarity," he says. An awareness of the forward and backward movement of life applies to our personal struggle with mortality. Since our health is generally better in youth, we often fail to heed the message of progress and regress until it resides in our own bodies.

Serious illnesses cause elders to reassess their lives on personal and social levels. But the creative outcome of such stocktaking is the ability to fold the physical problem into an ongoing life context. Hector Leuterio, a Filipino immigrant to the U.S., has undergone two heart operations. These intimations of mortality teach him to plan realistically for death. He and his wife have purchased a burial crypt with their names already inscribed. Yet his physical setbacks do not discourage him from pursuing wider concerns. "I think we all have a mission, a calling" he says, "and we keep searching to accomplish it despite our health problems." Leuterio finds himself moving into wider concerns in his later years. He follows his own advice of getting out of the house and relating to other people, "because it gets your adrenalin going." He directs a property-owners' association and serves on his county commission on aging. Margaret Traxler, a reformist leader among American nuns, notes that she has had to slow down after two strokes. As an attempt to limit her activities, she focused on women's shelter work. The latter has grown greatly, motivating her to leave more active roles to others. But despite her illnesses, she claims that "retirement belongs to another age. It belongs to people who don't like what they're doing. And that can be good, to quit and seek new options." Traxler wants to continue with women's shelters, even though her physical energies are lessened by age and illness. "We can always give tenderness to others," she says, "and help to empower them."

Physical impairments can act as catalysts for improving relationships among creative elders. Peter Kelley reflects in this light on his prostate cancer surgery a few years ago and ensuing arthritic problems. Each day that dawns became more valuable for him, and "I began to see that this body, my body, has only so much time left," he says. But he also appreciates more deeply his relationship with his wife which had reached an important level of reconciliation late in their marriage. A fall, resulting in a broken hip, became the medium for self-insight and new relationships for Clara Crook. Her need to become her own person through difficult marriages and career pursuits made her stress the importance of independence.

"The hip business has forced me to acknowledge my extreme position on independence," she says. She noticed that barriers to closer relationships came down when she found herself in a dependent role. "It was amazing," she says. "I learned that my friends really love me. It has always been easier for me to give than to receive." Not only was the hip incident a breakthrough in accepting the gift of love and care from others, it also moved her to a new awareness of why she isn't comfortable accepting love from others. "I think this is rooted in my lifelong attitude that poor, horrible me doesn't deserve love," she says.

Learn from Your Emotional Sufferings

The small deaths that life visits on our bodies as we age are not the only school in which creative elders learn about encountering their mortality. Emotional suffering can be just as catalytic for growth. The point here is not to glorify suffering, but simply to recognize that there can be little growth into deeper humanity without coping with sufferings of mind and heart. We emphasize "mind-heart" in emotional suffering to guard against a popular misconception that being emotional is inferior to being rational. Rather, the truth, as exemplified in the elders cited here, is that suffering on the level of feeling is both mental and emotional. And it may very well be this mind-feeling suffering that distinguishes elder wisdom from the less experiential insights of the young.

For some old persons, loss of status in society constitutes a level of emotional suffering that persists in subtle ways over long periods. Helen DeChatelet describes this feeling as that of being a "has-been." This comment forms an umbrella mode of speaking of status loss. The most obvious example of this mood relates to retirement from one's job. People who have derived considerable pleasure from their work, or at least from occupying a certain status niche in society, generally experience depression at being left behind or cast aside. Depression can result whether they were fired or whether their work time just ran out. In our technological society, the pensioner is a marginalized person, if he or she doesn't make special efforts to resist pervasive stereotyping. The depressed feelings that result from this aspect of our culture are not well-enough recognized in mental-health assessments. Some retired people offer their services as volunteers in tutorial programs or civic projects, only to find that they are not made to feel appreciated by the salaried staff. It is not hard to understand such neglect in a society that calculates people's worth by how much they are paid. Part of the feeling of being a has-been is that of no longer perceiving oneself as useful or needed. Older women who have dedicated themselves to family care for most of their adult lives are particularly susceptible to feeling unneeded.

Another form of affective suffering among the elderly, sometimes connected to status loss, is loneliness. Men and women who found the company of colleagues on the job a source of enhancement now face a curtailed circle of interaction. This can lead to feelings of sadness and alienation. Anne Eaton, who has worked with elderly people for many years, understands the plural causes of loneliness among the old. Loss of one's work status or of a spouse of many years can be an element of feeling dejected. Eaton, who lost her husband after a marriage of fifty-eight years, notes "that loneliness is a big problem for some people. It is mainly at night that people are lonely. You have to make up your mind to do something constructive about it. Talk to friends on the phone. Don't be afraid to call more than once. Read, watch TV." The loss of a husband who had been a good friend in a long marriage continues to be a source of loneliness, even for such a public person as Esther Peterson. "I miss friends who are dying," she says, "but especially my husband Oliver. I'm very lonesome for my husband. I think one reason I'm so busy is that I have to occupy myself. Having a good partner is the joy of life and was my strength." She remarks that her outside involvements also reflect the old Mormon questions that continue in her life: "Have I done any good? Have I helped anyone in need?" But her busyness is also a way of defending against loneliness, "and not focusing too much on my children. They've got to live their own lives."

A special level of emotional pain affects those who care for a spouse with Alzheimer's disease. Through years of home care for her husband, Harriet King understands the impact of this illness that robs a loved one of mental and gradually of physical facilities long before death. King recognizes that for valid reasons other people choose to institutionalize a family member with Alzheimer's.

But she chose to keep her husband at home as long as possible with the help of care-providers. She copes with this grief in a day-by-day mode, but instead of feeling sorry for herself, she finds solace from reflecting on "a long, happy marriage" that they had before the debilitating stages of the illness. She wants her husband to be surrounded for as long as possible by the love they long shared. "Even though he doesn't know what's happening most of the time," she says, "he will say 'yeah' at times that makes me think he's still able to connect with me at some restricted level. I'd hate to have him long for that moment of recognition and not be there for him." When asked if she would do over the many years of home care, she answers "yes, not because I'm some kind of saint; actually, it's the best way for me. I'm doing this for myself, too."

Struggling with the ordeal of Alzheimer's also taught King that she had inner strengths she did not know she had. She has attended support groups for Alzheimer caregivers, but the main benefit of these sessions has been to learn about community services rather than find emotional support. She knows that she will have difficult decisions ahead concerning involuntary feeding. "I just can't stand the idea of letting him starve to death," she says. And she realizes that the period after his death will be one of adjustment for which she hasn't yet given enough attention. But King is uplifted by friends and neighbors who make even small efforts to help her. Like Clara Crook, who learned the benefits of accepting kindness from others after her hip injury, Harriet King is elevated emotionally by receiving the kindness of others in her "injured" situation. Janet Ferguson, who also cared for a husband with Alzheimer's, says that although she has had other life-goals, "I have learned to be a caregiver, which is no mean task." As an only child, she cared for her parents in their declining years. Then she took care of her first husband who died of cancer and a second husband in the twilight years of Alzheimer's. Of all this time, she says: "I truly felt I had finished the race and kept the faith, and I was thankful it might be so." Ferguson elaborates on how she grew spiritually during these times: "These conditions helped me enlarge my patience, compassion, and wisdom, as I consistently felt divinely supported and led."

Some elders experience a kind of spousal loss through an unhappy marriage or an unexpected late-life divorce. The emotional pain from anger, resentment, and sadness that seeps into one over a long period of time can exact a heavy toll on mental and physical health. For complex reasons, some older people stayed with basically unsatisfactory marriages and, short of divorce, have learned to rearrange their lives to maximize creativity. We saw this in Virginia Davis who stayed in an unsatisfactory relationship. "Facing emotional pain is always hard," she says. "I'd much rather not think about how I made some very bad decisions in my life." She admits that she did not understand the depths of her marital problems and thought that she could restore the marriage by her devoted love. "I did not know the extent my husband would go to resist all who wanted to help him," she says. She also admits that "If I had it to do over, I would have gotten out of the marriage when my instincts told me it was time." Yet Davis has managed to raise children who care about and relate to her, and she has had considerable success as a playwright and theater director in her later years. It is an interesting coincidence that Charlee Lambert, who left a troubled marriage, has also written over twenty short plays and has taken a leadership role in the field of aging. Both Davis and Lambert have been able to use and transcend the pain of failed relationships, deriving from these disappointments keen insights into human needs and motivations.

The emotional suffering of the old is an acute reminder of mortality in a special way. Younger people have the sense that in time they can heal broken relationships and reconcile themselves to loved ones who may be alienated. But such hoped-for solace diminishes in old age. Not only is the time for reconciliation shortened, but a long estrangement can seem cemented in place and uncorrectable. Moreover, the negative emotions surrounding the break between mother and child, for example, may have been experienced for a very long time. Miriam Blaustein cites her estrangement from her daughter as the hardest thing about growing old. This alienation reaches into the next generation, as she "never gets to see her granddaughter." A powerful tension pulls her in opposite directions. On the one hand, she lives with the emotional pain and doesn't understand why her daughter won't talk to her, while on the other hand she "realizes that nothing will change." The best she can do is accept the limits of what to her is an intractable situation and "try to let go of it." She says that she wants to live her last years without the mourning and sorrow attached to this split from her only child. Aside from weighing any merits of parental expectations and children's choices, there is the reality of emotional pain simmering for many years in the elder. Such elders have found new outlets for friendship and service in later life, but the reality of a child's "loss" is still palpable to them. These problems also underscore the need for counseling among the elderly.

One of the greatest emotional pains carried by elders is the early death of their children or of abrupt, untimely deaths of other loved ones. In this regard, Rose Lucey talks about "a continuity of suffering" in her family. Not only did she lose a son to AIDS, but her granddaughter's husband was assassinated while on a good-works trip to Peru. Jane Dillenberger carries with her the memory of the sudden, "seemingly meaningless" death of her son in an auto accident. Mary Kunst's life has been marked in childhood, middle age, and elderhood by the losses of people closest to her. Her father was murdered as a bystander in a bank robbery. She found her husband asphyxiated in their garage, a suicide victim after a long depression. And her closest friend in later life died in an automobile accident. Kunst, herself a clinical psychologist, reflects on the importance of therapy in dealing with such major losses. Speaking of her psychoanalysis after her husband's suicide, she says: "It was a reliving of the good mothering I had from my mother. My analyst gave me a great gift to strenghten me to go on. She helped me reunderstand my whole life."

Another level of emotional pain for elders, one not frequently attended to, affects those who hoped to create a better world during their lifetimes. This might be called a form of internalized social pain. It emerges when elders are asked about their personal fears about getting older. The expected answer, which frequently occurs, concerning their fears of aging has to do with physical and mental decline. But a less expected response focuses on their fears for the nation or the world. Those who stay abreast of current events with their lists of domestic violence, foreign wars, economic and environmental exploitation sound like Tillie Olsen: "I'm very frightened about what's happening in my own country." William Sennett, who spent the first half of his adult life as a Communist organizer in the Midwest and the second part as a West Coast business man, carries forward his early social idealism. A turning point, both dramatic and traumatic for Sennett, was Khrushchev's famous speech in 1956 denouncing Stalinism. Although Sennett became successful in the trucking business, he continues to advocate the justice principles from his socialist days. "Even though it's clear to me where Marxism went astray," he says, "I believe that we should have a world in which everyone has the basics of life. I believe the rich are too rich; in one way or another, the wealth has to be spread." When asked about any sense of failure in his life, he doesn't talk about failed marriages or similar personal life issues, but rather "the failure to witness in my time the transformation of society into a genuine, democratic, socialist one." Yet these disappointments deeply felt in a number of elders do not make them indifferent or passive about trying to create a better community. Their passion for social justice arises in part from the painful experience of social wrongs. Rose Lucey expresses this well: "I have a great-grandson, and I'm not about to sit around and let this child grow up in a world that still believes in killing other people."

When elders point to social issues as a source of emotional pain for them, this frequently pertains to a cause in which they have been involved for many years. The Jesuit Joseph Fichter has not only crusaded for civil rights since the fifties, but has also advocated reformist positions within the Catholic Church. "Nothing frightens me personally," he says, "but I'm disturbed about the direction of the Vatican and church leaders. They refuse to face and talk about important changes that need to happen." On a broader social scope, Lillian Rabinowitz is upset by what she sees as a subtle but "monstrous" authoritarianism growing in our society. "I think we are moving into a kind of fascism, more sophisticated than Hitler, and that frightens me." Rabinowitz's apprehension about social authoritarianism may be keyed by her struggles to break free from oppressive family situations in her own past.

In a similar vein, Simon Greenberg echoes his lifelong adherence to meaning and order in the Jewish religious tradition when he looks about and finds disintegration and disorder in American society. "I fear the increasing loss of faith in our ability to cope with complexities, with diversity in national life," he says. "We are losing our underlying faith in a meaning for human existence." John Duryea has developed a great love for nature since he began climbing the Yosemite Sierras when he was a boy. "I fear for our continuing degradation of nature," he says. "There is so much destruction of natural habitats that is politically and economically driven . . . and that's tragic and painful to me." We catch something of Duryea's feeling for the natural world when he adds: "To me, nature is the expression of God that is the least complicated, the least burdensome." Emotional pain over continuing human destructiveness is especially acute for elders who have tried to make the world a little better during their long lives.

Reflect on Death and Dying

In contrast to the medieval tradition of "memento mori," being mindful of death, the modern temper finds such an attitude morbid. In some educational circles, courses in death and dying have somewhat rectified our aversion to the subject. And the AIDS epidemic with its numerous deaths of the young disturbs the culture of denial. But on the whole, death is still a taboo theme in a culture of technological mastery. This culture rests on order, control, and predictability. Its amazing mechanical, electronic, and resource capacities induce a sense of human mastery over existence. And yet death keeps creeping in around the edges of the modern mind, whether through images of war, starvation, and disease, or through the intimations of our personal demise. But we don't like to think or talk about it. One of negative dimensions of the word "aging" in the popular mentality is its association with decline and death. In some ways, it is unfortunate that "aging" has taken on this frightening hue, because it distracts us from conceiving of old age as a time for personal growth and new social contributions. And yet we need the goad of death at all ages to give us perspective on what really counts in life. We want to examine two questions in this section. How do creative elders react to the prospect of their own deaths? And how do they respond to issues surrounding the dying process?

By far the greater majority of elder participants in this inquiry say they do not fear death. Only three persons expressed some fear of death itself. Dorothy Kearney voices it directly: "I still fear death, not just the dying process. I guess I just love life so much and want to see my grandnephews mature . . . that death frightens me." She thanks God every day for the gift of life, and she has a sense of life after death. "But that doesn't erase the physical fear," she says. Joanne Stevenson acknowledges her fear of death, but it isn't clear how much of the fear is of death itself and how much of the mode of dying when she adds immediately: "I would hope that my death not be violent. That's what I would be fearful of—violence." Stevenson lives in East Palo Alto, a community that has been wracked by drugs and violence for years. But in the quiet hills near Santa Cruz, historian Page Smith talks about his oscillating fears of death. "I think it bothers everybody," he says, "and one of the tasks of old age is coming to terms with one's own death." He notes that just when he thinks he has resolved his anxieties about dying and something comes along that might be fatal, he realizes that he hasn't made his peace with death.

When people say that they do not personally fear death, they often add a reason or an experience to clarify their attitude. One set of such explanations can be grouped under the rubric of accepting a natural and inevitable event. Why fear it, Anne Eaton admonishes, since it is just part of the process of being a mortal human? "Why would anyone fear a natural process?" asks June Singer. Others underscore death's naturalness in reference to birthing. When Virginia Davis says she doesn't fear death itself, she adds: "I look at it this way. I didn't know what it was like the first time I gave birth. Death may be the same way." Charlee Lambert expresses her lack of fear by saying that it will be like being "in the same place we were before we were born." Others indicate their lack of fear by declaring that the end of consciousness means the end of suffering or anxiety. "I have no fear of death," says Tillie Olsen, "because I won't know that I'm dead." This theme is re-enforced by Beatrice Schiffman: "I'm not afraid of it; when it comes, it comes, and then it's over." Implicit in these expressions is the conviction that death means the end of sentience and especially of suffering. Vera O'Keefe makes this explicit: "Death is not to be feared. It is often a release from pain, loneliness, and fear. It has a positive side."

A number of elders attribute their lack of death-fears to having confronted them in earlier sicknesses or in work that put them in the proximity of death. Sally Lilienthal says that since she has dealt with cancer before, she no longer has much anxiety about dying. Coping with potentially terminal diseases seems to lessen the terror of death for some people. Ella Mazel adds another element for

understanding a lessening of fear through dealing with serious illness. "I had a life-threatening sickness in recent years," she says,
"and I don't feel I must live to a certain age, or that I must live to
see my grandchildren do this or that. Whatever happens, happens.
I'm not going to worry about it." Her illness refreshed an earlier
conviction about the unpredictability of death associated with the
untimely death of her brother in early adulthood. "With my
brother's death," she says, "I felt it could happen to anyone, any-
time, and I'm not going to worry about it." As a medic during
World War II, Eli Wallach confronted death many times. He claims
that such familiarity with dying, coupled with his experience of
losing many friends over a long life, diminishes his fear of death.

Charles Weltner, who has died since the interview for this book,
talked about a remarkable experience in confronting his cancer. For
some time during the progression of his illness, his mind was focused on dying. A crucial conversation with a friend, then U.S.
Senator Wyche Fowler, convinced Weltner that a positive, purposive attitude helped many survive illnesses beyond medical expectations. "I decided to live for my two young daughters," he said,
"and my attitude toward death changed. I changed. I rose from the
dead, as it were. Since that time, I just haven't worried about dying." For Weltner, the change of attitude through purposiveness did
not provide a much longer life, but it seems to have altered the
quality of his final months by making him less concerned about
death and more focused on life with his family.

Other elders talk about their lack of death-fears in the context of
specific preparations for the event. Evelyn Ho has worked with the
elderly and has attended many funerals. "When I was a child, death
was frightening, but not now. My husband and I have made definite
plans for our dying, such as living wills and the other arrangements." The actual engagement with death through specific preparations appears to lessen anxiety about dying or it confirms an already
held attitude about death. "I'm not afraid of death," says Winona
Sample. "I already have a will, a crypt, and everything planned."
The Georgia feature writer Celestine Sibley speaks in a similar vein:
"I really won't mind dying when the time comes. I've got a living
will and I've paid for my cremation and funeral through a memorial
association. I just don't want to be kept alive longer than necessary." For Hector Leuterio not being able to afford a proper burial

seems to have produced a greater fear than any fear of death itself. He has confronted death twice through heart attacks and bypass surgery. "For a while I was concerned about death," he says, "but since I've made some money, I do not fear death. We have a crypt with our names already on it." Of course, when people speak about their lack of fear of death, they are not, with the possible exception of Charles Weltner, at death's door. Anthony Soto seems to make the distinction between an intellectual and an existential fear of death when it becomes imminent. He does this in the context of specific preparations: "Intellectually, I don't fear death. I've written directions for my funeral, made all preparations, and I have a living trust."

A number of elders indicate their lack of death-fears by envisioning death itself in a positive light. Some make explicit what others intimate about perceiving each new day as a bonus. Gene LaRocque voices this attitude: "I feel I have a reservoir of good life already lived, so each day is sort of a bonus. I've felt that way for many years." "I never expected to live this long," says Gregory Bergman who struggled with ill health from childhood, "so I don't dwell on death. I'm just grateful to have lived into my eighties." Others encourage reflection on death for its positive outcome on living a better old age. "Not fearing death is a big part of aging well," says Janet Kalven, who has confronted death in the course of serious illnesses. Lin Ludy highlights the relationship between death and living a fuller elderhood. "Thinking about death," she says, "makes me enjoy people, beauty, change. It makes me empathize more with pain, sorrow, and loss." Both Kalven and Ludy emphasize an old tradition about the value of meditation on death. This tradition in Western spirituality has been misused to frighten people into submission to authorities for fear of punishment. But the positive benefits of meditating on death were meant to enhance our ability to shape higher goals and meanings in life, and to pursue a richer ethical existence that would ennoble our own lives and build better communities.

Elders also transcend the fear of death when they describe it as a culmination of life or an adventurous transition or a time for celebration. This is not for them a Pollyanna mode of denying its finality in human terms or the suffering that often precedes it. Elise Boulding believes that life connects with life in a universal web.

With such a vision, she can say: "I look forward to death because it is a culmination of life. I have such a strong sense that there are such very special qualities to that journey to the end." The words "connection" and "journey" underlie this perspective on death and link it to the last section of this chapter where we will discuss views about afterlife. Elizabeth Howes ties into Boulding's sense of universal connection when Howes sees little to fear in death because life is enveloped in a wider purpose. "I'm not afraid of aging or death," she says, "because I believe that all existence is purposive. I know there's a deep purpose in every moment." And Luella Sibbald picks up on Boulding's view of life-journey when she depicts death as a milestone on an adventurous trip. "Approaching death is okay; I'm not frightened at all," she says, "because I think of it as part of an adventure, a transition to a new level of being." Rose Lucey adds a celebratory note that would accompany such a positive grasp of death: "I've prepared a celebratory funeral service for myself. I'd like to throw a huge funeral party to thank everyone for giving so much to my life."

But not fearing death does not mean absence of serious forebodings about one's dying process. On this point, Joseph Fichter quipped: "I don't mind dying. I just don't want to be there for the preliminaries." Among those preliminaries, elders worry about the social circumstances of their declining years. The specter of poverty and neglect in one's later years is a widespread concern. We hear frequent reports about the high cost of long-term care, which can devestate even substantial savings. John Duryea expresses his anxieties about being able to afford health care beyond limited social-security benefits. His modest income and family assets do not provide much of a buffer against catastrophic illness. He also worries about the financial picture for his younger wife and children in the event that he becomes seriously ill. Tillie Olsen wonders about the quality of health care she might receive in a medical system based on the profit motive. Gregory Bergman, who has known poverty and family hardship in his early life, rents a modest apartment and still fends for himself. But he worries about "not having a roof over my head" and about being exploited as an older person. The fear of being cheated or robbed as a single older person is all too real. Unscrupulous individuals and organizations swindle the elderly through all sorts of scams. Bergman fears these prospects more than he does ill health as he moves into his middle eighties.

Thoughts about the dying process conjure up many fears about incapacitating physical decline. Anne Eaton thinks it may be harder for people like her, who have enjoyed a long life of good health, to face serious illnesses. "People like me," she says, "who have been so well tend to be hypochondriacs. My only fear is that I will get very sick. I hope I drop dead." June Singer hopes that her final period will be without pain. Mary Kunst talks about the sad prospect of lying incapcitated by a stroke. Martin Marty speaks about how he would hate to lose his physical capacities. But Evelyn Ho links physical to the mental losses when she discusses the interlinking of hands and mind. "Although my worst fear is the loss of my mind, I also fear losing the use of my hands, because then I lose my privacy," she says. From working closely with the sick elderly, Ho appreciates the close relationship between physical impairments and psychological suffering. With the loss of privacy comes a resurgence of bodily shame and feelings of unworthiness.

The contemporary prospect of longer life for an increasing number of older people accentuates the fear of mental loss through various dementias. Alzheimer's disease has received so much publicity in our time that it stands as the symbol for other dementias. The high incidence of such illness is partially coupled with the greater number of people living into and beyond their eighties. The views of a few elders cited here stand for those of many others when confronted with the prospect of mental deterioration in old age. "I worry about my mind going out," says Sidney Brown, who complains about her memory not being as sharp as before. Even minor memory loss, which is not a sign of dementia, causes anxiety for elders who are enveloped today in what we might call the Alzheimer fear. Stating a similar fear positively, Tillie Olsen says: "I hope I can be conscious of myself and the world around me until the end." Others talk about their fear of mental incapacity in terms of being reduced to a vegetative state of near total dependence. In a society like ours where independence is held in high regard, dependency of any kind takes on fearsome proportions. Much more thought needs to be devoted to a creative balance between dependency and independence, between the values of receiving as well as of giving, of being in control as well as just being.

Not being a burden to others in one's old age, therefore, becomes a salient theme for many elders. "I'd rather go into a nursing home than impose myself on my kids," says Helen DeChatelet. Again, Patty Crowley echoes this theme: "I don't want my kids to take care of me. That really worries me." Anne Zimmerman sums up the anxieties of many: "I fear that I will be incapacitated and not be able to take care of myself, that I will have a lingering illness that will exhaust my meager income and make me more dependent on my daughter." An intense fear of dependence is all the more acute when we realize that these elders have good relationships with their children. It is not as though they would have to be cared for by alienated, hostile children, who could be inclined toward elder abuse.

From a positive perspective, the desire to be independent as long as possible contributes to the dynamism of these creative elders. They are self-starters, self-motivators who do not wait around passively for others to stimulate them. We sense this dynamism behind the words of Miriam Levy, a longtime crusader for human rights: "I do not want to live to the point where I would be a burden. I don't want somebody else to deal with my pain. I want to die with dignity." Yet in the rhythm of our lives, many of us will die slowly, as it were, over a long period of time. Have we exaggerated the need to be independent? Is a life characterized by quiet being as opposed to one of energetic doing to be considered a life without dignity? To what extent would we expect to deal with the pain of others, if we lived in a less individualistic society?

Yet on the other side of the ledger we can understand the dilemmas of staying alive in terribly diminished capacities through life-support technologies. We hear this fear of simply existing beyond our time when elders talk about the very old in their own families. "What would frighten me the most," says William d'Antonio, "would be to spend the last couple of years of my life like my father-in-law is now. He has had a number of small strokes and has lost the will to communicate." Claude Sitton has come to accept his own death, but he adds: "My mother died at the age of ninety-nine. I'd hate to be in the state she was in during her last five years." Many elders say they have living wills. These instruments may keep them from suffering the very final indignities of prolonged existence by artificial means. But short of that terminal state which we associate with "pulling the plug," there are many aspects of diminished existence that are not affected by living wills.

In light of this, some elders contemplate the prospect of terminal suicide. Esther Peterson says that she has signed a living will, but she knows that this may not be enough to cope with a prolonged dying process with a very diminished quality of life. "I think the time will come when I will want to die," she says, "and when that time comes and I can't participate in life, I'd be willing to take my own life. That doesn't bother me one bit." Peterson's broaching of terminal suicide brings up a controversial problem of ethics and law that promises to become more acute as an expanding elder population struggles with the balance between existence-sustaining technologies and judging what would be the minimum for an acceptable state of human life. Zalman Schacter-Shalomi, who is very familiar with this dilemma through his work with the elderly, has made a pact with three friends not to commit suicide without consulting them first. The rabbi wants to be aware of his dying and experience it. He fears dementia or a protracted coma. In face of such circumstances, he believes that suicide is justified. "Some people may have the vocation," he says, "to offer the sacrifice of bearing incompetence and pain. But I don't think that everybody has such a calling."

Two elders speak for many others when they confront the fears connected with the dying process. They hope to be able to rely on inner spiritual resources that will help them die with dignity. Gerda Blumenthal, who sees life as a process of weaving a tapestry out of the threads given us, reflects on her own fears: "I suppose what is frightening is the possibility that the physical travails might outweigh my spiritual capacity to weave them into the tapestry of my life, to deal with them creatively. If that vital impulse subsides, then you're all bits and pieces." In a similar context, Robert Handy says: "Without spiritual resources, it would be hard for me to face those final diminishments. I can't talk for everyone. But most of us fear the unknown in one way or another. Catastrophic illness is an unknown. It can strike at any time. I can't conceive of facing it without spiritual resources." These resources will differ in keeping with one's temperament and one's spiritual history. Some will find support in prayer, worship, and religious communities. Others may discover needed inner strength through meditation or psychological and spiritual counseling. Still others will find such resources in living an ethical life or in the love of family and friends. Most of these elders will probably combine in varying proportions inner qualities that arise from traditional and nontraditional, inward and outward sources.

Viewing the Afterlife

A belief in the afterlife can be a spiritual resource for some elders, although it is very hard to judge how much influence such belief has on dealing with the major problems of aging. Responses to belief in an afterlife range across a spectrum from denial to a firm belief attested to by personal experiences that elders link to life after death. Eli Wallach summarizes the viewpoint of those who hold no hope for an afterlife: "The thought of it is a placebo; we get only one trip through." Others simply say that they have no belief in a continuance of life or consciousness after death. Ella Mazel couples her rejection of afterlife with being free from fears induced by religions. This would seem to mean that traditional religion, in fostering belief in reward or retribution after death, inspires unreal hopes or inhibiting fears. An academic like Bernice Neugarten finds that concepts about afterlife don't fit a scientific world-view. "I think we're the outcome of an evolutionary biology that is creating its problems as well as its benefits," she says. "I don't see a guiding spirit. I'd like to think there was one, but it doesn't fit."

Two elders who have spent many years working within religious Judaism are not sure about afterlife, but they open themselves to the possibility and find some comfort in it. After he notes that his morning prayers have prepared him for acceptance of death, Simon Greenberg says: "I find some comfort in feeling we're not going into a complete emptiness or futility. If there is a future, fine. If not, you're not going to know about it anyway, so why worry?" Norma Levitt connects her perplexity about afterlife to a matter of faith or trust. "I wish I had the faith that there was something after death, somebody welcoming you, embracing you, but it isn't there yet for me. I have a hard time accepting help from or being dependent on another. It has to do with trust, but I'm working on it." The Catholic nun Margaret Traxler seems closer to Levitt when she says: "I don't know that there's life after death. I have never talked to anyone who came back from the grave. I accept afterlife on faith. And if there's not, I will be grateful to God for the life I have lived." Yet both the outright deniers of afterlife and those who entertain a glimmer of hope for it face death with considerable equanimity and courage. Both groups fear the physical and mental losses of the dying process. But it seems that a creative process of aging has brought them closer to their last days with peace of mind.

A number of elders hold firmly to a life after death based on their understanding or image of God. A theologian like Martin Marty finds hope for an afterlife in the character of God which is relational. "It would go against that quality of God," he says, "to cease relating to us at death." For John Dillenberger, the divine is immersed in all of life that we have experienced on earth. "For me," says Dillenberger, "life after death would be no more unthinkable than life itself." Robert Handy believes in life after death, even though he doesn't know how this will take place. "The eternal one has designed us to be finite," he says, "and death with all its apprehensions just happens." But he envisons God as saving all that is of value in the history of creation. "If there is something in our life not worth saving," he says, "it will not be saved." Beneath this faith in the saving dimension of God is a conviction of the profound interconnection between past and present, between what we know in this world and what we intuit by faith. Elise Boulding speaks to this interconnectedness: "For me, a key discovery in life is the interconnectedness of the cosmos. I love to meditate on molecules floating from other galaxies into ours and being breathed by me. Also the interconnectedness with other people. Life has meaning as life connects with life." With elders like these, one has the sense that relationship or connection with God continues in some form beyond death. "God does not die when we do," says Boulding. "Exactly what our relationship might be to the cosmos after death is not clear to me, and it doesn't have to be clear."

Most elders who believe in life after death leave the particulars of that state to God. "I believe in life after death," says Claire Randall, but I leave it in the realm of religious mystery." Others express a longing to experience the journey beyond the grave. "I look forward to a face-to-face meeting with God," says Paul Schweitzer. Estelle Bierley echoes this perspective, seeing the phase beyond her death as an adventure: "When I die, I'll go to the Lord, and that will be the greatest adventure of all." Some talk about a positive curiosity concerning the life to come. Janet Ferguson represents this sense of calm expectancy: "I believe we continue to exist in some way, so I really am curious about what comes next." Two priests and a nun testify to how long lives, conditioned by the Christian promise of life everlasting, affect their outlook in late life. Katherine Forsyth, who has been a Catholic nun for over sixty years, not only believes in an afterlife but would feel "betrayed" without such continuance. "I feel it would be a betrayal of who I am to just cease to exist," she says. "It wouldn't be enough to just be remembered by God." In a less personalized way, Joseph Fichter, reflecting on death, finds that religion gives him a meaning system that bridges death and afterlife. "Over the years, I've helped and prayed with the dying, so I'm not caught without some answers when I get sick and feeble." Gerald Taylor reminds us of Ella Mazel's stricture about religion's tendency to induce fear of retribution in the afterlife. Taylor's own personal struggles with alcoholism and the image of a punitive God are the backdrop for his more hopeful attitude in late life. "I'm not as fearful of death and especially of facing a punishing God as I used to be," he says.

Some elders have a specially powerful sense of the afterlife based on what they see as psychological and spiritual experiences of the existence of a realm beyond this world. Although she does not claim such a personal experience, Sidney Brown tells how her own belief in the afterlife is confirmed by the near-death experiences of others. "I have a very, very strong belief in life continuing," she says. "I know people who have almost died and have experienced the goodness beyond." Barbara Payne-Stancil recounts her own transbodily experience and how it influenced her view of death and afterlife. "When I fell down a flight of stairs and landed face down, I almost died," she says. "But at some point in that event, I had an out-of-body experience, looking down calmly on the efforts of many to save me. I learned that I, Barbara, will always be Barbara. Much of my fear of death faded away." Theresa Hill finds confirmation of life beyond death in an almost palpable experience of her husband in the hallway of their home shortly after his death. Lin Ludy's personalized reflections bring us back full circle to the theological comment of Martin Marty about a relational God: "I've had enough of those overwhelming experiences that people can't really talk about," says Ludy, "to know that there's something more than myself to which I'm related." Ludy expands on her intuition of life beyond death: "Sometimes that relationship is very warm and loving, sometimes it's not quite that. But the relationship is there, and I don't have anything to do with it. And I assume that my stopping to breathe isn't going to affect the relationship, because it's so much more than physical."

Summary Reflections

These elders teach us how to embrace inevitable losses with patience and kindness toward ourselves, so that we do not waste our valuable energy in useless recriminations. They may not be able to drive at night or hear as well as they used to, but they try to stay focused on what Elise Boulding called the irrepressible and continuing younger self in the body of an elder person. We are invited by Janet Ferguson to work around energy losses to find creative modes of involvement. Even specific illnesses or disabilities, harbingers of our mortal state, do not destroy a courageous spirit. We have seen these people cope with chronic diabilities like polio and arthritis, as well as the setbacks of cancer, heart trouble, strokes, and physical accidents. Without romanticizing their illnesses, they perceive them as occasions for learning deeper lessons about life. These physical hardships teach them to appreciate the present more fully, to cherish relationships, to be more tolerant of themselves and others, to value beauty above material riches, and with Margaret Traxler, to realize that they can, regardless of their physical conditions, give kindness to others. Their attitudes challenge us to ponder how we deal with our own mortal limits. As we age, each of us experiences similar losses or the prospect of such hardship. How will we learn from our specific mortal conditions to become more fully human?

These elders also ask us to walk with them into the zone of emotional sufferings that enters all lives. Such losses are also harbingers of mortality. They know how it feels to experience status loss, to be marginalized and made to feel unimportant or useless. They know the loneliness that accompanies the loss of spouses and long-time friends. A number have been through the emotional roller coaster of divorce, having to reconstruct their lives in middle age. Some of them even experience the gnawing pain of estrangement from their own children. Others know the emotional diasppoint- ment that comes from seeing their hopes for a more just and peace- ful society not realized in their lifetimes. The important message for us is how these elders deal with the emotional "deaths" that life visits on them. They would be the last to say that they are paragons in coping with such trials. But it seems that they teach us to ap- proach our fears, angers, and depressions with a kind of merciful awareness, not rejecting these experiences but letting them soften our spirits so that we become more sympathetic toward ourselves and compassionate toward others. They invite us to examine the ways in which we handle our own emotional pain on the journey toward elderhood. Do we receive our negative feelings gently, trusting that these experiences, too, are vital for our creative becom- ing in later life?

Although a few of these elders talk about fear of death, most seem to have transcended such fear of death itself. Perhaps this has something to do with the ways in which they have rehearsed for death in dealing with losses mentioned above. Sally Lilienthal and Ella Mazel tell us as much when they say they have already encoun- tered death in other life-threatening situations. But it is good to hear Dorothy Kearney and Joanne Stevenson acknowledge their fear or trepidation about death. It is natural to be anxious about this unknown passage and to feel sadness about leaving behind the world we have known. Most of the elders, however, do not fear death itself. Some respond like Stoics of old when they talk about not fearing death because it is no more than a natural process or a state without awareness and therefore not to be feared. But a sig- nificant number of elders put death in a positive light by expressing gratitude for the many years of life they have enjoyed. This senti- ment seems to say that those who have relished life, and even a bonus of years, are more able to accept death without fear and resentment. Lin Ludy and others move beyond the fear of death by grasping its near presence as a stimulus to live each day with intensity and appreciation. And elders like Rose Lucey and Elise Boulding speak of death in the language of culmination and celebra- tion. We do well to ask ourselves where we stand on the spectrum from fear of death to understanding it as the culmination of life.

On different days and for a various reasons, we probably experience a mixture of attitudes and emotions concerning our own deaths. Yet a major message from the responses of these elders urges us to incorporate meditation on our own death into the patterns of our life. Rather than depress us, such meditation can encourage us to live each moment as fully as possible. In this sense, death becomes a goad for living with zest, appreciation, and altruism.

But if death itself does not appear to frighten the old, the dying process raises many troubling apprehensions. These range from concerns about financial destitution, exploitation, abandonment, and lack of care to the incapacities of mind and body. They do not want to be burdens on their families and they resist being kept alive artificially when the quality of life has permanently eroded. Some like Esther Peterson and Zalman Schacter-Shalomi converse about the desirability and the ethics of terminating their own lives when dignity and quality drain away from personal existence. These elders, not naive about the dying process, face it with normal worrisome anxiety. As models of creative aging, they give us permission to reflect on our own dying process with some fear and perplexity. But they also offer us hope that we can find the spiritual resources, however we understand such sources, to transcend our fears of the dying process. One has the impression that these elders will have found in their aging journey the courageous wisdom to adapt to life's final blows and let themselves go into the mystery of death. If we achieve this much, what more can we ask?

Some elders are consoled by their belief and hope in life after death. Martin Marty and Gerald Taylor base their hopes on an image of God as a relational and sustaining entity who does not allow anything of value to be lost. Elise Boulding speaks of her experience of interconnectedness with a wider web of existence as a herald of life beyond death. Others refer to related events that underscore the reality of a continuance of life in another form. Simon Greenberg and Margaret Traxler hold open the possibility of life after death, but whether it exists or not, they remain committed to God and grateful for the gift of the life they have known. Still others say they are convinced that afterlife is only wishful thinking. Bernice Neugarten exemplifies such a person; she would like to believe in a guiding spirit encompassing life and death, but her scientific mentality precludes such outcomes. It would seem that those who believe strongly in an afterlife, without fears of a punishing deity, approach the end of their lives with a positive element of hope and expectation, despite their trepidations about the dying process. But it would be hard if not impossible to conclude that such believers face life or death more blessedly than the creative elders who hold no hope for continued existence beyond death. Many other factors discussed in this book help to determine the peacefulness with which we will accept the end of our lives.

The creative elder knows no easy answers to the physical and mental sufferings of life. He or she confronts personal mortality to lessen fears of death and to enhance the mystery of the life that is known. As the Buddha and other religious savants understood from their own experiences, the path to spiritual awakening lies across a field of suffering and renewed awareness in the face of death. There are no authentic shortcuts. In the next chapter, we discuss different patterns of developing one's spirituality. We should remember, however, that all genuine religiousness arises in large part from contemplation of our primordial finite condition, from the recurring awareness of our inescapable death. Each elder must grapple with this closing event in his or her own way.

CHAPTER 7

Developing Personal Spirituality

Saying Yes and No to the Past

"I wish no one had taught me about Jesus; then in my seventies I'd be free to understand him." In her eighth decade, Virginia Davis speaks this enigmatic line. As we have seen, she is a late-life playwright in Wilmington, N.C., mother of five caring adults, survivor of a difficult marriage, and a lapsed Catholic.

Davis catches a key feature about the religiousness of creative older persons. Their spirituality is in the making. It is a dynamic search for meaning based on real life experiences. We tend to think of older people as religious according to traditional observances. We imagine them as solid church members who like things done the good old way in theology and ethics. Of course, one can find such people, but what stands out in these conversations with creative elders is the variety of responses about spirituality. Elders often question the authority of religious institutions and strive to shape a personalized religiousness. Davis is saying that she has had to unlearn the religious teachings and behaviors of her past to be able to strike out in new and more authentic spiritual directions.

A number of Catholics who lived through the Second Vatican Council challenge the religious structures of their past. Edna

McCallion, an ecumenical activist, refers to the council declaration on religious liberty as a clarion call for her own religious liberation. "The pronouncement on religious freedom meant so much to me," she says. "It unleashed what I always felt. One church doesn't have all the truth. By appreciating other traditions we come closer to our own religious truth." Yet McCallion criticizes the church for failing to implement the true spirit of Vatican II in the years since the council. She thinks that people have gone along with liturgical and other changes without understanding their implications for their own spiritual freedom. For her, the hierarchical church has merely substituted a new set of rules and observances for the old ones, without touching the deep need in people for finding their own spiritual center and for building authentic religious community.

Standing against the given ways of religion is usually not the result of a single event. It is a gradual process through which rules and doctrines clash with personal experience. For Virginia Davis, the collapse of the "rhythm" system of birth control came in 1960, the year of the pill for her, when her fifth child was born. Her doctor told her to take the pill, the church be damned. But her priest insisted that if she claimed to be a Catholic, she had to abide by the rules. Otherwise she would be a hypocrite. But the clinching· moment came when her first-born was about to take first communion. The seven-year-old brought home a booklet on the Ten Commandments. In addition to questions about adultery and coveting a neighbor's wife, there was a query about having impure thoughts. Virginia approached her priest after Mass and began to speak calmly about the questionnaire. He shouted back at her about sex and berated her for questioning the church. Then he asked her: "Do you believe God exists in other churches?" When she answered affirmatively, he said with contempt: "Well, you're no Catholic then."

Yet it is not only through such "horror stories" that older persons have developed a critical stance toward religion. Patty Crowley was a well-known name in Catholic circles in the forties and fifties. She and her husband Pat, as we have seen, were national leaders in the Christian Family Movement which reached thousands of people across the country. They were viewed as the ideal, large Catholic family promoting the church's teaching against birth control, as well as fostering an obediential spirit toward the hierarchy. The eyeopener for Crowley was the experience of being part of the commission in Rome that advised Pope Paul VI to change the church's stand against birth control. It became clear to her on both theological and pastoral grounds that the old teaching was wrong. "When the pope clung to the old doctrine," she says, "I was upset. Now they lump abortion and birth control together. That's hypocritical." This is strong language from a kindly woman whom few would have seen as a radical critic. Crowley was not only reacting to a problem in her church. She was in the process of developing a more independent spirituality.

Beneath this questioning attitude is a reappraisal of institutional control in one's life. Anthony Soto spoke of himself as an institutional man in his earlier years. "My attitude was closed," he said. "You had canon law, dogma, the directives of superiors . . . everything was settled, no need to question." Of course, many factors go into changing one's mind. For Soto, two key elements of change were the conciliar ferment of the sixties and love for his wife, Phyllis. "I became open to other possibilities," he says. "It was disconcerting and unnerving. I was developing religious answers for myself. But it was exciting." Soto maintains that he is not against the institutional church when he says: "Today I feel I am as religious as I have always been, but in a noninstitutional way." Soto has become a leader in an alternative religious community. He still goes occasionally to his parish church, but he feels spiritually undernourished there because he sees himself reduced to a spectator of a rote performance.

Janet Kalven, a convert from Judaism to Catholicism at the University of Chicago in the 1930s, presents a powerful tableau of change and challenge. She became one of the early founders of the American branch of the Grail. Joining this laywomen's movement upset her family, as one of her mother's greatest fears had been that her daughter would become a nun. Kalven was in the forefront of organizing Catholic educational programs at Grailville, Ohio, and was among Grail's international leaders. The most important agent of religious change for Kalven was the women's movement. Although she always strove to foster women's work, she recalls her opposition to Betty Friedan's *Feminine Mystique*. She wrote a pamphlet in the sixties countering Friedan and insisting on the role of woman as virgin or mother. Gradually, however, the women's movement brought her to see the link between patriarchy and the institutional church. Today Kalven takes a much more critical view of her church than she would have held earlier. "Church patriarchy is too painful," she says. "I get my spiritual nourishment from women's groups." She understands herself as a noninstitutional Catholic who "can't even pray in the old formula, because I can't get 'Lord' past my lips anymore." 'Lord' in her mind has come to mean a dominating male image of God.

Since these elders with Catholic backgrounds lived through the changes of Vatican II, their experiences of struggle with old ways might seem more clearly defined. But the critique of religion can be found just as sharply in elders from the Protestant heritage. Frances Pauley remembers her earliest questioning of the ways of the Methodist Church. Her mother had been chosen as a delegate to a major church convention, but lost her appointment when she refused to vote against racial integration. Both her bishop and her pastor were adamant segregationalists. This episode made the young Pauley critical of the church's stand on race relations. Later when Pauley in the 1930s set up a hot-lunch program for poor school children, her Methodist preacher refused to come to a benefit for the program, because he saw it as taking money away from the church. "Even today," she says, "the churches are too busy building edifices rather than feeding the hungry." Pauley, who has developed her own understanding of the teachings of Jesus, goes to services at an alternative Christian community that feeds the poor and homeless in Atlanta.

Claude Sitton is disappointed because the churches are so oriented toward brick and mortar that they neglect deeper personal and social problems. "There are too many boring preachers," he says, "because their sermons don't relate to current events and to the real needs of people." Esther Peterson, whose grandparents were married in Utah by Brigham Young, learned even as a young woman to stand against the doings of her Mormon Church. Her brother was sent on a mission to Liverpool where he experienced great difficulties with the attitudes of the church in face of the appalling living conditions of the working people. When he made his criticisms known, he was banned by the church. Yet her parents defended him, saying he had a right to independent thinking. "In confronting the narrowness of Mormonism," she says, "it meant a lot to me that my parents said you can be different; you can stand up for what you believe."

Esther Peterson's remarkable career in Washington, working with presidents from Roosevelt to Johnson, gives us valuable clues about the factors that go into shaping one's own religiousness and ethics. It is a gradual process through years of learning to say no and yes from one's own concrete experiences. As a graduate student in New York, she met her husband, Oliver, a dedicated Socialist who as a child had experienced hard-scrabble poverty in North Dakota. It was Oliver who introduced her to the plight of the poor during the Depression when Esther was raising their four children in New York. She began to teach cultural activities for labor unions. Later in Boston when she was teaching women's night classes at the YWCA, she noticed one evening that none of her students showed up for class. They were on strike. Esther went looking for her students in the slum areas where they lived and was astounded by the living conditions she found. "That's when I really changed and decided to become an advocate for the left-out people," she says. Peterson took up her students' cause by joining them on picket lines.

Peterson was doing the wrong thing by Mormon standards. She had married a radical Socialist who smoked. But in the process of saying yes and no to events in her life, she was growing spiritually. One such event was meeting Eleanor Roosevelt while Esther was teaching courses for a women's union. She had already become involved in political campaigning. She would sing (indulging her Mormon love of hymn-singing) at street corners to gather a crowd; eventually Eleanor Roosevelt and Frances Perkins would come by to address the audience. Peterson became the first woman lobbyist for labor and later became a leader in consumer affairs for Presidents Johnson and Carter. Even though she broke with what she saw as the narrowness of Mormonism, she insists that "I was really living what I was taught." She was developing her own spirituality as life events taught her what to retrieve from her family religious tradition and what to discard. It is interesting to note this kind of love-hate relationship of older people toward their earliest religious formation.

Joseph Fichter echoes this struggle with one's religious institution in still another way. Fichter, after completing his doctoral studies at Harvard in 1947, became a crusader against racial bigotry in New Orleans. He obtained his archbishop's approval for a serious study of racial attitudes in a local Catholic parish. When the study was done and about to be published, the parish pastor read it and disapproved. He prevailed on both the archbishop and Fichter's superior to demand a halt to publication. Representatives of the University of Chicago Press came to New Orleans to try to persuade the clergy leaders to respect a work of scientific research. It would be to no avail. "The nonpublication of the book," says Fichter, "was irrational and immoral. But I was too obedient then. Instead of rolling with the punches, I should have been a lot more angry and aggressive. I regret that now." Fichter, throughout a renowned career, has learned to challenge both church and society by his religious commitment to truth as it manifests itself in serious research.

Although the critique of one's religious past stands out in most creative elders, other patterns should be noted. There are those who resemble William James's once-born personalities. They do not deviate from the chosen or given course in religion. They are little bothered by religious doubts and anxieties. Edwin Hayden, a conservative Protestant minister in the Midwest, portrays such an elder. Long-time editor of the *Christian Standard*, pastor, and teacher, Hayden never doubted his faith, as he put it, in any important ways. "I've considered the alternatives," he said, "and found only uncertainty, negativity, and cynicism." He attributes his long and happy life to holding firm to the traditional biblical world-view of his childhood.

Still another variation on the theme of one's religious heritage appears in Herbert Karp, an Atlanta neurologist and geriatric specialist, who grew up in a secular Jewish home. His parents, like many immigrants from eastern Europe, had committed themselves to socialist causes which promised to better humanity. In their minds, the religion they knew had become an obstacle to social progress. Karp characterizes most of his earlier life as guided by ethical, humane motives. Only much later in life did he discover the Jewish religious experience in prayer and community. He became president of his synagogue. He attributes this return to religious Judaism to his reaction against the disappointment of his parents when their secular hopes failed. "They did not have a transtemporal aspect to their lives," he says. "I wanted to avoid that."

Journeying Inward

Yet this winnowing process for creative elders in shaping their spirituality means more than just standing against old rules and structures. Positive patterns for understanding religiousness also emerge in later life. In the interviews, people spoke about their spirituality in a variety of ways. Sometimes they would refer to what gave their lives deepest meaning. Other times they would refer to ethical dimensions of religiousness or to experiences of the presence of a personal diety or energy larger than themselves. Hardly any of the responses fell into merely traditional categories. In a general way, these perspectives can be summed up under the terms of inward and outward religiousness. Moreover, as elders discuss their spirituality, they speak in depth with their true voices. The creative aging process is a breaking of stifling silences by listening to important inward voices and expressing a more authentic outward voice.

The aging process brings about important changes in attitudes, images, and views about God. Gerald Taylor spoke about his transformed images of God in terms of his own difficult life struggles. Reflecting on his problems in coping with childhood abuse and later alcoholism, he says: "My concept of God gradually changed from a vindictive, punishing deity to a compassionate, forgiving God." For Rose Lucey, images of God altered in keeping with her own life experiences. She referred several times to her negative self-understanding in childhood as a "Dago-Wop kid from South Boston who wouldn't amount to much." Yet through the blessing of a long, constructive marriage to Dan Lucey, she was able to find her own voice in many ways. "As I grow old," she says, "my picture of God has changed. No more a long-bearded male on a throne controlling every act of my life. God's not a vindictive judge. God is now for me beyond gender, beyond my imagination. God just is an empowering mystery that I can't describe on this side of death."

For elders who claim a relationship to God, the divine image seems to change in positive directions as they age. But the dark side of God also appears in their reflections. Elizabeth Howes is indebted to her therapy under Carl Jung for appreciating the dark aspect of God as seen through her own insecurities and negativities. For the most part, she relates her experience of God to her journey toward centeredness and wholeness. But it was particularly remarkable to hear this octogenarian underscore the importance of being in touch with the dark sides of oneself and even of God. "Part of wholeness," she says, "is holding the polarity, a balance between light and dark." This theme of God's darkness takes on different emphasis in the expression of anger toward God. Speaking one's negative feelings toward God has a long heritage in Judaism, but it less known in Christianity. Gertrude Wilks, however, was intensely angry at God after the death of her two sons. One died in the drug culture, the other died early in life from heart disease. The latter had made his way from his mother's alternative school in East Palo Alto to Harvard medical school. Of course, anger toward God does not define Wilk's whole image of the divine, but it does bring out a human trait that many religious people tend to deny.

The journey inward in later life manifests not only changed attitudes toward God. Another important characteristic is a sense of the divine as mystery and presence. Maggie Kuhn speaks of this as an experience of the Holy Spirit in the whole created order. Kuhn is well known for her political activism as an elder. Yet her social involvements stem from "my greater awareness of the Holy Spirit in the world," she says. "This leads me to quiet meditation, prayer, and regrouping my energies for self-healing and for insight about moving in new directions." Elise Boulding talks about retrieving in old age an experience she had as a three-year-old of deep reverence for God as the interconnectedness of all things. Like Kuhn, Boulding insists on the need for meditative solitude to revive that sense of mystery and presence. At one point she retreated to a place of solitude in the Colorado mountains for a year to cultivate the inner journey when she felt herself "flattened out" by activism. In her hermitage, she rediscovered interconnectedness with other people and the mysterious presence of the divine connecting life with life.

After a long time as a career diplomat's wife, Lin Ludy has become a spiritual counselor in Washington, D.C. She strongly underlines the experience of the presence of God. "I don't remember growing up in the Presbyterian Church that we ever talked about the presence of God. We expressed everything about the divine through right doctrine and service." But in later life her spirituality is marked by an intense feeling of mysterious presence. Her words seem to capture graphically what other elders intimate. "When I feel God's presence," she says, "I experience a physical feeling of inner light, inner warmth and comfort. Sometimes there is a deep sense of joy that is beyond pain and sorrow. It's indescribable. It opens up a wonderful sense of awe." Ludy also stresses the importance of finding even brief times for solitary meditation, "those centers of silence where we find peace in the presence."

But Ludy adds another dimension to the inward experience, its physical and aesthetic aspect. She and her husband have become semiprofessional clowns. She defends this strange move in later life by citing the medieval mystic Meister Eckhart: "God laughed and brought forth Jesus. Jesus laughed and brought forth the Holy Spirit. All three laughed and brought forth us." For her, laughter is the gift of God's healing. One might think that her mystic spirituality is removed from the physical realm. But, as we might expect from a clown, she emphasizes physical contact, the need for human touching. "Hugging is vital," she says. "We're all skin-hungry. But it's deeper than that. We honor who we are by embracing. When you do it with care, compassion, interest, it can be very healing and energizing."

The experience of mystery and presence characterizes the spirituality of June Singer. She does not see herself as religious in a traditional sense of participating in religious institutions. Her long career as a therapist put her in touch with a powerful inner and outer presence of the transcendent. "As far as the spiritual goes," she says, "I experience a great presence, that is, being supported by something far beyond my ego." She doesn't want to be told what to believe by religious authorities. Prayer, for Singer, is a preparing of herself for relationship to the totality. "I have a sense of energy moving, that there is some kind of order under the apparent disorder in our world," she says. "Life has a direction and some kind of intelligence beyond ours." Luella Sibbald echoes this sense of spiritual presence, connecting it to her experience as a three-year-old. She has a distinct memory of divine presence when as a child she walked down a dark hallway to light a candle. Her mother was too tired to light it. Now in her eighties, she cherishes that childhood memory as a symbol of her spirituality. Although she has walked through many dark places in life, she has felt the protecting presence of the divine. She has learned to light her inner candle. "The planet is in a dark time," she says, "because people don't explore their inwardness, their connection to the whole. This brings on great discouragement."

A subtle relationship exists in older age between the ability to find peace inwardly and not being discouraged by evil and suffering in the world. When we are young, we expect things to get better in our lifetimes. Somehow, we think, the idealism and vigor of our generation will solve the problems of humanity. But to approach the end of our days in a world of famine, war, and other social ills can be disheartening. We feel this not only for ourselves but also for the seemingly bleak prospect facing our posterity. Such a vision at the end can lead to what Erik Erikson described as a state of personal despair. Paul Schweitzer, who had a long and notable career as an educator in New York, expresses this important link between a sense of mystery in one's spirituality and the avoidance of despair. "I think it is a terrible world, but a good world," he says. "I'm not optimistic about great improvements. But I don't have to have the answers to all this. I'm much more aware now of being surrounded by the mysterious presence of a Mother-Father God. There are no simple answers. I've become more receptive to mystery, to seeing things as they are and accepting greater pluralism of ideas and lifestyles."

The experience of mystery, of a benevolent presence pervading the world, expresses itself in a renewed sense of something larger than one's individuality. Moreover, this presence calls the elder to embrace a wider vision, a more spacious tolerance of others. Martin Marty speaks about his own experience as partly that of Christian particularity. Christianity is his primary story, his root source of metaphors. "But at its depths, every profound religious involvement leads one to transcend its own particularity as a step toward the universal," he says. Dorothy Kearney talks about her long search for her own spirituality, a search that led her into widening rings of understanding about how humans are spiritual. Kearney gratefully acknowledges her parents and others who introduced her to the life of the black church. But her vision of religiousness has expanded over the years. "I think everyone is spiritual, at least potentially," she says. "By spiritual, I mean a person who at a deep level has a loving concern for life, for creation, for relating to people. A spiritual person may not identify with any organized religion. At the center of a spiritual person, there is a faithfulness, a truthfulness, and an ethical awareness that operates no matter what the situation is." In her work of spiritual direction, she tries to be a "prayerful presence," helping each client cultivate the seeds planted within from the beginning of life.

Sometimes this widening of religious perspective shows itself in the blending of specific religious traditions. Gerda Blumenthal has lived as an "exile" by her own reckoning. She grew up a Jew in Germany, fled as a child to Russia, entered a profession dominated by men, and became a convert to Catholicism. She finds sufficient linkage with her Jewish tradition through the Hebrew Scriptures which are maintained in Christianity. Clara Crook came to Christianity from Judaism by marrying a Protestant minister. She was able to make the adjustment to her husband's congregations without great difficulty. Bertram Gross looks for ways of expanding the Judaism of his birth with his wife's Hinduism. He explores the ways of Vedanta and Gandhi, stressing nonviolence and introspection. All three of these elders note, however, that their original commitment to Judaism was more ethnic or cultural than religious. It may well be that those more strongly rooted in one religious tradition would find it harder to enter into another faith community. Yet it may be too easy to conclude that one proceeds from a weak commitment in one group to a stronger one in another. It is perhaps more likely that these elders have developed toward a stage of spiritual cosmopolitanism. This means an ability to feel at home in more than one faith community, drawing insights and inspiration from multiple traditions. This attitude is characterized by Winona Sample who is able to blend her Catholicism with the spirituality and rituals of her Chipewyan tribal background.

Another way of tapping into the inward spiritual experience of creative elders was to ask what gave their lives its deepest meaning. Psychotherapist Singer sums up a perspective that characterized others: "Being open. Going into experiences without expectations, without demands, open to what happens, and flexible enough to go with it." Her statement also summarizes a major Buddhist insight about developing mental peace by gradually overcoming ego cravings and false expectations. This trait of staying open was also expressed in other terms, like fostering curiosity, wanting to turn a new page in the book of life, being receptive to the new, and willing to be surprised. But this openness is to be experienced in the present. It is not a postponing of life to some future point when one will feel better or when someone else will bring happiness to these elders. Lin Ludy says it well: "Don't be good. Don't be bad. Just be in the present. It's wonderful to look back and to look forward. But what really counts is being open in the here and now."

Yet this positive inner growth in spirituality is related to coping with sufferings and disappointments. Theologian Marty made this point well in terms of religiousness when he reflected on the course of his life. Alluding to Jacob's struggle with the angel, he spoke of accepting the polarity of wound and blessing. For Marty a major wound was the death of his first wife from cancer. He makes the point that the suffering and the blessing are not detached from each other. Rather, in religious development these are organically joined. It is not that one seeks sufferings directly; that would be a form of masochism rather than authentic spirituality. Life inevitably brings us physical, mental, and emotional trials. What counts is how we process these experiences. They do not automatically lead to a deepened spirituality. Suffering can freeze and harden the soul as well as soften and expand it.

Suffering can be both physical or psychological and is often a combination of both. It can be induced by what happens to oneself or to those around one. If Gertrude Wilks were to point to the hardships in her life, they would exemplify most of these categories. She has lost two sons as young men, one in the violence of the drug culture, the other through early heart disease. She tries to cope with other family problems. And as she "slows down" in elderhood, her fear of violence in the streets increases. She has learned to use her pain for spiritual growth through religion and psychotherapy. Wilks talks about her faith in God, as "an unseen power you're able to connect with." The church has been another source for coping with the trials of life. But she also credits psychological counseling for helping her grow as a spiritual person. When her second son died, she sought professional help because she thought she was "going crazy." Psychotherapy affirmed that it was normal to feel the torrent of negative emotions going through her, and to express her anger at God. These sufferings have tempered and strengthened her, making it possible for her to reach out with greater understanding and compassion. "I've tried to use up my life," she says. "I know I've made a difference in lives. That makes me feel good, like my life has been more whole."

Gerda Blumenthal has experienced a lifetime of living with physical disabilities and discomfort. Although she overcame paralysis from childhood polio to shape a distinguished life as a university professor in French literature, the hardships of the disease have expanded in later life. She experiences considerable pain in her hips and back. Her condition tends to isolate her more now than when she was young. "In our culture, to be an older woman who is disabled makes you an invisible person," she says. "I experience that every time I go shopping. People don't talk spontaneously to me. It wasn't that way when I was young. And it makes me feel more lonely." Nor is she naive about the capacity of her physical problems to overwhelm her spirit. "What is frightening," she notes, "is that my physical travails might outweigh my spiritual capacity to deal with them creatively." Growing old involves a new form of problem-solving for her. "How do I handle a day when I really feel bad?" she asks. "Do I rage or do I accept it quietly, hoping that tomorrow will be better?" Blumenthal's own pain and disability have taught her to accept the givens. She speaks of learning to live with less freedom. Yet in these sufferings, her prayer is to "be sufficiently receptive to God's love to enable my vision to turn outward, away from myself, and not be turned in on myself." Again we see in this sensitive woman the daily struggle to weave one's suffering into a more excellent tapestry of life.

Gerda Blumenthal also opens up another avenue for elder spirituality through the arts. Music not only gives her pleasure, but it also connects the finite world with the infinite. Just as painting links the invisible dimension with the visible, so music puts her in touch with the incarnation of God in the sensible. She speaks of her favorite instrument, the piano: "With a limited number of keys, you open up infinity. It's the mystery of the incarnation. Through the materiality of sound, a Mozart or a Bach reveal the transcendent world. Great music in church is like a huge eye that helps you to see the divine." Music not only puts us in contact with the riches of imagination, but it also allows us to feel our own emotions. Burt

Sparer, formerly a city planner and now a consultant, underscores the importance of music for aiding him to connect with his deeper, hidden feelings and thus with his true self. Psychological therapy helped Sparer understand some of the sources of his acute depression and low self-esteem in the context of his overdemanding and suicidal father. He speaks of his real spirituality not in traditionally religious terms, but as a process of keeping in touch with his true feelings. This builds his self-esteem, shows him his limitations, and allows him to relate to others. But music is a key means for this inner work. His day is incomplete without a hike with his Walkman playing classical music or a contemplative period at home listening to music.

Art as a medium for deepening one's spirituality stands out in the reflections of Jane Dillenberger. Throughout her life as an art historian, immersion in artistic beauty was a principal catalyst for her spirituality. "Art startled and perplexed me," she says, "and ultimately redirected my life." In this statement we see the potential in artistic expression for engendering those experiences that are akin to religious conversion. Here conversion is understood not as a unique event, but as a continuing series of experiences that draw us toward new levels of insight and existence. It is also particularly interesting that she associates art and religiousness with traumatic events in her personal life. Art provided her with "emblems of suffering" when her son was killed in what was otherwise a sudden, random accident. It helped her see his death within a larger context of tragedy in human life. She speaks of art's importance to her when the ending of marital relationships brought her much pain. Dillenberger sums up her religious experience through art: "Art has again and again sustained me, summoning me to my true self and grounding me in the common past of our humanity and our faith. It has given a cohesion, a pattern to what otherwise might be random occurrences in the flux of time. It is not that art is my religion, but I feel religion most deeply in art."

Journeying Outward

Spirituality or religiousness among creative elders manifests a powerful outward dimension. For some, this aspect of spirituality is referred to as an extension of one's traditional religious commitments. For others, an ethical focus itself constitutes their religiousness or philosophy of life. Those in the latter group, for a variety of reasons, do not link themselves to traditional religions. Their families of origin may have nurtured them in secularized environments, or these ethical religionists consciously broke with the creeds and observances of their prior religious histories. We will attempt to honor this division among participants by acknowledging it, since many do not see themselves as religious people in the ordinary sense of the term. In common parlance, being religious connotes explicit adherence to a church, synagogue, or other institution. But in sophisticated theological circles, religiousness is not narrowly confined to explicit religious beliefs and actions. If we understand "religious" in the primal sense of that which both opens us to transcendent experiences and links us to the best ethical instincts of our nature, we could also call nonexplicitly religious persons religious or spiritual.

Joseph Lowery locates his religiousness within the Christian church, but he joins it closely with ethical concerns. A dramatic story from his Alabama childhood brings out the point. As a ten-year-old walking peacefully into a store, he was gratuitously punched in the stomach by a white policeman. He went home to get his dad's pistol to kill the officer. By some unusual coincidence, his father came home from work early and found Joseph going out with the gun. After reprimanding his son for touching the gun, his father complained about the officer's assault to the police chief, who said that nothing could be done. Lowery finally came to terms with this experience, recognizing that white people who act like that were products of their own homes and society. But this insight did not come easily. "I struggled a lot with the Christian imperative to love and the temptation to hate," he says. It was only later as a close companion of Martin Luther King Jr. that he understood the full implications of the childhood event. "The battle for justice is religious, spiritual, not just political and social," Lowery says. "A moral issue like that must be resolved at a religious level in our hearts." Twenty years after the run-in with the policeman, Lowery learned yet another lesson about the potential for inner transformation. While the young preacher was visiting his mother in his home town, the same officer, now turned postman, happened to be delivering mail as Lowery was leaving. The two men recognized each other. After a tense moment, the former policeman apologized and asked for forgiveness.

A similar theme about linking inner and outer life in one's spirituality is echoed by Henry Clarence, a former Benedictine priest, who has long been active as a married minister. In his later years, Clarence finds himself deeply involved in the pursuit of a contemplative life, largely through Hindu and Buddhist meditative practices. "The East helped to make sense of Jesus for me," he says. He strongly urges the development of an interior life among elders. "This is necessary to joyfully and graciously experience the passage through life," he says. "It also diminishes physical and psychological pain. Older people need to know that this is possible." Yet despite his movement from an external to a more interior spirituality, Clarence cautions against "putting the cart before the horse." We must first commit ourselves to ethical issues in the world, he insists. Such commitment opens us to a more authentic interior life. Our spiritual potential blossoms when we see justice and other virtues exercised by people in their ethical struggles. Meditation can bring us to an undisturbed point of quietness and insight, but we first become sensitized to spiritual life by the virtues of those around us.

Charles Weltner was only a few months away from his own death by cancer when he reaffirmed the link between the spiritual and the ethical. He spoke of his belief in God as found in the human spirit, especially as it manifested itself in works of justice. He dedicated much of his tenure on the Georgia Supreme Court to strengthen ethics in the life of public officials. For Weltner, those who held public office were not to use their positions to enrich and empower themselves. Rather they held such posts as a sacred public trust. Thirty years earlier he witnessed to such dedication when he gave up his seat in the Georgia House of Representatives rather than compromise himself by supporting what he perceived to be the racist platform of the then Governor Lester Maddox. Weltner, like Atlanta's former mayor, Ivan Allen, came to see how social structures were racially unjust. Both men struggled to educate their fellow southerners toward the civil-rights cause. Allen, in ways less dramatic than Weltner, guided his city through the angers and demands of the early sixties. He held a controversial civic dinner honoring Martin King Jr. when the latter received the Nobel Prize for Peace, and later he was conspicuously prominent in Dr. King's funeral services in Atlanta.

The journey of widening one's spirituality in later life sometimes revolves around intentional communities. The latter are more clearly defined, face-to-face smaller groups that meet for inner sharing, worship, and sometimes service activities. A growing number of people have become disenchanted with the impersonal and routine religion of institutional churches. These persons seek spiritual environments with others who want to experience a deeper sense of community and a fuller sharing of their lives with friends. Such communities are also freer to incorporate religious wisdom from a broader spectrum of sources than are usually allowed in traditional religious institutions. A remarkable example of such a community, which we noted earlier, is the house church movement of Anthony and Phyllis Soto in San Jose. Although the Sotos were in the formative leadership of this community, they would caution against exaggerating the role of any leader. The ethos of such communities calls for a discipleship of equals in contrast to the hierarchical religion experienced in their Catholic tradition.

"My spirituality today," says Anthony Soto, "is based in good part on our small, home-centered community." This group meets twice a month in different homes of members where bread and wine is shared, and women and children frequently lead the liturgy. Members get to know one another and feel free to share their needs, problems, joys, and hopes. Soto insists that this kind of spiritual community is an alternative to, not a rejection of, institutional religion. "I still go to church on occasion," he says, "but I feel very undernourished spiritually. I sit like a bump on a log in a spectator situation. The priest is up there going through a formula that I know." Small religious communities have vastly expanded in recent decades as an offshoot of the "base ecclesial community" movement in Latin America. Brazil, for example, has thousands of such communities; most of them have been influenced by liberation theology which calls for a more communal and participatory form of spirituality. Soto says that his home-centered religiousness has led to deeper spiritual growth for him. "I meditate more, commune with God in nature. . . . It's more genuine than what I knew in the church structures."

Janet Kalven's involvement with the Grail movement provides another example of an intentional community on a larger scale. She was one of the American leaders of this women's organization that sought to do missionary work for the Catholic Church. She was interested in women's issues from the beginning, but a major shift toward contemporary feminism went in hand with a radical critique of the patriarchal Catholicism to which she had converted in her student days in Chicago. Kalven is still committed to the postpatriarchal Grail, but she does not see herself connected with the institutional church. Its patriarchy is too painful for her. "I rarely go to a parish for worship," she says. "Rather I get my nourishment from women's groups. In the old days, I thought of the sacraments as channels of grace out there. Now I encounter the holy within a community of caring and serving people." She talks about building such face-to-face communities, especially among women, and then ritualizing that experience, rather than repeating a prescribed, rote ritual. "This has some of the same qualities that the sacramental moments used to have for me," she says.

The connection between religiousness and social ethics manifests itself among many elders who are less directly related to intentional communities. Some of these older persons associate their other-oriented spirituality with the explicit mandates of their traditional religious backgrounds. Although Frances Pauley is critical of Christian churches for their brick-and-mortar mentalities, she finds her "passion for justice" motivated by the teachings of Jesus. Her ethical reading of the New Testament inspires this octogenarian to work with AIDS victims and to help feed the homeless at a church-related hostel. The core community of the homeless shelter has actually become a religious support group for Pauley. She is also acutely aware of racism among her fellow residents in a retirement community in a more comfortable section of Atlanta. "If I had known that, I wouldn't have moved in; but they have a right to their own opinions," she says.

"I'm religious but not pious; I've gradually come to embrace the spirit of Christianity, not the letter," says Gregory Bergman. His own awakening to a social ethic came as a youth when he got a low-paying job delivering papers for the Hearst chain in San Francisco. "I saw Hearst exploiting workers at home while he was over in Europe buying all that expensive stuff." Similar experiences drove him toward social radicalism and involvement with the Communists before World War II. His return to a more explicitly Christian movtivation for his ethical religiousness happened later in life after the shock of his wife's sudden death, which we noted earlier. He explains how she was going to teach a class in Stockton; he was driving only minutes behind her for a doctor's appointment. "There was an awful crash scene. I was going to drive by it. But I looked up, and there was my wife, hanging dead, killed by a drunk driver." This launched a long, painful process of recovery for him. Among those who assisted his healing from depression was a Methodist minister who counseled him to "turn the arrow outward," that is, to involve himself in service to others. Well into his eighties, Bergman continues to live by that prescription, at once psychologically and religiously healing. He turns the arrow outward through his continuing publication of social-justice essays. A few years ago, he was honored by the American Society of Aging for his lifetime dedication to social justice.

Service in the world for God is a major dimension of Estelle Bierley's religiousness. At eighty-eight she works as a lay Catholic minister in a nondenominational retirement community in Cincinnati. After a failed marriage in the late 1920s, she started her own small business and raised two daughters. Both became nuns, a life toward which Estelle also aspired. But in the mid-fifties, just as she planned to enter a convent, one of her daughters left her order with problems that required her mother's care. Much of Bierley's life has been devoted to taking care of family members in need: not only her daughter, but her father and sister. "I chose a nondenominational retirement center," she says, "because I'm dedicated to the secular world, which means I am to serve in such a place rather than in a religious retirement center." Yet her religiousness doesn't become ponderous. With a smile in her eyes, she talks about her comic modeling for television commercials. "We need to be of service not only to people," she says, "but also to the environment of God's earth and its creatures. If we don't get outside ourselves like that, life becomes boring."

Simon Greenberg, now in his nineties, represents another example of a religiously motivated ethical spirituality. Greenberg reflects on a long life spent as both rabbi and educator. Growing up in an observant Jewish family, he met a group of educated rabbis who inspired the young man toward a life of study, teaching, and administration. He speaks of a decision made when he was only sixteen in answer to the question of whether life has real meaning. His affirmative response set the course of his life. "It's an absolutely crucial point," he says. "Do you want to live as if the world had no meaning?" Meaning for him was sustained by daily prayer, Scripture study, and other observances of Jewish religious communities. Yet all of this traditional religion orients Greenberg outward toward ethical considerations. "The main role of the Jewish people, and of any people, is to represent the fullness of the ethical law as much as possible in their daily practices."

Unlike the above elders, some older persons do not associate their religious-ethical orientations to specific traditions. Some of these, when pressed, would credit early religious education with partial influence for the strong ethical concerns they reveal in later life. But others see themselves as humanists, whose relation to either Judaism or Christianity is ethnic or cultural. Miriam Levy is a good example of such a perspective. This San Francisco social activist has been intensely dedicated to human-rights causes, not only as related to Judaism, but also to Asian-Americans, Africans, and African-Americans. She has been honored with a number of civic citations for her work in human rights. Levy says that she does not pray or meditate in any formal sense. Yet when she speaks about the driving motive for her human-rights activism, she sounds almost biblical: "The road of wisdom for me has been to know my limitations, and to do justly, to love mercy, and to walk humbly with God." Again, it is difficult to sort out the explicit and the implicit influences from religious traditions. Two concrete experiences stand out in her memory as related to her life focused on social justice. When she was five years old in Minneapolis, she recalls her father protecting his black barber by standing in front of his shop when a menacing KKK group formed on the street. A second major event for her was *Kristallnacht* in the late thirties when the Nazis smashed the windows of Jewish shops in Germany. She talks about her religiousness as a kind of instinct for doing the right thing. "You know when it's right and just . . . whatever God is, I'll take my chances that the divine is a good life force."

When asked about her religiousness, Lillian Rabinowitz calls herself an atheist. But she has a good deal to say about her spirituality of doing good works and how the latter involvements changed her self-identity. Her self-esteem had been badly hurt by a childhood which left her with few happy memories. It was further damaged by two "disastrous" marriages. Most of her working life was spent as a teacher while she raised two daughters. Outside of music, which she loved, there seemed to be little consolation in life until her retirement at age sixty and her encounter with Maggie Kuhn. Before this meeting, Rabinowitz had moved into health care and advocacy for the elderly through a Jewish senior center in the Berkeley area. When she attended a workshop led by Kuhn, "It was like being hit by a bolt of lightening," she says. "It was a transforming experience." Rabinowitz organized the largest Gray Panther chapter in the country, and has been very active working on behalf of the elderly, especially with health issues, day-care clinics, and residential facilities for the old. "This is the most enjoyable time of my life," she says, "and working with elderly causes has, as a byproduct, restored my own self-esteem. My work now is not a career; rather, it's a mission that helps others and transforms me."

An ethical spirituality not only seeks to help others; it also fosters personal growth. Arthur Stark exemplifies such a religiousness. His parents moved away from traditional Judaism and became interested in the Ethical Culture movement, enrolling the young Arthur in its school. "I consider myself religious because I'm committed to an ethical way of life, and because of my aesthetic appreciation," he says. In his work as an arbitrator, he has been much in demand, not only for his skills in the field, but also because of his sense of justice and fairness. Both sides to a dispute have confidence that they are putting their cases into the hands of a sensitive and honest judge. Stark sometimes regrets that he wasn't exposed to traditional Judaism. He has no conscious reference to a transcendent God. "But, I'm dedicated to high ideals," he says, "and I want to do good for others. That's religious. I've always felt that way, even though I don't go church or synagogue, except as a sightseer."

Eli Wallach hails from a fairly typical background of immigrant Jewish parents who fled from the anti-Semitism and pogroms of Poland. They set up a small candy store in New York's "Little Italy." His parents observed major Jewish festivals, but he drifted away from traditional religion into liberal, humanitarian causes. About as close as Wallach came to a church door, as it were, was the public controversy in 1956 with Cardinal Spellman of New York over the release of *Baby Doll* in which Wallach starred. The film's romantic scenes were offensive to the Catholic Legion of Decency. When asked about his spirituality, he sums it up: "I've tried not to hurt anyone, and I worked to bring people pleasure, the best tonic in the world." He has also tried to bequeath ethical principles to his children: a sense of justice and of unselfish giving.

Just as Wallach continues his acting career with pleasure into his seventies, so in a different way does Gene LaRocque pursue ethical-spiritual commitments. This retired sailor has gone a long route from being a war militant in World War II to being a peace and nonviolence advocate. As a young officer, he commanded ships that saw action in the Pacific. LaRocque is not a pacifist, but he is dedicated to curbing militarism as a solution to world problems. His spirituality is still another version of ethical religiousness oriented to helping people solve conflicts. LaRocque is a good example of personal change through important life experiences. His secular spirituality derives in part from reaction to early experiences of having a narrow version of Catholicism imposed on him in Midwestern schools. "They taught that you couldn't get into heaven unless you were baptized a Catholic," he says. "We couldn't go into a Methodist church, which was insane. Religions have divided people into warring cults."

Yet LaRocque's spiritual-ethical development continued through his military experiences to the extent that a few years ago he was advising the American Catholic bishops about their pastoral letter on war and peace. He attributes his transformation to peace advocate to his travels as an adminstrator of war colleges, and especially to his seven years as a war planner in the Pentagon. The tragedy and evil of a war politics turned him around. "The more I planned, the more I realized that we were committing suicide," he says. As early as 1967, he advised President Johnson to leave Vietnam. "A few years ago, I told the Catholic bishops that nuclear war was a theological-moral concern, even more than a secular problem," he says. "I urged them to come out with a statement, despite what the pope says, that possession of nuclear weapons with intent to use them is immoral." LaRocque's is a spirituality of averting war and promoting nonviolent solutions. "I don't think there are any just or good wars. We ought not to be killing other people," he says.

Since Admiral LaRocque lists President Jimmy Carter as one his heroes, it seems fitting to conclude this section with a few insights into the latter's spirituality. Of course, much has been written about the Carters' philosophy of life, but the interview with him revealed perspectives that draw together themes in this chapter on developing a personal spirituality. As a Southern Baptist, Carter brings together both religious commitment to traditional Christianity and an intense ethical spirituality. "Whether one believes or doesn't believe in details of the Bible," he says, "the teachings and example of Jesus offer an ideal set of priorities for being human. The teachings of Christ have helped shape my own moral standards, from which I frequently depart, by the way." But for statements like this to become deeply rooted in a person's lifestyle, it usually takes coping with life-shocks that become life turning points.

For Carter such a turning point came long before his disappointment at losing the presidency in 1980. Fourteen years earlier he went through a spiritual crisis when he lost the governorship of Georgia to Lester Maddox. "I didn't understand how God could let this racist beat me in the election," he says. "It was quite a blow to my ego and my standards. It was much worse than in 1980." His sister, Ruth Carter Stapleton, became the catalyst for his spiritual transition. She told him that the priorities we set for ourselves in life are frequently opposed to those of Christ. She mentioned three such priorities: to live as long as possible, to become economically secure, even wealthy, and to gain social prestige and power. She reminded him that Jesus died at thirty-three, abandoned by friends; he was homeless, poor, and powerless. She made the point that he needed to stay open for unexpected opportunities. She said: "You should thank God for the disappointment, because it gives you a chance to reassess your life; you may find a better path if you submerge your ego." "That was the most profound turning point in my life," Jimmy Carter says.

The Carter example underlines two points that in various ways run through the stories of other creative elders who are in the process of shaping their own spirituality. First, there is an element of faith involved. This faith can be characterized as a trust that life or God, in the more traditional expression, will bring new, unexpected possibilities. In the case of Carter, it was a secular event that challenged his ego enough to open him to new insight. Secondly, inner growth in spirituality is intimately linked with an ethical expansiveness toward those in need. With President Carter, we see this later-life expansion in his other-oriented involvements regarding poverty, disease, homelessness, and peacemaking. He speaks of breaking the encapsulation that impedes our altruism:

> I really think most Americans want to do something altruistic. The most difficult thing to me is crossing that chasm of encapsulation. We want to live in a cozy environment, preferably among people like ourselves, for whom we don't have to be responsible. But we must learn to break through our encapsulation to respect human diversity and serve human need. To penetrate the rest of the world, even on the basis of dealing with minutiae, visiting one family or something can be exciting.

Summary Reflections

As we look back on experiences that elders call religious, we notice a spiritual quest that is dynamic and personalized. We might have expected otherwise if we went along with popular images of the old as religiously traditional and resistant to change. But in fact we find very little cookie-cutter religiosity. On the contrary, these elders have worked through their own processes of saying yes and no to inherited religion. Edna McCallion sums up this quest by saying that people need to find their own religious centers rather than conform to external dictates. Usually this does not mean a total rejection of their religious past, but rather a dynamic of agreement and disagreement, of rethinking, retrieval, and renewal. Their inner growth as spiritual persons proceeds in keeping with concrete life experiences. Virginia Davis is thwarted by a priest and by certain church teachings. Patty Crowley and Janet Kalven encounter blockages in their patriarchal church and are inspired by new modes of women's spirituality. Frances Pauley and Joseph Fichter struggle with their churches over racial integration and move on to new insight and action. One senses that these elders have become freer in later life to negotiate their own journeys in the spiritual realm. We would do well to ask ourselves about important transitions in our own spiritual histories. Have there been specific experiences that have especially drawn us in one direction or another? What have we discarded and what have we retrieved from our spiritual past? What insights and lifestyles are compellingly new for us as we try to shape a viable religiousness in later life?

Many elders speak of religiousness as an inner journey rather than a conformity to religious externals. Or put another way, they find the outward forms of religion helpful if they contribute to deeper inner awareness. Even their images of God change in conjunction with new life experiences. And these changed images of the divine mirror developments within elders like Gerald Taylor and Rose Lucey. The former gradually comes to envision God as compassionate rather than vindictive, and the latter rejects a patriarchal God for one of undescribable mystery. Paul Schweitzer finds himself less sure of answers and more receptive to the mystery of a Mother-Father God. Elizabeth Howes and Gertrude Wilks, each in her own way, are willing to stand before the dark side of God. Another strong theme among some elders is an uncanny sense of the presence of the transcendent in almost palpable forms. Jane Dillenberger finds this in art; Elise Boulding in a cosmic network of connections; Lin Ludy in an awesome feeling of inner light. How have our images of God changed over time according to our own life experiences? What do these reformulations of God within us say about the paths we have walked, the people we have encountered, the events, sometimes traumatic, of our lives? How do we experience the transcendent mystery today?

Another quality in the spirituality of these elders is two-sided: a greater tolerance for different beliefs and practices, and an openness to experience enlightenment in the present. Martin Marty understands the particularity of his Christian commitment in a way that leads him to honor and learn from other traditions. For him the particular opens to the universal. Dorothy Kearney, a spiritual director from the heritage of the black church, sees spiritual potential in all people inasmuch as they all live by some faith, seek truth, and live ethically. Some elders live comfortably by blending traditions: Christian, Jewish, Hindu, and American Indian. They look beyond confined categories to find deepest meaning in openness to present experience. Against the stereotypes about the old, these elders are, in the words of June Singer, willing to go with their best experiences in the present. But also, like her, their experiences in late life are tempered by sufferings. They have developed their spirituality amid painful losses. They know with Gertrude Wilks that sufferings can soften or harden one, and with Martin Marty that all life is both wound and blessing. Gerda Blumenthal speaks for many of them when she struggles as an elder to weave the pain creatively into the tapestry of a whole life. We might ask ourselves about our openness to diversity of religious manifestations. Are we aging with an expanding respect for the multiform spiritual expressions? Despite our personal suffering and losses, are we able to discover rich meaning in our lives as the present unfolds itself to us?

For creative elders a crucial part of spirituality revolves around ethical or moral concerns. But the journey outward, as Henry Clarence reminds us, is linked to a deepening of inner life. Some elders are motivated toward ethical action by traditional religious backgrounds. But such general motivations are brought to life in concrete circumstances. Long involvement in the civil-rights struggle shapes the ethical spirituality of Joseph Lowery. Charles Weltner and Ivan Allen devoted a good part of their careers to public service with its constant demands for ethical awareness. Frances Pauley carries her understanding of the ethic of Jesus to the poor and homeless. With similar motivation, Estelle Bierley quietly serves the needs of elderly people in a retirement community. Anthony Soto and Janet Kalven experience the holy in small communities that inspire them to reach out to others in need. Others find ethical spirituality without direct ties to traditional religions. Arthur Stark sees himself as religious because he tries to be sensitive to ethical considerations in his work as an arbitrator. Miriam Levy relies on her "instinct for doing right" for direction in a life dedicated to human-rights causes. But all of these people seem to have learned the lesson of Gregory Bergman, "to turn the arrow outward," that is, to convert the losses and griefs of life into positive energy toward valuable causes. And these elders reflect the experience of Jimmy Carter in that they have learned to submerge excessive ego and move in later life from encapsulation to altruism. These older people summon us to reflect on our own spirituality in the eldering process. What would it take for each of us to "turn the arrow outward," to envision a spirituality for our elderly years that drew us away from ever-narrowing concerns and toward lives of compassion and altruism?

• ◆ •

CHAPTER 8

Crafting Your Own Elderhood

U p to this point, we have been reflecting on the experiences of creative elders to help us appreciate the many ways of aging well. But reflecting on admirable seniors, though profitable for our vision of older age, is not enough to transform our own thinking and action in ways that change us. To accomplish that goal, we need to explore our own lives for insights and directions that will foster creative aging for each of us. In this chapter we are moving from conceptual knowledge about aging to starting a personalized process that can bear specific fruit in our individual and group lives. We began this process in the short summary reflections at the end of chapters. The exercises that follow invite us to deepen this work by using the teachings of wise seniors as a launching pad for a journey into discovering our own elder wisdom. Each person ages within the context of his or her own story. Although we will follow the structure of preceding chapters in formulating questions for our own inner work, patterns for wise aging will probably differ from those arrived at by people cited in the book. We should honor this diversity of outcome because it will represent the different ways by which we, as individuals and groups, experience life. We want to respect plural modes of aging well.

We use the phrase "crafting your own elderhood," for a number of reasons. Craft derives from a Germanic word for power. To craft something is to exercise creative energy or power. Implicit in the chapter title, then, is the conviction that we can and should be about the task of shaping our own elderhood. We begin doing this from our earliest years, but middle and older age are especially good times to focus on this crafting. In midlife we have a better grasp of our limits and potentials, and we have established a more independent identity. From our multiple experiences, we have had a longer time to deepen our insights about the things that count. In middle age, we start to feel the foreshortening of time; before long, we will be old. Those already in their later years will want to intensify the crafting of their lives. As they greet each day as a bonus to be lived to the full, they will want to ask: In the context of my own experiences, what will bring about a life more personally satisfying and socially contributory?

Yet the notion of crafting one's own elderhood brings up problems. The word "craft" might be misunderstood to mean that we can do whatever we want in shaping our present and future. Of course, that would be a mistake, given the limitations of our physical, mental, emotional, and social circumstances. But within our network of limits, and sometimes because of them, as we saw from elders in previous chapters, we have the power to change much about the way we think, feel, and act. Another problem with the idea of crafting is that it may sound too active and external. We think of a person doing crafts as manipulating something outside of the individual. But this is a superficial view of crafting or creating. The external activity of the artist is driven by inner power to understand and feel in a way that creates beauty, that helps us see the ordinary in ways that challenge and move us. Crafting of our own elderhood calls on each of us to become creative artists of the last phase of life. Worthwhile crafting must build on a reflective and contemplative spirit.

To encourage a contemplative environment, we suggest that before doing the particular exercise suggested below, participants as individuals or in groups do a preparatory, brief meditation. Before each set of questions, we will present an optional meditation joined to the practice of sketching images appropriate to the subject under consideration. Meditation involves both body and mind, linking them in ways that help us to deepen our reflections. To achieve such unison, we advise some stretching exercises followed by getting in touch with one's breathing in silence. The meaning of breath in

Greek and in other languages is connected with spirit or the spirit of life. Encountering our breathing as our life-spirit not only relaxes us with its rhythmic cadences, but it also guides us beneath the surface of our often scattered mind. When we join breathing awareness with silence, we can better appreciate the stages and issues in our story as aging persons. During or after the reflective exercises, we strongly encourage some form of writing and drawing. It is useful to have a journal for these exercises where thoughts and impressions can be recorded before they are lost to memory amid the distractions of daily life. Moreover, the very process of journal-writing elicits new insights that wouldn't have come to us if we hadn't put pen to paper. Drawing summary images, realistic or abstract, for each set of exercises can be very evocative and rewarding. Put aside the I-can't-draw excuses. Unless physically disabled, anyone can make designs with colored pencils or crayons. These drawings are frequently enough more pregnant with meaning than cursive writing. Drawing and writing stimulate each other in reciprocal ways. If these exercises are done in a group, it can be useful to reserve some time to allow participants to share in twos or threes what they have written and drawn. A few people can be invited to present their drawings to the whole group. Finally, it doesn't matter if some questions overlap with others and draw out similar answers. Just as our minds and bodies are united, so also our lives are a continuum of memory, feeling, and thought. Thus a similar theme may reappear whether the topic be family, work, or friends.

A. Family

A natural place to begin a life-review for creative eldering is with your family of origin as well as with families formed in adulthood. The questions below should stimulate your reflection on how parents, siblings, relatives, spouses, and children impacted on the formation of your personality. As you reflect on your families from the vantage point of later life, some of this influence may be positive and some negative. Whatever the balance of benefit and deficit, family influence remains profound. It is crucial to assess it as we attempt to craft a more satisfying elderhood.

Meditation: Before starting the meditation, do some easy stretching exercises standing in place. Next, sitting comfortably but erect or walking slowly in a quiet place, become aware of your breathing. Breathe deeply a few times to sense the full and penetrating infusion of your inhaling and the slow return of breath in your exhaling. Realize how you are not an isolated being, but rather how you are connected with the whole environmental community through your breathing. This breathing began in your earliest family life, linking you biologically to your parents. It is better not to do a lot of thinking in this phase of the exercise. For a few minutes, just enjoy the quiet relaxation of your breathing, gently bringing your drifting mind back to the calm rhythm of inhaling and exhaling.

With your eyes partially closed, imagine that you are looking through an album of family photos. You see pictures of yourself in childhood, of your parents as they were then, and of your siblings. What thoughts and feelings are evoked by these mental pictures? Perhaps the context of the photos is as important in awakening your reflection as the persons pictured. Don't try to decipher specifics; just let the album elicit a mood for you. Then see as graphically as you can the house (or main home) where you grew up. Remember the arrangement of rooms, the furniture, the traffic patterns, the sounds and smells, the feelings associated with important rooms. It may help to sketch the house both outside and inside.

(After a few minutes of quiet meditation, recollecting the scenes and impressions of family life, address some of the questions below. Remember, this is not a test; you don't have to finish; no one will grade you. The questions are meant to stimulate your own reflections. You are drawing the threads of the past into the tapestry of your present life. When we do autobiographical work, we never image earlier happenings exactly as we experienced them in childhood or in an earlier adult stage. We interpret from where we are in the present, consciously or unconsciously blending in later knowledge and wisdom. But that is what makes autobiography interesting as a creative act in which we incorporate the dense mix of experiences over a lifetime. In this sense, we are crafting new interpretations of who we are from earlier experiences.

It may be helpful to have a journal or writing tablet at hand. You can make some preliminary entries in brief phrases to help you remember thoughts as you move from one question to another. Later you can write complete sentences and paragraphs from these notes. If you become stuck in the process, close your eyes, return to easy breathing exercises and especially to the images of home and family. The images will aid you to once again start the process of reflection and interconnection.)

QUESTIONS

* How does parental influence from your family of origin continue in your life at present?
* Who was the most influential parent in terms of your development? How and why?
* Who provided warmth and nurturance in your childhood? To which parent were your closest? In whom did you confide?
* What patterns of relating to other people do you carry forward from your family of origin?
* Who was the most powerful person in your family? How did you relate to him or her?
* How have relationships with siblings and relatives affected your adult development?
* How do you assess the strengths and weaknesses of your family of origin? Have the same qualities persisted in your own life?
* What was the emotional environment of your family of origin? How has this affected you in later life?
* What was the financial environment of your family of origin and its general attitude toward money? How has this influenced you in adult years?
* What were the main conflicts and problems in your family of origin?
* What were the overt and the hidden rules and expectations of your family of origin? Did you continue the same pattern in your adult family?
* Were you loved as a child? How did you know? Where have you experienced the most important love in your life?
* What fears did you form early in life? Do you still deal with them?
* How is your world-view or philosophy of life the same or

different from that of your family of origin? Has your world-view changed through the experiences of your adult family?

• Reflect on the family (families) you formed in adulthood. Where appropriate, apply the same questions from your reflection on your family of origin.

• What are the best aspects of your adult family (families) both in themselves and in terms of your own development as a person? Think of specific relationships and events.

• What have been for you the hardest dimensions of life in your adult family (families)? Again, be specific and give the reasons for your views.

Final drawing: After you have reflected on your family of origin and your adult family, draw an image or images that integrate some of the main lines of all your reflections on family. Use colors whenever possible. Make the drawing large enough (at least an 8-by-11-inch page) to be easily seen. These drawings can be representational or abstract. It may help to review some symbols from the natural world like rivers, mountains, trees, animals, oceans, stars, clouds to find the right combination for you. Or you may want to work more abstractly with color and form. Perhaps you may want to join both the representational and the abstract. If you are working in a group, it is helpful to share your drawing with one other person or with the whole group as you talk about the impact of family on your eldering process. (Some of the questions on Family, Work, and Turning Points were drawn from the very helpful volume: *Guiding Autobiography Groups for Older Adults* by James E. Birren and Donna E. Deutchman [Johns Hopkins University Press, 1991], pp. 67–71.)

B. Work Life

Our working lives occupy most of our waking hours. Work or career can be understood loosely in this exercise. Some may have had one or two main careers in business or professional realms, occupations that filled their years until retirement. Others may have raised families and only later entered the world of salaried work.

Still others may have balanced career and family throughout life. Again, one's life work can be understood as being a parent or spouse, perhaps combined with volunteer work in community activities. Some people work for organizations, while others work privately as artists, musicians, and writers. People can have different careers or a sequence of careers in a particular field. But whether paid or not, we all work. Even homeless and jobless persons work at the hard task of staying alive in difficult surroundings.

How would you describe your main work or works? Remember that the purpose of this exercise (and all the others) is not to reminisce mainly for the sake of leaving a document or tape for posterity. Rather, the goal of the exercise is to help us as elders or as middle-aged people learn from our past involvements in order to work now and in the future in more rewarding ways. Since work is part of the humanizing and developmental process, we presuppose that people need to work in some capacity as long as they are alive.

Meditation: Begin this exercise with some relaxed stretching. Have materials at hand for writing and for drawing images. Start the meditation in your chosen position by getting in touch with your breathing. Don't rush into thinking and writing. Focus in a relaxed way on your breathing. Notice how good it feels to breathe fully and deeply. The working life of your body and mind depend on this vital but taken-for-granted activity. As you imaginatively place yourself back in each main workplace of your life, try to come back regularly to your breathing. When you put yourself in each work environment, notice how the benefits of that work may have enhanced your life's breath, and sense, too, how the stress, physical and mental, of a particular workplace may have injured your breathing, recalling that breath also means spirit, life-force. Dwell on the concrete scenes of each workplace and the feelings you connect with them. See again the faces of people who were important to you in your working life. Perhaps there were crises associated with one or other of these persons. Some may have been special mentors for you. Others may have formed an important support community in your life. Allow the people, places, thoughts, and moods to flow across the screen of your memory.

(Repeat the format for jotting down insights in short phrases as you dwell on the questions below. Later you can write full entries into your journal. Also remember that images and feelings are crucial for getting deeper into your thoughts. If you are operating in a group, you may wish to share your drawing with others at the end of the exercise.)

QUESTIONS

• Did particular people or events specially influence you in the choice of a career or line of work? How did you get into your work?

• How important is work to you? Is it more meaningful to you than relationships or some other activity that wouldn't be classified as work?

• Have you had to balance career and family? What have been the difficulties and rewards of such balancing?

• What has been your principal life-work (or works)? How much do you identify your self-worth with such work?

• What has been special for you about your work? What did you really like about it? What did you dislike?

• Was your work chosen or was it the result of accident or necessity?

• Do you now wish that you had changed earlier to another line of work? Why didn't you? What can you do about it now?

• What have been the ups and downs, the successes and failures of your work life?

• How do you evaluate the years of your working life?

• Are you still involved in work that is meaningful to you? If yes, tell why it's important. If no, reflect on reasons why.

• Are you pleased or disappointed about your overall involvement in your work? Why do you answer as you do?

• Does your work express who you really are? Is it important that it do so?

• Do you still enjoy your work? Is it important to have meaningful work to do after one's official retirement? On what do you base your views?

• If you could live your life over, what would you do differently about your work? Whether you would do otherwise or not, try to formulate why. If you would have changed your work, can you still incorporate some of that change into your life now?

(Remember to draw in color an overall image of your working life as a symbolic and metaphorical way of picturing it to yourself and discussing it with others.)

C. Turning Points

We can think of our lives as flowing streams from birth to death. As these streams meet hills or other objects, they alter their flow. Most of us have changed the course of our lives at various places on our journeys. Some turning points are fairly routine, such as graduating from school, while others affect our lives more dramatically. In chapter 2 we saw some of these changes relating to divorces, deaths of loved ones, and unforeseen career opportunities. In light of the changes we have seen in these readings, let us explore our own lives to better understand important shifts that continue to resonate in our personalities.

Meditation: After following the same preliminary stretching and breathing procedures for contemplations described above, we begin this meditation by remembering the most dramatic turning point in our lives. Put yourself back in the circumstances of that event. Who was with you at that time? What were the issues over which you were struggling to make a decision? What was your emotional state during this period? Did the turning point involve a conflict of values for you? Such discursive questions are only preliminaries in a meditation. At some point, put analysis aside and quietly observe and feel the images that circulate around that event. Stay in this receptive mode for a few minutes before you go on to the next stage of meditative drawing. When you are ready, take out a blank piece of paper and draw a long straight line representing your life from your birth to the present. Then mark the line off in decades. As you seek out the main turning points from childhood to the present in your silent meditation, mark an "x" at the ages when these events took place. Remember that we are looking for the most important turning points of your life, so you will probably not end up with more than a few. Give each turning point an apt title and write it near the "x's." As a final part of the meditative drawing, before you follow the journaling procedure on the questions below, draw a curving line at the "x's" that goes either above or below the straight line. The height or the depth of this curving line cutting through the straight line should indicate the mental and emotional intensity that the turning point had for you. If the turning point was mostly positive for you, draw the curve above the chronological line; if negative, draw it below the line. This will serve as a preliminary graph of turning points and their relative impact on you.

QUESTIONS

• Did any of the turning points affect both your personal and familial life as well as your career? How would you rate these turning points as to overall importance for your personal development? How do you rank them in order of importance for you?

• Who were the people most involved in these turning points? For example, were they family members or work associates? What roles did they play in each of the major shifts?

• How did the turning point impact on you emotionally at the time it occurred? Would you characterize your feelings at that time as positive, negative, or mixed? What were the specific feelings? What was the intellectual component of the shift for you, that is, what did yor learn from it?

• Now that you most likely have some distance from these events, has your assessment of them changed? In what ways?

• In what ways do these turning points continue to have an effect in your life today?

• What degree of choice did you have in the turning point? Was it something that you elected to do, or was it largely imposed on you? For example, an illness or being forced out of a job would be examples of the latter. Does the relative importance of choice or necessity in these happenings say something about your character?

• Can you foresee to some extent new turning points in your life? For example, the death of a spouse or close friend, or the inability to do the kind of work that now gives you pleasure? Is it valuable or counterproductive to imagine future turning points and your possible reaction to them?

(You have already done a life-line drawing about your turning points. But at the end of this exercise, choose one or two turning points at most and render them symbolically in colored images.

Again, if you are going to talk with others about your turning points, it is very useful to share the drawings as you discuss the events. It is not unusual for a listening observer to have insights into the drawings that you might miss.)

D. Empowering the Elder Self

Understanding later life as a time for personal development is still a foreign notion in our culture. At best elderhood is seen as a holding action against the vicissitudes of age. It is as though elders must hold their fingers in the dike of decline, lest they be swept away by the final flood. The older people who speak in chapter 3 give us a different perspective on aging. They portray an elder population that is seeking to live to the fullness of its powers. They invite us to take into ourselves their vision of empowerment. This exercise intends to draw us into deeper reflection on ways to empower ourselves as older people. We have an opportunity to redefine the power dimension of "crafting your elderhood" as largely an interior power, based on our inner resources. From this restored inner well of energy, we will be able to choose and act more skillfully in the outer world.

Meditation: As a way of starting your meditation, stand in front of the longest mirror you have. After you do some stretching and breathing exercises, stand in a comfortable but erect way and look at yourself for a more extended time than you ordinarily would. What you see may not conform to the dictates of fashion magazines and fitness ads. But appreciate the physical qualities of your body at whatever age you are. Notice your bodily abilities to see, sense, smell, touch, and breathe. Close your eyes and be grateful and pleased with these basic powers, as you get in touch again with your breathing. Sway gently from one side to the other while you stand in place. This will remind you of your power of physical motion and of your bone and muscle structure. Visualize your vital organs, such as heart, liver, and brain, working in splendid coordination to sustain your life. Admire and be grateful for the organism that you are. As you see yourself in the mirror, move beyond the purely physical dimensions to acknowledge your mind and character. Resist the temptation to belittle yourself by comparisons or by rerunning old scripts about your unworthiness. For these moments, recognize your intelligence, goodness, and other virtues that have been manifest to others for all these years. After dwelling on these positive aspects of yourself for a few moments, conclude your meditation by repeating interiorly a simple mantra of gratitude (such as "I admire and am thankful") coordinated with slow and easy breathing.

QUESTIONS

• Become aware of some social stereotypes about getting old, such as physical weakness and unattractiveness, mental incapacity, excessive dependence, uselessness. In what subtle or overt ways have you incorporated these stereotypes into your mind and into your lifestyle?

• What positive steps can you take in very concrete circumstances of your life to reject these stereotypes and replace them with true and positive images of yourself?

• What are you doing to empower your own bodily health? Are you too passive about it, overly dependent on medications, excessively worried about health, and forever discussing your aches and pains with others? Or do you take responsibility for your physical well-being by doing enjoyable and sensible exercise, eating and drinking wisely, getting enough rest, avoiding harmful drugs like nicotine, managing stress, and in general developing a doable fitness strategy?

• Looking back on your life, what were the wisest things you did to foster your physical health? How can you retrieve and adapt that wisdom for the sake of your health today? This question gives you a chance to recall social environments, such as walking companions or other group activities, that enhanced your health.

• How important are material possessions and money for your sense of self-esteem? How was your attitude toward wealth and things fostered by your early family background and subsequent experiences? How much is your philosophy about material things guided by the prevalent views of society? What relationship does money have to love in your life?

• If you think that your attitude toward money and things is skewed in some way, that is, that your attitude does not empower true self-esteem, what steps might you take to change your approach on this subject?

• Does worry about money and possessions overburden you and put strains on your family? Can you simplify your life in this area to lessen these concerns? Would living more modestly have an adverse affect on your self-regard and your network of relationships?

• Do you think you have inner resources for shaping a creative elderhood for yourself? Or are you more or less backing fearfully into older age? Is the idea of an inner journey alien to you? What might be some ways for opening contemplative spaces in your life? If you can begin to get in touch with your inner resources, how would you describe them? How could they be put into play in ways that would enhance your self-esteem and help others?

• Have you ever thought it useful to get in touch with the shadow or dark side of yourself? This is an important part of the eldering process. It helps us deal with our prejudices and our demonizing of others. This contact with our shadow side also aids us to redirect energy in more beneficial ways. How would you discuss your shadow side?

• Self-reliance is an important quality in aging well. Do you consider yourself a self-reliant person? A brief examination of your personal history can be instructive. How have you dealt with serious losses or major changes in the past? At these times, were you able to tap into your inner resources to cope, without being overly dependent on others? Imagine a loss in the present: financial, physical, or interpersonal. How well could you cope on your own? What steps can you take to become more self-reliant? Be specific, and remember that these steps can be small ones.

• Creative elders seem to achieve a high degree of self-acceptance and self-esteem. Explore how much you allow false expectations, either imposed by yourself or by society, to hinder your self-acceptance. Or perhaps you think that you need to control everything around you, lest disorder or even chaos threaten you. What would it take for you to let go of false expectations and an excessive need to control in order to enjoy the serenity of self-acceptance? If you were more inner-directed, would your self-esteem improve?

• Why is a sense of humor and a spirit of playfulness vital for empowering the self in later years? How alive is your inner child? When did you last show that delight or playfulness of your inner child? Do you know how to laugh both at and with yourself? How would you rate your sense of humor? List a few things you really enjoy doing and ask yourself when was the last time you did them. Do you take a little time to celebrate the small and the large events of life?

• Boredom can be a serious affliction in older age. It is the opposite of vital interest and motivating purpose. When interest and purpose are internalized, they empower the elder self. Have you set some achievable goals for yourself in different areas: for example, intellectual or social or recreational goals? How can you turn the skills and achievements of your past into new purposes that would interest you? Interest and purpose lead to productivity. Do you see yourself as a productive person in later life?

(At the end of your reflection period, devote a little time to making one or two overall drawings related to the above issues. Don't try to cover everything. Rather, choose those questions that resonate more deeply for you. Attempt to express your thoughts and feelings in the symbolism of line and color.)

E. Expanding the Elder Self

Few people in our culture think of older age as a time for expanding into new dimensions of life. Yet we have seen in chapter 4 how people move beyond the confines of their histories and biological condition to widen their life-experiences. The question then becomes: How can each of us, in our own circumstances, extend our capacities to engage and enjoy life? A preliminary query would be to ask ourselves, whether in midlife or elderhood, how satisfied we are at present with our lives. Have we settled for a safe haven in which to mark time, buffering ourselves against personal change and development? Do our fears, nurtured over many years, keep us from realizing our many potentials? The following meditation and questions are geared toward inviting us to envision our own older age as a period of expanding horizons. Yet this rewarding task also involves dealing with our hesitancies and fears about venturing forward. There is no magic way to accomplish this expansion. Each of us must do the ongoing work of opening new paths from where our journeys have brought us at this moment.

Meditation: As you begin your meditation, remember to put yourself in a comfortable but erect position, after you have done some light stretching exercises. Do some deep breathing, then return to your normal breathing pattern. For some moments, get in touch with your breath, letting go of all pressures about how you are going to do this exercise. Simply observe your breathing in a quiet and relaxed way. Gradually realize how your breathing expands your chest, lungs, and abdomen. In its involuntary way, breathing expands us into the world. We continue to draw the world in through our nostrils to energize our life. If we stopped this interconnecting and expanding process, we would die. Our biology is already a lesson in expansion.

Imagine yourself walking in a forest on a pleasant, clear day. You are at ease because you know this place. The light breeze, the sounds of birds, the rustling leaves are all familiar to you. Suddenly you come to a clearing that looks out on an extensive meadow, inclining up a hill to another forest opposite you. You pause before the sight because it is new to you. As you observe more closely, you realize that sounds in the new forest are unknown to you, and the trees are of a different kind. In the distance, you hear bird and animal calls that you haven't heard before. And in the farthest distance there seems to be a sound of rushing water, perhaps a river or an ocean inlet. Do you go forward to explore, or do you stay where you are? If you move ahead, it will mean climbing the meadow and walking into a forest you do not know. You could go back and stay with the familiar. In some ways that choice would be easier. But you are also drawn toward the new. You would like to inspect the different trees, listen to and see the new birds and animals, and eventually make your way to the edge of those beckoning waters. Nothing compels you; the choice is yours. Stay with this imagery for a few minutes before you take up a pen and turn to the questions below.

QUESTIONS

• Do you live mainly in the past, the present, or the future? How do you use your past? Is it for enjoyment of memories or is it for the repetition of unhealed hurts with their emotional baggage of guilt and resentment? If the latter, what are the main examples of such repetition? Do you live in the past as an escape from present realities? Can you think of ways in which you employ wisdom from past experiences for coping with present problems? Give specific examples. Do you think you have a future? If not, discuss why this is the case. If yes, expand on it a bit. What keeps you from making the most of the present?

• Do you continue to educate yourself? In what ways: e.g., taking courses, worthwhile reading, traveling to learn, involvement in new ventures? Are you able to learn from your failures? Do you stimulate your curiosity about things? Do you think there is a relationship between physical health and a vital, inquiring mind? Is the unexamined life worth living? How is wisdom related to lifelong learning?

• How open are you to change and new possibilities? Perhaps you are open in some realms but not in others that could lead to a richer elderhood. Can you note where you are open and where closed? Can you get in touch with the fears that restrain you from pursuing new options? When you address the last question, do it in terms of specific possibilities that you thought would be good for you. Have you been able to turn setbacks, whether physical, relational, or job-related, into potentials for new and better choices? Can you "accept what is given, and go from there"?

• What are you going to do with the rest of your life? The answers to this question are not only in the zone of security for later life, but also of adventure and exploration. Try imaging optimal futures for yourself. What would be the components of such futures? Is your planning for the future only in terms of physical and financial security? What other aspects of the future would help you "live with passion"?

• Do you connect older age with greater freedom? Consider freedom from and freedom for. From what burdens do you need to liberate yourself? These might be excessive worries, negative psychological scripts that you repeat compulsively, passive aggressiveness, destructive self-images, enervating relationships, social idolatries, and related burdens. Why carry all this weight into your later years? By releasing some of this load, you ready yourself to be free for positive contributions and experiences. Are you free enough to speak in your own voice, to communicate from your depths? Are you free to live a life of increasing benevolence and service?

• One elder in his nineties says that he lives in a sea of gratitude. Is your older age marked by thankfulness? Can you be grateful even amid hardships? Make a brief list of the things for which you are most grateful. These can be small happenings as well as major items. What simple ritual (for example, a phrase repeated silently to yourself) might you devise to bring conscious gratitude into everyday living? The opposite of living with gratitude is to exist in an atmosphere of excessive demands and expectations.

What does gratitude have to do with your aging well?

(Conclude this exercise by drawing a summary image, depicting in symbol your grasp of the dynamics of expanding your elder self. If it is appropriate, share this drawing with others who are working on the same theme. It can be helpful to keep the drawing in front of you as you elaborate on these topics in your journal.)

F. Reaching Out from the Elder Self

Old people need to rethink their social image as senior citizens. The latter term connotes passivity and disengagement. A senior citizen, in the popular mind, is someone to be taken care of, to be offered financial discounts, and to be relegated to a park bench. Or senior citizens are viewed as potential consumers, as a market to be exploited. They are pictured as outside the mainstream, except when a voting issue touches their entitlements. Society's message is to retire to the periphery of life and not seek active social engagement. The senior citizen's day is done. In contrast to this vision, the vibrant elders in this book deliver a different message. They see themselves as "elders of the tribe," as persons called upon to contribute their skills and wisdom to the greater causes of humanity. Their many life experiences have prepared them for a new vocation of reaching out in important spheres. They reach out in creative ways not despite their age, but because of it. The circles of their outreach move in ever-widening rings from family and friends to planetary concerns.

Meditation: As you begin your meditation, place yourself in a quiet and comfortable position. Breathe deeply a few times and then return to normal breathing, but with you attention focused effortlessly on your inhaling and exhaling. When you feel relaxed and at peace, see yourself being led to the top of a beautiful mountain by a spiritual guide. If you can, imagine a favorite mountain place, one with vistas and sensations that are known to you. Choose any spiritual guide you wish, such as Black Elk, the great Sioux shaman who, as an elder, projected a marvelous vision of nature and humanity. Your guide leads you through the last clump of trees and out on to a rocky point whence you can see vast distances. You are both quiet, because you have traveled a long way to come to this point and the climb has been both wearying and exhilarating. But you are also stilled by the magnificence of the view on all sides. Distant mountains fold into one another in tiers of different blues. In the foreground, rivers and streams run through verdant valleys. You can make out towns and roads along the water routes. Overhead clouds drift along and beautiful birds glide by on the updrafts.

You and your guide sit for a long while in silence observing the vista. Then he or she speaks gently to you. "This is not an ordinary excursion. I have led you here to help you understand something crucial for your new calling as an elder of the people. From this place, nature teaches us to cultivate a panoramic view of reality. Nature entices us to come this long road by the gift of its incomparable beauty. Through an immense evolutionary journey, the earth had brought you here both to behold the vision and to grasp your responsibility as an old one for all that you see. Now that you are an elder, this ritual initiates you into a new phase of meaning and service. Through sufferings and joys, you have learned much about the ways of humans and the needs of Mother Earth. You are ordained to elderhood. This means reaching out from your wisdom to inspire peace and reconciliation among all creatures, respecting their special natures and their needs. The old ones must crown their life-journeys as peacemakers, as advocates for those things that will enhance all life in the one great web of the universe. Return to the places of your regular life, but now go as an old one who seeks to transform yourself into a reconciler, to live out your final season as an elder whose life will bless the tribe and the earth." The guide places both hands on your head and smiles at you. Then the guide disappears and you are left alone before the panoramic vision. You choose a mantra to commemorate your new vocation. Before you descend the mountain, you sit in silence. You do not know the particulars of your new commissioning, but you are ready to be led and to lead as an elder.

QUESTIONS

• An important part of reaching out in elderhood concerns one's own family. What experiences from your family of origin impact on your ability to reach out to others and to wider human needs? Think of each person in your immediate family from your spouse to your grandchildren. As you bring each person into consciousness, reflect on your place in that individual's life. Is the relationship with him or her blocked in ways that seem insurmountable? If communication is reasonably good, how can it be improved in terms of your reaching out? Do you enjoy the lives of your children without interfering or demanding too much from them? Are you able to relate to your family members with the same qualities (some are mentioned in the next group of questions) you would show to a good friend? If not, why is this so? If you live as an elder couple, do you encourage each other to reach out in service beyond the issues of your immediate family?

• Is loneliness an important problem in your life? How do you understand its causes? Do you cultivate friendships as one remedy for it as well as for the value of the friendships themselves? Are friends more meaningful in your life than immediate family members? Would you say that the best outcome of your marriage is the creation of close friendships with family members? Here are a few qualities that make for good friendship: availability, nonjudgmental attitudes, deep listening, respecting autonomy and otherness, and benevolence. When you think about your best friends, or about those with whom you would like to be closer, how well do you exercise these qualities? If you have friends of long standing, to what do you attribute the success of these relationships? Do you believe that friendships need to be worked on or that they are automatic? Are you adaptable in a friendship without being overly dependent? Do you have (or seek to have) intergenerational friendships? How does continued learning and mental stimulation enhance friendship? Do you seek out groups or organizations where you might meet new friends?

• In addition to family and special friends, intentional communities have been helpful to older people. These groups can have many purposes from recreation to good works. Are you part of an intentional community, even though it has never called itself by such a title? What benefits do you derive from such a small group? How important do you think an intentional community could be for persons in later life? If you could form such a group to suit your own needs, what kind of people would be in it? How often would it meet? What sort of things would it do; what issues would it address? After you have sketched out the qualities of an ideal support community for you, where might you find something similar in your area? If it doesn't exist, what could you, and possibly a few friends, do to start one?

• In what ways does your life embrace the world? At first, this question may seem forbidding or impossible, because it appears to imply influence on a worldwide scene. But everyone's life can have influence on the world, even if we operate in modest and local ways. Think of this in terms of the ripple effect, as when we throw a rock into a still pond. By raising children, your influence extends through them to many others. What contribution do you make to your local community through gardening, tutoring, recycling, and supporting causes for health and education? What might be some ways by which you embrace a wider world than your local community? Perhaps you could review some fields of your involvement that would elicit clues about your wider engagement: aesthetic, political, religious, educational, commercial, and so forth.

• How "holistic" is your outreach, that is, how integrated are your activities in pursuit of what you see as worthwhile goals? Are you discouraged from continuing your commitment to causes when they seem too hard to achieve or when there are setbacks? Do you allow yourself to be mesmerized by TV sitcoms and "groupthink"? As an older person, do you feel freer to speak out on wider issues that concern you? Are you willing to take risks that would have frightened you earlier in life? In considering wider causes for yourself, do you look to your own resources or do you denigrate yourself by comparisons to more influential people? When you help people, do you try to give them confidence in themselves, or are you altruistic in controlling ways?

• Among the many valuable ways to embrace the world is commitment to environmental or ecological movements. In what ways do you feel connected to the natural world? Has this sense of bonding with nature increased with age? Can nature teach us important lessons about aging? Do you think that elders have a special calling to work for environmental integrity? What reasons for such a calling would you give? What roles can elders play in this movement?

• Whatever worthwhile cause you choose to embrace as an elder, it implies that old people are linked to the future. Since the lifespan of elders will probably be less than most younger people, how would you explain that old people have a future?

(As you look back over your notes on these questions, return to a more meditative mode. After mulling over your replies, do a drawing that depicts the highlights of your insights. Be sure to draw what wells up in you, as pertaining to you, and not as a message for other people. End the whole exercise with a smile of gratitude.)

G. Encountering Mortality

Thinking about death and dying is a morbid experience for many people. It is also a frightening reflection for most people when it brings up the dying process with its physical and mental losses. These anxieties and fears are normal and should be recognized. Our human condition is profoundly marked by being animals who know well ahead of time that we must die and don't like the prospect. The experiential sense of our mortality seems to come home to us mainly by midlife. The signs of aging stare back at us from the mirror, and our inner clock pushes us to count the years from the end rather than from the beginning, as young people do. Yet all the wisdom traditions of the world, through their poets and philosophers, encourage us to reflect on death and dying for beneficial reasons. Such meditation can help us gain perspective on what truly matters in life. It leads us to examine our values and motivations. And it pushes us to reassess our relationships: How are we behaving toward others and how are we being treated by them? In short, meditation on death can inspire us to live at a deeper level, to question superficial values, and to enjoy a fuller elderhood.

Meditation: As you begin your meditation, sit quietly in a comfortable but erect position or walk slowly in pleasant surroundings. Focus again on your breathing. Draw a few deep breaths, holding briefly, and then releasing slowly. If you are sitting, you might find it helpful to partially close your eyes and fix your gaze at one point a few feet ahead of you. This can symbolize your movement inward and minimize surrounding distractions. As you breathe normally, visualize your inhaling and exhaling as the sustaining rhythm of your life. Your breath is spirit, vital energy drawn into you from the wider web of life. As you exhale, you are returning breath to be revitalized. Visualize a breathing world where humans, other mammals, birds, fish, plants, and many other creatures share in the great dynamic of cosmic life.

Imagine yourself walking alone in a quiet wooded place. The sun is shining and the environment is pleasant and beautiful. After some time in this forest, you hear the sound of moving water in the distance. Before long you come out of the trees on to the banks of a wide river where you sit and watch the flow. You notice the ever-shifting composition of the water as it glides by. In one place, it is turning white as it splashes against boulders; in other places, it rushes along fast and strong, while near the shore, it swirls in circular eddies. As you observe the river, it seems to look more or less the same on the whole, but it is forever changing as it adapts the volume of its flow to the surrounding terrain. You realize that the river mirrors the rhythm of all life and of your personal existence. All creatures follow the pattern of death and rebirth, of perishing in some ways and being renewed in other modes. In this sense, your embodied self, in all its thinking and doing, resembles the river. Your cells are in motion, dying and being reborn in the flow of your personal time. You understand that the cadence of dying is inextricably connected to the dance of life.

The river teaches you the central lesson of the life-death pattern of all beings. It also awakens you to a core truth of your own existence. Your life is transitory but it can have meaning in the overall web of living. The river tells you not to hold on at every turn as though you could stay there forever. If you cling too hard and defend vigorously against the current of life, not only will you be carried away, but you will not have experienced the fullness of the journey. You will be so concerned about your own preservation that you will miss opportunites to help others understand the river. As an elder, you are called to delve deeply into the mysteries of the river so that you can assist others to navigate its waters. And since you are the human eyes and mind of the river, it depends on your wisdom to keep its watery sources from destruction. As you sit on the shore concluding your meditation, you ponder the river's meaning in your own life. In what ways does your mortal condition call for letting go? How can you find peace and joy in a world of constant death and rebirth?

QUESTIONS

• Have you experienced physical "small deaths" in any way? Perhaps there are impairments that keep you from doing things that were important to you. This could have to do with sight or mobility or a health condition. How are these small deaths both warning signals and beacons lighting new directions for you? Do you rebel against these givens or use them as catalysts for new ways of living? Some people have found that unexpected physical limitations have changed their lives in positive directions. For example, they worry less about health or they question a prior life of excessive striving or they cultivate new values and involvements or they make more of relationships. Does any of this resonate for you?

• What have you learned from the small deaths of your emotional sufferings? Perhaps retirement or the sudden loss of a job caused a period of depression? Do you mourn the loss of your youth? The loss of friends or a spouse can lead to prolonged emotional crises. Divorce is frequently the source of deep mental upset for at least one of the parties. Others live in relationships blighted by addictions or by coldness and cruelty. Some have become alienated from their children. Others are afflicted by sadness over violence and suffering in the world, despite their efforts to improve the human condition. Sometimes these emotional losses are connected with important turning points in life. Spend a few moments reviewing the pattern of emotional small deaths over your lifespan, and return to the initial question of this section: What have these experiences taught you?

• Do you fear your own death? For the moment, put aside fears of the dying process which we will take up below. Just focus on the knowledge that one day you will cease to be alive. What sadness, fear, or anxiety arises in you? Perhaps these feelings are provoked by a network of losses: family, friends, important involvements, and a general enjoyment of the world. Do you think it is valuable to recognize such feelings, if you are to reform your way of living in the face of death? Can even our negative feelings about our own deaths be part of a process of personal growth? In terms of relating to others, enjoying each day, revising one's priorities? What concrete preparations have you made for your own death, such as a living will, a legal will, instructions on where things are for your survivors, dispositions for your funeral and burial or cremation? Would you want your friends not only to mourn your passing but also to throw a party in celebration of your life?

• The dying process can be long or short; it can be relatively painless or it can involve considerable suffering. This may be the most difficult prospect to face in life. What are your deepest fears or anxieties about the end of your life? For some, it may be poverty or isolation in a nursing home. For others it will be a combination of physical suffering and mental incapacity. Do you worry about being a burden to your family when you can no longer live independently? Would you be concerned about elder abuse and neglect in your situation? What is your position on a living will that may prevent you from being kept alive on machines for an indefinite time? Would you consider terminating your life, if you judged that its quality had declined drastically? Although no one can predict the trajectory of his or her death, what do you do to promote your bodily and mental health? Do you engage in physical fitness activities in a regular way? Do you avoid smoking and excessive drinking and other addictions? Are you knowledgeable about preserving your health through better nutrition? Do you think that some form of counseling or therapy could help you enhance your life? We have already reflected on a number of areas like cultivating friendship and purpose that foster one's total well-being. But in the end, we must each face our own dying. Are you developing spiritual resources that will help you die in peace? How would you characterize these resources for you personally?

• Do you believe in some form of afterlife or of reincarnation? What is your rationale for such belief? Does such belief have a strong, positive influence on how you live now? Or are you among those who are less sure about life after death? If you are in this group, does your understanding of afterlife affect how you live? If you do not believe in an afterlife, do you think such a position has any impact on how you live or how you face your own death?

(As you conclude this exercise, return in imagination to the river setting of the previous meditation. Sit again by the river of life, and let the thoughts and impressions of your work on the questions flow along the river current. Simply observe them without judging. Allow the impressions and insights to surface at their own pace. When you are ready, draw a design that captures for you the most important aspects of your work on this topic.)

H. Developing Personal Spirituality

We use the word "spirituality" in this context to avoid the narrower meaning of the term "religion" in the minds of most people. The two words are certainly not opposed to each other, and often they overlap for many people. As we have seen, a number of elders find a spiritual home in traditional religious communities, while others find different paths to a personalized philosophy of life. By underscoring personal spirituality here, we are searching for that changing network of meaning and motivation that empowers older people at the deepest level. Where do they find a sense of transcendence and broader interconectedness that affects every aspect of living? And we emphasize "personal" because we want to discover what has been and continues to be truly meaningful to each elder person. What have we retrieved from one or possibly more traditions and from unique life-experiences to formulate a personal spirituality that supports and influences our thinking, feeling, and acting? We are also concerned with how one's spirituality continues to grow and change through the experiences of later life.

Meditation: We can begin a meditation on this topic by doing some preliminary exercises for relaxation such as stretching and bending or by taking a short walk. Find a quiet place that is pleasing to you and sit in a comfortably erect and centered position for meditation. Breathe deeply and slowly a few times, sensing the expansion and contraction of your chest and abdomen as you inhale and exhale. Then breathe normally, focusing gently on your breathing process, allowing your mind to free itself for a while from pressing concerns. After you have dwelled on the physical rhythm of your breathing for some minutes, recall that the word for breath is also related to the word for spirit. Imagine that your inhalation is an in-spiriting, drawing into your chest around your heart all the spirits that energized you in different periods of your life. As this breath-spirit fills the center of your chest, imagine that it becomes a warm, bright light, a golden circle within you. Stay with this inner sun for a while, basking in its light and warmth. You notice how this spiritual light within is being continuously fed by the oxygen of your breathing. The central sphere within now opens to reveal images important to your spiritual formation in early years. Observe these images from your past as they move across the inner circle. Perhaps the images are of places or of people who influenced your early spirituality. Continue to watch and experience as other images unfold with your aging process. What other people, movements, or events appear within the frame of the golden circle as you review your life in chronological order? Do not seek to analyze or criticize the images depicting the formation of your spirituality. Simply observe closely and let whatever affective valence the images produce stay with you. Even though your spirituality may have changed many times over your lifespan, you carry forward into the golden light some elements from the past. When the images have passed, the circle of light within returns to its original undifferentiated shape. You notice again how the circle pulsates with your breathing. As you feel warmed and enlighted by the golden ball, you see it begin to expand and gradually fill all of your body. Then the light moves out beyond your physical dimensions and suffuses the spaces and entities around you. It spreads in ever-widening circles of light to embrace the world. You feel joined in spirit to all beings. Without any discursive thought, you stay immersed in the light and warmth of the circle within now become the all-suffusing sun without. Listen for whatever response comes from your heart and quietly express it as a repeated mantra as you conclude your meditation.

QUESTIONS

• What were the main vectors of your spirituality as a child? What were the most influential factors (persons, teachings, institutions, events) in shaping this early spirituality?

• Try to formulate important turning points in your spirituality. What experiences caused you to change your religious or spiritual outlook and action? Can you divide your life into periods characterized by different spiritualities? What was carried forward at each turning point? What was left behind?

• If you believe in God or some form of transcendent energy or being, how have your images of the transcendent changed over time? Is there any contrast between your youthful images of the divine or the transcendent and your present understanding? Express any contrasting images or beliefs from different phases of your life in reference to God or to spiritual principles.

• How do you factor into your spirituality the problems of evil, injustice, and other destructive aspects of life? Are you aware of your own shadow side? How do you deal wisely with that part of yourself?

• Would you say that your spirituality as an older person is simpler or more complex? Or perhaps it is both at once; how do you explain this?

• If you belong to a particular religious tradition, how do you understand it in reference to other spiritual traditions? In this regard, has your attitude become more pluralistic and tolerant? Can you live with integrity between or even outside of given traditions? How do you understand and explain this?

• Have you ever had spiritual experiences that were so intense and unforgettable that they marked your life to this day? Can you describe any of these?

• Do you feel freer as an older person to shape your own spirituality, regardless of what other individuals or groups might think? In what way is this freedom related to the aging process?

• If the words "spiritual" or "religious" have either no meaning or negative connotations for you, how do you express your deepest philosophy of life? What are its principles, its virtues, its goals, its actions? You could apply a number of the above questions to the changes and development of such a philosophy of life.

• How is the development of your spirituality related to personal sufferings, physical or mental? What upsetting events in your life challenged the spirituality you had when they happened?

• Do you think there is a close relationship between an enlightened spirituality and ethical or aesthetic awareness? How does your spirituality extend outward in ethical or other directions? If you do not associate your spirituality with your understanding of ethics or morality, perhaps you can connect it to ways in which you serve other people or organizations.

• What aspects of your spirituality do you think need development? You might think about interior or external dimensions. What concrete steps might you take to develop what is lacking?

(You are invited to conclude your reflections and writing by sketching images that draw together aspects of your own spirituality. Before you do such drawing, spend a few moments in quiet meditation, returning to the imagery of the inner circle of light and to an awareness of your breathing. Let the images you choose to draw emerge from such contemplation. If you are working on this exercise with others, you may want to share your drawings and their meanings for you.)

◆ ◆ ◆ ───────────────────────────────

CHAPTER 9

Sharing Gifts of Wisdom

Throughout history creative and generous elders have given gifts or blessings to those younger than themselves. The older people who share their experiences and insights in this book also want to leave a legacy to the young. When asked what constitutes the best of life for the individual and for society, these elders thought back on their own experiences to come up with answers that are gifts to the young. More specifically, they were requested to answer this question: If a young person asked you how to live a good and satisfying life, how would you respond? The answers differed in form but had a remarkable similarity in overall meaning. The responses tended to cluster into two groups: those directed toward individual development and those aimed at social living. In this concluding chapter, we present a representative sampling of views on what is most important for living a satisfying and contributory life. Of course, the answers of the elders were meant to be general and would need to be adapted in many ways to individuals in their particular environments.

Looking Inward

The advice of a number of elders concerns deepening one's self-reflection and strengthening one's inner life. Helen DeChatelet talks about "being honest with yourself and finding out what you really want to do." But such self-discovery implies what Elizabeth Howes calls exploring your own inner maps, your special personality patterns. In this way, she says, a younger person will find the freedom not only to do something valuable in the world, but also to be what he or she is supposed to be. Anthony Soto points in the same direction when he counsels the young to "develop your own gifts and liberate yourself from mental and social structures that hinder this development." But an important aspect of knowing oneself in an honest way is the ability to trust oneself. Mary Erlanger, who emphasizes self-trust, admits "that it takes a lot of living to do that."

When Eli Wallach urges the young to confide in themselves, he doesn't mean a self-enclosed confidence that ignores advice and experience from without. Rather, he is affirming the need to take responsibility for one's own life and not allow oneself to be swayed this way and that by family or society. His advice is echoed by Gertrude Wilks who says: "Take control of your life." Only then can you decide what you really want to do and do it, says Wallach. Only then can we make use of the advice of Celestine Sibley: "Try to find what you like to do and work at it." By gradually learning how to go inward and confide in oneself, a person can "enjoy what's available to him or her," says Sally Lilienthal. Yet real self-knowledge and self-trust are closely linked to self-esteem. When Charlee Lambert counsels the young to "like yourself," she knows that loving oneself is not a command that can be executed as one might perform a physical chore. It took Ross Gritts a long time to incorporate into his own life the advice he gives to those who would live a satisfying life: "Think well of yourself."

Another dimension of healthy inward living concerns the ability to live each day with intensity and curiosity. Sidney Brown tells the young: "Don't take things for granted. Each day is a new day. Don't just say, 'Well, it's another day.' Ask questions. Be curious." This theme is reaffirmed by Mary Thoits: "Live each day with keen awareness," and by Charlee Lambert: "Live today with passion, and don't be afraid to take some chances, some risks." This advice is repeated by Lin Ludy who counsels the young to live intensely in the present and not be be overly concerned with the past or the future. More than one elder associates this living in the present with fostering one's educational abilities. Living in the now can stimulate the mind to think and get excited about ideas, says Bertram Gross, who reiterates Brown's imperative: Be curious, ask questions. The young tend to live in a fantasized future, which is not all bad. Their imaginings are part of the process of discovering new paths for themselves. But if they confine themselves to familiar childhood emotional patterns or to dreams about how much better life will be in the future, they miss much of real value in the present. This is why Earl Brewer exhorts them to: "Dig in where you are and make the most of opportunities available to you. For what seems little and less important now can become powerful and influential. Be open to small gifts along the way."

Edna McCallion encourages young people to get to know their inner selves, or as she says, the child within. She would like them to realize who they are in their uniqueness. Environmental and cultural factors also influence who we are both externally and internally. But beyond these forces, we also experience a unique component, a special clustering of conscious and unconscious life that marks our personality in special ways. Too often we suppress or betray that unique inner personality in order to conform to the pressures of our immediate world. McCallion reminds us that it is virtually impossible to live a truly satisfying life if we are out of touch with what another elder, Dorothy Kearney, calls our inner blueprint. This does not mean that a young person is programmed like a machine to follow given lines. Rather, to find our inner child is to discover our particular gifts and potential, as Soto advocated. These gifts are open to a wide and self-liberating range of applications. Thus by working out of our unique configuration of talents, we free ourselves to choose life directions that are compatible and rewarding. When Simon Greenberg tells young people to answer a question about meaning ("Do you want to live as if the world has no meaning or as if the world has meaning?"), this meaning is not simply something outside oneself. It must also correlate with the inner patterning of each person. Yet this personalized meaning that drives a satisfying life requires a spirit of faith or of trust. One's meaning world cannot be constructed quickly by just thinking about it or willing it. It is accessed gradually, as Martin Marty insists, by embracing the wounds and blessings of existence that constantly interface with each other.

Yet the advice to look inward is not only for itself, but it is also a preparation to reach outward toward other people to serve the welfare of the planet. If young people are helped from childhood to appreciate their personal gifts and develop honest self-love, they become more disposed to giving and receiving love in the wider world. Robert Handy maintains that the essence of a satisfying life is to be able to give and receive love. And Page Smith reiterates this goal of the good life: "I think the capacity to love and the experience of love are the most essential things, and the most needed, and often the hardest to achieve." But this network of love is far more than an infatuation or a warm glow. John Duryea talks about the good life as one in which love means caring and benevolence that manifests itself in daily deeds. And Susan Carlton Smith, who also sees love as the center of the good life, refers to "big love" that has to do with kindness, generosity, consideration, and consistency. Although love can be manifested in many ways beyond the intimate couple, elders also point to the great value of having a close companion. Barbara Payne-Stancil talks about finding someone "to love and be loved by." And Arthur Stark tells young people to "try to find a compatible partner for life." Beatrice Schiffman broadens this theme beyond the image of a couple: "Find a loving environment in which to live. It's important to know that you are loved."

Reaching Outward

In the last paragraph, we already see the close relationship between the inward focus of the advice for a satisfying life and the need to move beyond the self. The theme of moving outward toward other people and important causes is prominent in the wisdom legacy of these elders. In this section, we will divide the general theme of reaching outward into two topics: direct involvement with other people and commitment to causes. This distinction is somewhat arbitrary and loose, because one is usually directed toward other people when one pursues causes. And we don't want to force the advice of elders on this subject into overly narrow confines. But we also want to respect a distinction that seems to come out of the comments of the elders when they are asked to advise younger people on how to enjoy a worthwhile life. It is really a matter of emphasis. Some stress individual persons first as a focus, others stress important social causes. Both aspects of this advice are interrelated and very important, to judge by the frequency of the responses on this theme.

Estelle Bierley urges the young to be of service to other people directly. "If we don't get outside of ourselves in this way," she says, "life can be very boring." According to William d'Antonio, who spent his career in university teaching, young people can avoid some of the pitfalls of drifting along without meaning by using their talents to serve other people. "Doing work that serves others gives meaning to life," he says. Jack Etheridge adds a related note about pursuing wealth that recurs in the advice of a number of elders. The point is not to make the accumulation of money a life-goal. Here's how Judge Etheridge puts it: "Learn as much as you can. Make money to keep the pressure off. Believe that you're lucky, and go where the action is. But above all, life-meaning comes from the love you have for other people." Mary Kunst and Bernice Neugarten stress the cultivation of friendships and interpersonal ties as the most satisfying aspects of life. "Invest in other people," says Neugarten, "in fostering their welfare. . . . I think the good life consists in meaningful interpersonal ties that grow over the years." Admiral Gene LaRocque says that helping other people produces the greatest satisfaction in life. Winona Sample adds an enjoyment angle on reaching out to others: "Do something you enjoy when you try to help other people. If you like to fish, take someone with you."

But helping other people, as the elders tell us, has its own dangers. Sometimes we think we are assisting others when in fact we may be merely trying to control them for our own purposes. Ella Mazel is aware of this when she offers the noninjury rule: Don't hurt anybody. And Mary Thoits states the positive side of the non-injury rule when attempting to help others. Thoits reminds us that authentic altruism respects the boundaries of the other and encourages others to pursue options that they choose for themselves. And Hector Leuterio asks us to test our good works for others by examining our motivations. Does our helping proceed from genuine affection for the other person or from self-centered motives? When Mabel Broom at 106 urges young people to do right by others, she warns them to be careful of "false people." Her advice would probably please a Bodhisattva: "Protect yourself from them, but don't get mad at them; just smile and say something nice to them." President Carter offers still another challenging counsel for those who would help others. He tells them to get to know people who are different from themselves, to break across clan barriers in one's altruism. This is particularly important advice in our era of racial, ethnic, and religious divisions.

Commitment to valuable causes is often mentioned by elders in advising the young about living a satisfying life. These causes can be local or worldwide, little-known issues, or matters of general concern. Robert McAfee Brown, who has dealt with seminary and university students throughout his career, announces this general theme: "Find something to which you can wholeheartedly commit yourself. This can be many things: art, family, religious faith, but it needs to be something that keeps you from being too much turned in on yourself. Commit yourself to the integrity of other people. If you concentrate just on yourself, you are going to become very unhappy." The Jesuit priest Joseph Fichter returns to the topic of pursuing material wealth within the perspective of seeking the good life: "Do what you feel God wants you to do with honesty and integrity. And instead of aiming only at making money, commit yourself to social service of some kind. You have to have concern for people who are in need."

We hear the same theme from cardiologist Willis Hurst, who also underscores the element of joy in supporting causes: "Seek a joy that is not self-serving both in private and professional life. Select a profession you enjoy and throw yourself into it without regard to money or other material good." Again, journalist Claude Sitton guides the young around the stumbling block of making money one's chief pursuit: "Prepare for something that interests you. Get into that field and give 100 percent. If you like it, stick with it no matter what. Don't worry about financial rewards. Respect humankind." Charles Weltner, both as U.S. congressman and Georgia Supreme Court justice, tried to live out the advice he gives the young for a good life. His death shortly after the interview adds the aspect of a special testament in the following statement to warn the country's youth against the all-pervasive quest for wealth: "Don't try to make a lot of money. Do whatever you're interested in to serve the public purpose. I think that if a person ends up working for him- or herself solely, that person will be miserable."

Pursuing causes is to seek purposes that are larger than oneself. William Sennett speaks from his own experiences as a long-time Communist organizer and then as a successful businessman: "Develop purposes in life that are bigger than your own narrow interests. This will make living meaningful. It will bring a sense of satisfaction and accomplishment." But reaching out in valuable causes, Janet Kalven reminds us, is not an individualistic endeavor. She advises the young to work out of communities of like-minded people in doing good works. If they can operate with a small community that pools and shares its gifts, she insists, the end result will be better, both for those who are served and for the individual's own growth. Although the award-winning, human-rights activist Miriam Levy considers herself a secular Jew, she speaks in biblical language about the virtues the young need to engage in causes: "Do justly and love mercifully as you devote yourself to vital issues. Try to keep a sense of balance and proportion in working for causes so that the outcome will produce more amity than hostility." And Ike Saporta, who through a lifetime of engaging in causes from resisting the Nazis to planning better cities, points out to young people the healthiest underlying motive for embracing any cause: "Develop a zest for life, love it and love its beauty; then you will be ready to enter into imprortant movements, and you will find deeper happiness."

Interfacing the Inward and Outward

In this last section of the chapter, we listen to those elders who in their comments linked the inner and the outer dimensions of living a good life. They remind the young that life to be lived well needs a balance of self-reflection and action in the world. It is a matter of interfacing our inner needs and longings with our outer involvements. In all of the following admonitions, we hear this rhythm as the core song of worthwhile living. Esther Peterson exhorts the young to be true to themselves and find out what gives each of them inner joy. But she hopes that "service to others comes with finding that inner joy." She wants them to remember that life has its disappointments and traumas, "but know that if you are down one day, it will pass," she says. She counsels the young not to be discouraged because they can't solve all the problems of the world: "I can't change history, but I reserve the right to put the stubborn ounces of my weight where I'm convinced they ought to go." We notice a similar cadence in Gregory Bergman's advice. He has experienced crushing inner sorrow and he knows that the tragic is part of human existence. "You can't think 'why did this happen to me,'" he says. "You have to transcend it and move on. You do this by turning outward and loving someone or something."

Elise Boulding has devoted a considerable part of her career to causes of peace and justice. In her admonitions to the young about living a good life, we notice the interplay of inner and outer factors. "Help to build community," she says, "but you must build from an inner abundance. You can't do anything for others unless you have this inner abundance. But you can't develop inner abundance by sitting in a corner. You discover it in the very process of learning how the social and biological processes work where you live." Norma Levitt expresses the same polarity in her advice to the young. Part of what Boulding called inner abundance is the cultivation of one's own integrity. Levitt knows the costly journey of that search for her own authenticity and for a deepening of her faith. "In the life rhythm of love and work," she tells the young, "seek your own integrity, deepen your faith, and serve causes bigger than yourself." Therapist June Singer has counseled numerous people in their quest for a more satisying life. In therapy each person must dwell on the specific aspects of his or her own life. No universal statement will satisfy all needs and desires. Singer reminds us of this, but she also gives general advice that links the inner and the outer dimensions of good living. "I think you have to strike a balance," she says, "between taking care of yourself and taking care of those around you. This is very important and covers a lot of territory. You must learn to do it in three important areas: work, health, and love."

It is noteworthy that so many elders from different backgrounds gave similar responses to what the young should heed to live a satisfying life. Physicians, teachers, social workers, diplomats, and business people seem to agree that wealth and fame are not the secrets of a worthwhile life. This is a particularly important insight in an era when young people feel fiercely driven by their fears of perceived economic insecurity. The elders urge the young to mitigate this fear and pursue goals that interface inward growth with outward commitment. We hear this message in the following statements by diverse elders. Former Governor Lester Maddox encourages the young to "discover your God-given gifts and talents and serve other people with respect." Evelyn Ho, a Chinese-American, tells the young that to have a good life they should stay open to learning, respect themselves, and reverence others. The founder of the Gray Panthers, Maggie Kuhn, also advocates that the young pursue lifelong learning and "reach out to those in need, bonding with many people." Rose Lucey, a bookstore owner and mother of a large family, echoes the refrain of other elders about the good life: "Learn to love yourself in a humble but honest way, receive love from others, and open yourself up to the world."

Two elders gave longer responses that incorporate the inner-outer rhythm and elaborate it in telling ways. Quaker social activist Janet Ferguson invites a young person to "accept yourself, accept all parts of yourself as a gift from God, a gift from life. Embrace life, say yes to it, savor it, immerse yourself in it. You have unrealized potentials you never imagined. You will be so filled with love and gratitude that you will want to pour yourself out in service to others with joy and compassion." And playwright Virginia Davis first demurs from giving advice to the young "because life is an individual learning process." But then she adds: "If a young person really wanted to hear some advice, I'd say: Take good care of your body. You're responsible for your own health. Don't lie, cheat, or steal. Fight for what is important to you. Hold on to what is precious to you. Discover who you are, but don't be stingy with yourself. Avoid pettiness like a plague. Set a good example for others. Laugh. Enjoy. Contribute your talents to help others. Love passionately. Do right and fear not."

These legacies of the old to the young reflect the hard-won achievements inscribed in the faces and minds of the elders themselves. They know that younger people will have to determine for themselves the rightness of this advice in the ebb and flow of their own living. The old are not asking the young to believe them unquestioningly just because they are old. Rather the elders invite future generations to stop periodically and meditate on what constitutes the good life. Perhaps these guidelines, when confirmed by their own experience, will inspire the young to envision their own elderhood as a season rich in joy, gratitude, hope, and service.

It seems fitting to conclude this book with these gifts of the old to the young. For all of these creative elders are givers. We have seen in these chapters that there exists an elder wisdom, a wisdom not bought easily, but one purchased dearly in the orbit of joy and pain that shapes human life. These are elders who have known in their own flesh the words of the Roman poet who spoke of *lacrimae rerum*, the tears of human affairs. But they understand with Martin Marty that the wounds and the blessings are interlinked. Time has etched lines of wisdom in their faces, and time has gentled them into a deeper humanity where they have come to love themselves and care about others. In the end, they have learned, as educator Paul Schweitzer says, "to stay open to the mystery of existence." They have understood how to listen to the river of life. They have struggled to overcome their silences and make their voices heard. Their wisdom holds out a special hope for all of our elderhoods.

Appendix A:
Questions for Interview

Participants did not necessarily answer all these questions. They are directed toward opening up other dimensions of the interviewee's life and thought.

1. What do you feel have been the important successes in your life? The frustrations or failures?
2. What were the important turning points in your life? Describe.
3. What have been the most influential experiences of your life? Most influential people?
4. Are there periods of your life that you remember more vividly than others? Which ones? Why?
5. If you were writing the story of your life, how would you divide it into chapters?
6. What sorts of things frighten you now? When you were in your 60s? 40s? 20s? In childhood?
7. What kinds of things give you the most pleasure now? When you were in your 60s? 40s? 20s? In childhood?
8. If you could live your whole life over, what would you do differently?
9. Do you feel differently about yourself now from how you felt when you were younger?
10. If a young person came to you asking what's the most important thing in living a good life, what would you say?
11. What do you think has stayed the same about you throughout life? What do you think has changed?
12. How can one prepare for old age?
13. How do you feel about growing old now?
14. If you were going to live 5, 10, 20 more years, what would you do?
15. What is the hardest thing about growing older? The best thing?
16. What do you look forward to now?
17. Do you think about death?

Note: The above questions are adapted from *The Ageless Self* by Sharon R. Kaufman, p. 192.

Appendix B
Participants in the Elder Wisdom Project

1. Allen, Ivan, 82 (Atlanta, GA) Former mayor of Atlanta, businessman
2. Baker, Woolford, 102 (Atlanta, GA) Biology professor, ecologist
3. Bergman, Gregory, 85 (Berkeley, CA) Writer, peace and justice activist
4. Berry, Thomas, 79 (New York, NY) Ecologist and cultural historian
5. Bierley, Estelle M., 89 (Cincinnati, IL) Businesswoman, lay minister
6. Blaustein, Miriam, 80 (San Francisco, CA) Community activist, educator
7. Blumenthal, Gerda, 72 (Washington, DC) Professor
8. Boulding, Elise, 73 (Boulder, CO) Professor of sociology, conflict resolution
9. Brewer, Earl, 79 (Atlanta, GA) Sociologist of religion, aging specialist
10. Broom, Mabel, 107 (Atlanta, GA) Homemaker, clerk
11. Brown, Robert McAfee, 73 (Palo Alto, CA) Professor, theologian
12. Brown, Sidney, 71 (Palo Alto, CA) Organizer for second careers
13. Carter, Jimmy, 70 (Atlanta, GA) Former U.S. President, Governor of Georgia
14. Clarence, Henry, 70 (Berkeley, CA) Married priest, salesman
15. Cook, Douglas, 78 (Atlanta, GA) Minister, missionary
16. Crook, Clara, 83 (Santa Mateo, CA) Educational administrator, aging consultant
17. Crowley, Patty, 80 (Chicago, IL) Catholic lay movements, women's movement
18. d'Antonio, William, 67 (Washington, DC) Sociologist, professor
19. Davis, Virginia A., 72 (Wilmington, NC) Playwright, director
20. De Chatelet, Helen, 87 (Dayton, OH) Teacher, counselor
21. Dillenberger, Jane, 77 (Berkeley, CA) Art historian
22. Dillenberger, John, 75 (Berkeley, CA) Theologian, administrator
23. Dodd, Lamar, 84 (Athens, GA) Artist, professor
24. Duryea, John, 74 (Palo Alto, CA) Married priest, bookstore agent
25. Eaton, Anne Marie, 86 (Atlanta, GA) Aging center organizer
26. Erlanger, Mary, 70 (Athens, GA) Therapist
27. Erlanger, Michael, 78 (Athens, GA) Businessman, artist, poet
28. Etheridge, Jack, 65 (Atlanta, GA) Judge, alternative dispute resolution
29. Ferguson, Janet, 79 (Atlanta, GA) Teacher and volunteer
30. Fichter, Joseph, 85 (New Orleans, LA) Priest, sociologist
31. Forsyth, Katherine, 88 (Chicago, IL) Nun, educator

32. Greenberg, Simon, 92 (New York, NY) Rabbi, educational administrator
33. Gritts, Ross, 59 (San Jose, CA) American Indian activist, entrepreneur
34. Gross, Bertram, 81 (Moraga, CA) Federal government, professor
35. Handy, Robert T., 75 (New York, NY) Professor, Baptist minister
36. Hayden, Edwin, 80 (Cincinnati, IL) Evangelical minister, editor
37. Hill, Theresa, 78 (Dayton, OH) Homemaker, volunteer for elderly
38. Ho, Evelyn, 74 (Burlingame, CA) Social worker, organizer for elderly
39. Howes, Elizabeth B., 86 (Berkeley, CA) Therapist
40. Hurst, J. Willis, 73 (Atlanta, GA) Cardiologist, administrator
41. Johnson, Jan, 74 (Atlanta, GA) Artist
42. Kalven, Janet, 80 (Cincinnati, IL) Grail movement leader
43. Karp, Herbert, 71 (Atlanta, GA) Neurologist, professor
44. Kearney, Dorothy Gentry, 70 (Washington, DC) Librarian, deacon, spiritual director
45. Kelley, Peter, 68 (New York, NY) Theatrical-TV agent
46. King, Harriet, 76 (Atlanta, GA) Homemaker and volunteer
47. Kuhn, Maggie, 88 (Philadelphia, PA) Founder of Gray Panthers
48. Kunst, Mary, 89 (Chicago, IL) Child psychologist
49. Lambert, Charlee, 71 (Atlanta, GA) Social work, playwright, elder abuse work
50. Laplaine, Jean, 66 (Ottawa, CAN) Canadian government, musician
51. Land, Philip, 82 (Washington, DC) Priest, social justice scholar
52. LaRocque, Gene, 75 (Washington, DC) Admiral, founder: Center for Defense Information
53. Leuterio, Hector, 77 (Berkeley, CA) Computer programmer
54. Levitt, Norma, 76 (New York, NY) Jewish women's organizations, UN involvements
55. Levy, Miriam, 77 (San Francisco, CA) Human rights activist
56. Lilienthal, Sally, 74 (San Francisco, CA) Plowshares Fund, nuclear activist
57. Lowery, Joseph, 71 (Atlanta, GA) Minister, President: Southern Christian Leadership Conference
58. Lucey, Rose, 76 (Oakland, CA) Bookstore owner, peace activist
59. Ludy, Lindsley, 71 (Washington, DC) Spiritual director
60. Maddox, Lester, 78 (Atlanta, GA) Former Governor of Georgia, businessman
61. Marshall, E. G., 83 (New York, NY) Movie actor
62. Marty, Martin, 65 (Chicago, IL) Church history professor
63. Mazel, Ella, 75 (New York, NY) Publishing business
64. McCallion, Edna, 74 (New York, NY) Catholic ecumenist, UN involvements
65. McClendon, James, 66 (Los Angeles, CA) Theologian, professor
66. McDonald, John, 71 (Washington, DC) U.S. ambassador, founder of institutes for peace and diplomacy
67. Neugarten, Bernice, 77 (Chicago, IL) Professor, scholar on aging
68. Nguyen, Lien, 76 (San Jose, CA) Vietnamese community leader
69. Odum, Eugene P., 80 (Athens, GA) Professor, ecologist
70. O'Keefe, Vera, 78 (Atlanta, GA) Health training coordinator
71. Olsen, Tillie, 81 (San Francisco, CA) Writer
72. Payne-Stancil, Barbara, 73 (Athens, GA) Sociologist, aging specialist

73. Pauley, Frances, 88 (Atlanta, GA) Political and social activist
74. Peterson, Esther, 87 (Washington, DC) Consumer affairs leader
75. Rabinowitz, Lillian, 82 (Berkeley, CA) Teacher, aging work
76. Randall, Claire, 74 (New York, NY) Church leader
77. Sample, Winona, 76 (Santa Clara, CA) Educator, American Indian leader
78. Saporta, I. E., 83 (Atlanta, GA) Architect, educator
79. Schachter-Shalomi, Zalman, 69 (Philadelphia, PA) Educator, rabbi, aging work
80. Schacht-Lavine, Lillian, 69 (Atlanta, GA) Therapist
81. Schiffman, Beatrice, 80 (El Cerrito, CA) Senior center organizer
82. Schweitzer, Paul, 86 (New York, NY) Educator
83. Sennett, William, 79 (San Francisco) Social activist, businessman
84. Sibbald, Luella, 86 (Berkeley, CA) Therapist
85. Sibley, Celestine, 76 (Atlanta, GA) Journalist
86. Singer, June, 75 (Palo Alto, CA) Therapist
87. Sitton, Claude, 67 (Atlanta, GA) Journalist, editor
88. Smith, Page, 76 (Santa Cruz, CA) Historian, professor
89. Smith, Susan Carlton, 69 (Athens, GA) Artist, librarian
90. Soto, Anthony, 72 (San Jose, CA) Married priest, sociologist, job training leader
91. Sparer, Burt, 67 (Athens, GA) City planner
92. Stark, Arthur, 75 (New York, NY) Labor arbitrator
93. Stark, Dorothy, 80 (New York, NY) Sculptor
94. Stevenson, Joanne, 80 (Palo Alto, CA) Teacher
95. Taylor, Gerald, 69 (Dayton, OH) Priest, navy chaplain
96. Thoits, Mary, 70 (Los Angeles, CA) Educator
97. Torrance, E. Paul, 78 (Athens, GA) Professor, creativity specialist
98. Traxler, Margaret Ellen, 69 (Chicago, IL) Nun, social work leader
99. Tutu, Desmond, 62 (Atlanta, GA) Anglican archbishop
100. Wallach, Eli, 78 (New York, NY) Movie actor
101. Ward, Judson, 81 (Atlanta, GA) Educator
102. Weltner, Charles, 65 (Atlanta, GA) Georgia Supreme Court Justice
103. Wilks, Gertrude, 65 (Palo Alto, CA) Educator
104. Zimmerman, Anne, 79 (Chicago, IL) Nurse, official for nursing groups

Index

Advice, from elders to the young, 223–32
Afterlife beliefs, 162–64, 167–68
Ageism, mandatory retirement as, 59
Ageist stereotypes, 3, 64–66, 83–84, 87, 134, 148–49
Aging, 1
  ambivalence about, 81–82
  association of, with death, 154
  creative, themes of, 5–9
  energy loss in, 142–43
  fears about, 159
  image of God and, 175–76
Allen, Ivan, Jr., 115, 184–85, 194
Altruism, 49, 130, 135, 192
Art, 79, 93–94, 181–82

Baker, Woolford, 116, 137
Balance in life, 230
  between dependence and independence, 159–60
  between family and career, 38–42
  between family commitment and independence, 35
  between humanistic values and material possessions, 68
  between intimacy and world experiences, 35–36

between physical and psychospiritual health, 66–68
Beauty, love of, 146, 165
Bergman, Gregory, 12–13, 34, 77, 85, 90, 109, 139–40, 144, 157, 158, 186–87, 194, 230
Berry, Thomas, 135, 136, 140
Bierley, Estelle M., 133–34, 140, 163–64, 187, 194
Blaustein, Miriam, 94, 104, 120–21, 133, 134, 138, 140, 151–52
Blumenthal, Gerda, 77, 85, 90, 93, 110, 138, 143, 161, 179, 181, 194
Boulding, Elise, 28–31, 35, 102, 112, 142–43, 158, 163, 166, 167, 176, 193, 230
Brewer, Earl, 90, 119, 136, 225
Broom, Mabel, 71, 84, 98, 111, 116, 227–28
Brown, Robert McAfee, 107, 112, 118, 127, 228
Brown, Sidney, 118, 120, 127, 138, 159, 164, 224
Buddhism, 44–45, 127–28, 179–80, 184

Careers, 37–53
  balancing home and, 38–45, 60–61
  turning points in, 45–60, 61–62

Caregivers, 73, 120, 138, 149–50
Carter, Jimmy, 3, 52, 53, 96, 111,
    130, 140, 173, 191–92, 194, 228
Catholic Church, 24, 72, 105, 153,
    169–72, 186
    Angelo Roncalli Community, 56
    birth control teachings, 21
    changes in commitments of
        religious professionals, 54–58
    Christian Family Movement,
        20–21, 23, 127, 170–71
    friendships of religious
        professionals, 123, 124
    intentional communities of, 126,
        128–29
    patriarchy of, 58
    social-justice teachings of, 21
Celebration, 80, 86
    death as time of, 157–58, 166
Clarence, Henry, 127–28, 139, 184,
    194
Clown, message of, 26, 80, 177
Commitment, intense, 62, 81, 86, 184
    to wider concerns, 88, 129–37,
        139–40
Communities, intentional, 6, 125–29,
    139
Contemplative mode, 69–70
Cook, Douglas, 99
Cousins, Norman, 76–77
Crafting your own elderhood, 7,
    195–222
Crafting your own elderhood
    exercises, 197–222
    Developing Personal Spirituality,
        219–22
    Empowering the Elder Self, 205–8
    Encountering Mortality, 215–19
    Expanding the Elder Self, 208–11
    Family, 197–200
    Reaching Out from the Elder Self,
        211–15
    Turning Points, 203–5
    Work Life, 200–3
Creativity, inner resources for, 68–71,
    145

marital relationship and, 27–28,
    150–151
Crook, Clara, 17–18, 34, 65, 84, 92,
    118, 123, 138, 147–48, 150, 179
Crowley, Patty, 20–22, 35, 127, 160,
    170–71, 192
Curiosity, 93, 94

d'Antonio, William, 81–82, 86, 227
Davis, Virginia, 8, 15–17, 34, 91,
    117, 137, 142, 151, 155, 169,
    170, 192, 231
Death and dying, 7. *See also* Loss(es);
    Mortality, encountering
    belief in afterlife and, 162–65
    fear of, 154–55, 161, 166, 167
    as goad to achieving perspective,
        154, 167
    meditation on, 157, 167
    perspectives on, 80
    reflections of elders on, 154–68
    spiritual resources and, 161–62
    transcendence of fear of, 154–58,
        162–65, 166
DeChatelet, Helen, 67, 84, 95, 111,
    124, 148, 160, 223–24
Dependency, 159–60
Depression, and status loss, 148–49
Dillenberger, Jane, 144, 152
Dillenberger, John, 163
Disabilities. *See also* Health problems
    mental, fear of, 159
    physical, coping with, 143–44,
        145–46, 165, 181
Dodd, Lamar, 93–94, 111, 145
Duryea, John, 54–56, 62, 129, 137,
    139, 142, 153–54, 158, 226

Eaton, Anne, 120, 124, 138, 149,
    155, 159
Eckhart, Meister, 177
Ecology, interest in, 46–48, 135–37
Elder wisdom. *See* Wisdom, of elders
Emotional suffering. *See* Suffering,
    emotional

Empowerment, self-, 64–86
elimination of ageist stereotypes and, 64–66
financial security and, 68
humor and, 76–80
inner creativity and, 68–71
interests and, 81
physical health and, 66–68
purpose and interests and, 80–83
self-acceptance and self-esteem and, 74–76
self-reliance and, 71–74, 84
Energy loss, 142–43, 165
Erlanger, Mary, 27–28, 65, 71–72, 76, 84–85, 111, 224
Erlanger, Michael, 26–28, 35, 97, 145–46
Etheridge, Jack, 115, 129–30, 227
Ethical concerns, 182–92, 194
Exercises. *See* Crafting your own elderhood
Expansion of elder self, 87–113
through embracing new possibilities, 97–103, 112
through expressing new freedoms, 107–9, 112
through integration of past into present, 88–93
through intellectual stimulation, 93–97, 111
through living with gratitude, 109–10, 112–13

Family, marital. *See* Marriage
Family of origin
cultivating friendship bonds with, 137–38
positive and negative influences of, 9–19, 34–36, 115–16
Family histories, integrating, 9–36
Fear(s), 161
of being cheated or robbed, 158
childhood, letting go of, 15–17
of death or dying, 154, 166
financial, 156–57, 158–59, 167
of physical decline, 159

Ferguson, Janet, 76, 90–91, 136, 143, 150, 164, 165, 231
Fichter, Joseph, 72, 84, 123, 153, 158, 164, 173–74, 192, 228
Financial problems, 66, 68, 73
fears about, 156–57, 158–59, 167
Forsyth, Katherine, 91, 94, 107, 112, 123–24, 164
Freedom, of creative elders, 60, 71, 87–88, 103–9
from burdens of past, 103, 104–8, 112
inner liberation, 103–8, 112
Friedan, Betty, 171
Friendship(s), of elders, 6, 165
adaptability and, 121, 122–23
intergenerational, 125
in marriage, 119, 138
new, cultivating, 119–25, 138
Future, for elderly, 92–93, 101–2

Gift-giving, 7–8
Goals, need for, 80, 81, 86
God. *See also* Religion
changed attitudes toward, 175–78
concepts of, 175–77
Grandchildren, 63, 117–18, 153, 154
Gratitude, living with, 6, 109–10, 112–13
Gray Panthers, 100, 101, 125, 126, 132–33, 139, 189
Greenberg, Simon, 72, 81, 109, 121, 153, 162, 167, 187–88, 225
Grief, coping with, 149–52
Gritts, Ross, 10–12, 34, 224
Gross, Bertram, 98–99, 111–12, 146, 179, 225
Growth, personal, 69
ethical spirituality and, 189, 192

Hammarskjöld, Dag, 110
Handy, Robert, 161, 163, 226
Harding, Esther, 31
Hayden, Edwin, 98, 112, 174

Health maintenance
  empowerment of elder self and,
    66–68
  humor and, 76–77
  psychospiritual components of,
    67–68, 69
  taking responsibility for, 66–67, 84
Health problems, 73, 141–42, 143,
  147–48, 156, 165. *See also*
  Disabilities
Hill, Theresa, 164
Ho, Evelyn, 65, 156, 159, 231
Howes, Elizabeth B., 70, 84, 121,
  158, 176, 193, 224
Humanistic values, 68
Humor, 5, 76–80, 85–86, 146
Hurst, Willis, 95–96, 111, 228

Identity. *See* Self-identity
Independence. *See* Self-reliance and
  independence
Inner child, 77, 79–80, 85–86
Intellectual stimulation, 93–97
Interests, development of, 80–83
Interviewees, 3–4, 235–237. *See also*
  names of interviewees
Interviews, for elder wisdom project,
  3–4, 233–234
Inward journey, 69–70, 84, 128, 193,
  223–26
  spiritual growth and, 175–82

Judaism/Jews, 33, 69, 70, 174–75,
  179, 187–88
Johnson, Jan, 142
Journal-writing, 88, 197

Kalven, Janet, 67, 79, 83, 126–27,
  139, 157, 171–72, 186, 192, 194,
  229
Karp, Herbert, 81, 86, 136, 174–75
Kearney, Dorothy, 74, 154, 166,
  178–79, 193, 225
Kelley, Peter, 106–7, 112, 147
King, Harriet, 74, 91, 111, 149–50
Kuhn, Maggie, 58–60, 62, 64, 66,

81, 84, 97, 100–101, 119, 125,
  126, 132–33, 138, 139, 144, 176,
  189, 231
Kunst, Mary, 121–22, 138, 152, 159,
  227

Lambert, Charlee, 38–42, 44, 61,
  82–83, 73, 86, 102, 112, 138,
  151, 155, 224
Land, Philip, 109–11, 126, 139
LaRocque, Gene, 131, 136, 140, 157,
  190–91, 227
Learning, lifelong, fostering, 93–97,
  111, 138
Letting go. *See also* Loss(es)
  of false expectations, and self-
    acceptance, 74–75
  learning about, 24–25, 26
  of perfect health, 68
Leuterio, Hector, 124, 147, 156–57,
  227
Levitt, Norma, 32–34, 35, 162, 230
Levy, Miriam, 160, 188, 194, 229
Life
  awareness of impermanence and
    transience of, 44, 51
  Buddhist philosophy of, 44
  after death (*see* Afterlife)
  intensity of living, 51
  prolongation of, through
    technology, 160–61
  simplifying, 68
  yin and yang phases of, 75
"Life-harvesting," 89, 91, 110
Life history(ies), 5, 37, 62
  integrating family experiences in,
    9–36
Life review, 5, 88
  questions for, 199–200, 202, 204,
    206–8, 209–11, 213–15, 217–19,
    221–22
Lifespan, 2, 48–49, 159
Lilienthal, Sally, 114, 142, 155, 224,
  166
Living in present, 91–93, 111, 180
Loneliness, 119, 149, 165

Loss(es), 25, 142. *See also* Letting go
  change of attitude and, 44
  creative solutions regarding, 32
  through death, 121–22, 127, 152
  of energy, 142, 165
  through estrangement, 151–52
  of friends, 119
  integrating into lives, 141
  and openness to new possibilities,
    100–101
  as opportunity for reassessment,
    191
  self-reliance and, 71–72
  of spouse, 149, 150–51, 165
  as turning point, 32, 48, 51, 191
Love
  in marital relationship, 23 (*see also*
    Marriage)
  of self, 80, 231
  of life, 71
Lowery, Joseph, 116, 131–32, 140,
    183–84, 194
Lucey, Rose, 22–24, 35, 79, 86, 118,
    152, 153, 158, 166, 175, 193, 231
Ludy, Lin, 24–26, 35, 67, 80, 85, 86,
    94, 157, 164–65, 166, 176–77,
    180, 193, 224

McCallion, Edna, 74, 84, 169–70,
    192, 225
McDonald, John, 52–53, 62
Maddox, Lester, 130, 139, 184, 191,
    231
Marriage
  becoming own person in, 28–34
  beneficial relationships in, 20–28,
    35, 75–76, 108, 116, 122, 175
  and career, balancing involvement
    in, 38–45
  defining self-identity in, 28–34
  estrangement in, 151–52
  friendship in, 119–20, 138
  health problems and, 147
  independence within, 23, 25
  late-in-life, 120
  negative effects of, 189

  self-acceptance and, 23–24
  as turning point, 55–56
  unhappy, coping with, 150–51
Marshall, E. G., 92
Marty, Martin, 49–52, 61, 117,
    137–38, 159, 163, 178, 180, 193,
    194, 225, 232
Mazel, Ella, 44–45, 61, 108, 117,
    137–38, 155–56, 162, 164, 166,
    227
Meditation, 70, 127, 157, 163, 167,
    184
  life-review exercises, 196–7,
    198–99, 201–2, 203–4, 205–6,
    212–13, 216–17, 219–21
Memories, 6. *See also* Life review;
    Reminiscing
  childhood, retention of, 23
  difficult, facing, 19, 89
  harvesting, 89
  healing of, 89–90
Mental disabilities, 159
Mentors/mentoring, 2, 31, 49, 70,
    135. *See also* Role models
Middle age
  commitment to larger concerns in,
    130
  exploring creativity in, 68
  fostering friendships in, 123
  stereotypes of aging and, 2
Mortality, encountering, 141–68
Music, 181–82
Mystery, experience of, 175–78

Nature, love of, 153–54
Neugarten, Bernice, 48–49, 61, 76,
    79–80, 85, 117–18, 122–23,
    138–39, 162, 167, 227

Odum, Eugene P., 46–47, 49, 61,
    96–97, 111, 136–37, 140
O'Keefe, Vera, 75, 41–42, 44, 61,
    155
Olsen, Tillie, 8, 85, 103–4, 112, 121,
    152, 155, 158, 159
Openness, 179–80, 194

Passivity, advice against, 65, 66, 67, 86
Past
  importance of not focusing too much on, 91–92
  integrating into present, 88–93
Pauley, Frances, 78–79, 109, 118, 135, 140, 142, 172, 186, 192, 194
Payne, Ray, 41
Payne-Stancil, Barbara, 38–40, 61, 164, 226
Personality, 91
  family history and, 9–10
Peterson, Esther, 119, 138, 149, 161, 167, 172–73, 229–30
Peterson, Oliver, 173
Playfulness, 5, 77–80, 85, 146
Polarities, inner, recognition of, 70–71
Possibilities, openness to, 97–103, 111–12, 126–27
Prejudice, 10–11, 14, 22–23, 26
Present, living in, 91–93, 111, 180
Productivity, need for, 82–83, 86, 151
Protestants, religious professional, change in commitments of, 58–60
Psychotherapy, 43, 45, 61, 122, 180, 182
Purpose, sustaining, 80–81, 86

Rabinowitz, Lillian, 34, 65–66, 75, 82, 85, 104, 153
  family in life history of, 18–19
Reaching out from elder self, 114–40, 226–29
  through cherishing family, 114–19, 137–38
  through committing to larger concerns, 129–37, 139–40
  through cultivating friendships, 119–25, 138–39
  through developing intentional communities, 125–29, 139
Religion, 167–68, 183. See also Buddhism; Catholic Church;

Judaism/Jews; Protestants; Spirituality, personal
  and afterlife beliefs, 162–64
  changes in commitments of religious professionals, 54–60
  critical stance toward, 169–74, 190, 192
  faithful adherents to, 174–75
  family of origin experience and, 25
  patriarchy of, 172
Reminiscing, 110–11. See also Life review; Memories
  integrating past into present through, 88–93
Retirement, 53, 59, 60, 83, 86, 90
  ageist stereotypes and, 148–49
  loss of support in, 119, 124
Risk-taking, 60, 72, 132–33, 145
Role models, for aging well, 65
  interviewees as, 65–66, 97, 111
Ryan, John, 21

Sample, Winona, 82, 86, 156, 179
Saporta, I. E. (Ike), 72–73, 95, 111, 146, 229
Schacht-Lavine, Lillian, 42–43, 61, 66
Schachter-Shalomi, Zalman, 69–70, 84, 89, 91, 102–3, 110, 111, 161, 167
Schiffman, Beatrice, 94, 138, 142, 155
Schweitzer, Paul, 110, 163, 178, 232
Self-acceptance, 23–24, 74, 76, 85
Self-empowerment. See Empowerment, self-
Self-esteem, 17, 18
  increasing, 74–76
  playfulness and, 77–80
  prejudice and, 22–23
  self-acceptance and, 74
  serenity and, 76, 85
  success in work world and, 37
Self-expansion. See Expansion of elder self
Self-expression, freedom for, 108

Self-identity
  burdens of past and, 103
  defining, in marital relationship,
    28–34
  discovering, 75, 88
  and life-shifting turning points,
    54–60
  retirement and, 90
Self-image, reexamining, 84, 88–89
Self-love, 80
Self-reliance and independence, 39,
    84–85
  cultivation of, 71–74
  and family commitment, balancing,
    35
  freedom from fear and, 71–72
  within marital relationship, 23, 25
  resiliency and, 72–73
Sennett, William, 152–53, 229
Serenity, sense of, 76, 85
Sexual love, 119–20, 138
Sibbald, Luella, 76, 121, 158, 177–78
Sibley, Celestine, 92, 156, 224
Silences (Olsen), 8, 103
Silences, breaking, 8, 121
Simplifying life, 68
Singer, June, 30–32, 35, 84, 91–92,
    111, 155, 159, 177, 179–80, 193,
    230
Sitton, Claude, 73, 94, 172, 228
Smith, Page, 108, 112, 134, 155, 226
Smith, Susan Carlton, 66, 226
Social causes, commitment to, 20–22,
    28–29, 67, 129–37, 139–40, 173.
    See also Altruism
  experiences leading to, 12–13,
    28–29, 53, 57–60
  inner development and, 6–7, 69
  intentional groups and, 126–27
  love of family and, 118
  social pain and, 152–53
  spirituality and, 182–92, 194
Social ethics, 182–92, 194
Soto, Anthony, 75–76, 85, 110, 128,
    132, 139, 157, 171, 185, 194, 224
Spirituality, personal, 7, 169–94

  art and, 181–82
  coping with suffering and, 180–81
  dying and, 161–62
  ethical concerns and, 182–92, 194
  inward journey and, 175–82
  as personal search for meaning,
    169, 192
  psychotherapy and, 180–81
  versus religious teachings, 169
Stark, Arthur, 79, 108, 140, 189,
    194, 226
Stark, Dorothy, 79, 107–8, 112
Status loss, 148–49, 165
Stereotypes of aging, 64–66, 83–84,
    134, 148–49
Stevenson, Joanne, 67, 110, 155, 166
Suffering, emotional
  facing, with creativity, 13
  learning from, 148–54
  loss of status and, 148–49
  as mental and emotional, 148
  physical impairment and, 159
  social pain as cause of, 152–53
  spirituality and, 180, 194
Suicide, 161, 167

Taylor, Gerald, 104–6, 107, 112, 164,
    167, 193
Thoits, Mary, 73–74, 84, 135, 224,
    227
Tolerance, 76, 145
Torrance, Paul, 145
Traxler, Margaret Ellen, 55–59, 62,
    147, 162–63, 165, 167
Turning points, 5, 37, 62, 90
  in careers, 37, 41, 46–47, 50–51, 52
  life-shifting, and self-identity,
    54–60
  losses as, 32, 44, 48, 51
  marriage as, 55–56
  physical disability as, 145–46
Tutu, Desmond, 3, 64, 69, 72, 78,
    83, 84, 85

Unconscious mind, 31, 32, 35, 70

Volunteer work, 82, 130–31, 149

Wallach, Eli, 68, 70–71, 77, 84, 85, 156, 162, 189–90, 224
Weltner, Charles, 115, 156, 157, 184–85, 194, 228–29
Wilks, Gertrude, 13–15, 34, 129, 176, 180, 193, 194, 224
Wisdom, of elders, 2

facing reality and, 95
gifts of, to young people, 223–32
loop toward, 95–96, 111
maladies and, 146
sense of serenity and, 76
Work experiences/working life, reflections on, 37–53

Zimmerman, Anne, 73, 84, 100, 112, 118, 125, 160